£2.50

University Challenge

The First 40 Years

D0808862

£2.50

University Challenge

The First 40 Years

Peter Gwyn

Questions compiled by
Stuart Brumpton

GRANADA

First published in Great Britain in 2002

By Granada Media, an imprint of André Deutsch Limited
20 Mortimer Street
London W1T 3JW

In association with Granada Media Group

University Challenge is a College Bowl Company Inc format
The series is a Granada Television Production for the BBC

A catalogue record for this book is available from the British Library.

ISBN 0 233 05082 5

Typeset by E-Type, Liverpool.
Printed and bound in Great Britain

1 3 5 7 9 10 8 6 4 2

Contents

Introduction

The author of this book, Peter Gwyn, said he wanted a few words 'from the presenter's chair.' I have tried imagining myself into the state of mind of the black, mock-leather thing which once had wheels but is now firmly taped to the floor, (so that its occupant doesn't career around as if the chairman's desk on *University Challenge* really is the dodgem car it so closely resembles) but I have struggled in vain. The chair is mute, stunned into silence by the experience of listening to the 100,000 questions it has introduced during the last 40 years. You will have to make do with some reflections from its current occupant.

I should start with a confession. When Granada Television, who make the programme, first approached me to present the show I was shocked. The show had been part of the furniture of my early life, but had been off the air for several years. My feelings went 'hmm', then 'wow!', swiftly followed by 'you'd be a fraud if you accepted' (provoked by the hazy memory of the evening when half the college had rolled out of the bar to take part in the quiz which would choose our team: I fell at the first fence), until I finally answered 'I don't think so: it's Bamber Gascoigne's show.' The man from Granada responded with a lot of guff about how the *Zeitgeist* had changed and it was time for a different person and a different style. But I still declined, with a few suggestions of other people they ought to consider.

A couple of weeks later I happened to be in the Reading Room at the British Museum, looking something up. I spotted Bamber Gascoigne by one of the filing cabinets and approached him.

'We've not met,' I said, 'but I think you ought to know that Granada are bringing back *University Challenge* on BBC2. If you're interested, you ought to give them a call.' 'Oh yes,' he said, 'they called me about that *months* ago. But I don't really want to do it. Too much like hard work.' With my tail between my legs I rang the producer next day, saying that if the job was still going, I'd like to be considered.

I have seldom regretted a decision less. Someone with a better turn of phrase (and a much greater understanding of fashion) remarked to me the other day that '*University Challenge* is the little black dress of quiz shows.' The rules, developed by the game's Canadian inventor when devising a way to keep servicemen from their more conventional styles of recreation, are simple. There is only one correct answer. And the outcome is always decisive.

Over the last eight years I have seen hundreds of teams enter the studio. Periodically, someone will ask whether I have a prejudice in favour of one sort of team or another. I do. I like best the ones who want to play earnestly, while recognizing that it is only a game. There are a million things in life more significant than winning a match on *University Challenge.* But for the 30 minutes that the thing lasts, before they fall upon the cans of Boddington's and Twiglets that Granada's legendary 'hospitality' provides its contestants, it really matters.

And here's another secret. There is a pile of questions kept in a secret drawer in the dodgem car. Their distinguishing characteristic is that they are classed as 'easy.' Not quite at the level of 'who originated Heisenberg's Uncertainty Principle?', or the authorship of *Bleak House,* but not much more difficult. Occasionally, after a run of failures by either team to answer a single starter question correctly, I will pull one from the pile, because it's too boring to watch eight people sitting there getting things repeatedly wrong, and the viewers do not pay their taxes to have it demonstrated to them that the education budget has been mis-spent. But if more than one of these easy questions is deployed in a series, I should be surprised. For the truth is that, for all the times that irritating phrase 'dumbing down' is used about education, the best students are still astonishing. It is remarkable what they know. And what they don't know. In the days when the show first went on British television, a tiny proportion of young people went on from school to university. Now you can find a university somewhere, I have no doubt, offering a course in lawn-mower maintenance. Of course, if you take an average of the entire student body in the country, the general level of intellectual achievement has fallen. But the best of the students are as good as ever they were.

All knowledge exists in a cultural context. The question is not whether they know everything – no-one can know everything – but *what* they know. Certainly, today's students are much less familiar with classical mythology or the Bible than their parents' generation might have been. But equally, they know much more about science or information technology. When we ran a 'champion of champions' competition in 2002, a team from the 1960s was matched against one from the 1990s. The complaint from the 1960s team was that there was 'too much science.' The 1990s students moaned about 'too much Latin.'

But even an ability to regurgitate the entire contents of the latest edition of *Britannica* is no guarantee of success, for many of the most entertaining questions require an ability to think quickly, to think laterally, and to take a chance. Fortune favours the intuitive.

Jeremy Paxman.

1

University Challenge: The First 40 Years

It's heading for disaster. For some reason or other, Imperial College, London, have got off to a miserable start and are hopelessly trailing their opponents, Somerville College, Oxford, who have a healthy 150 points to Imperial's paltry 5.

And this is not an ordinary show. It's the half-way point of the final match in the 2002 series. Two hundred student teams wanted to get on the series; the top twenty-eight did so, and now only the brainiest two remain. In a few minutes, one of them will take the trophy, and the title of "Series Champions". These are two very bright, very well-matched teams, but the scores are telling a different story.

Up in the production gallery, the producer and assistant producer are groaning. They don't care who wins, but the last thing they want is the anti-climax of a trouncing in the final match of the series. Everyone is expecting an excellent game, the studio audience wants to be gripped and Jeremy Paxman is wearing a darker suit than usual to convey the gravity of the occasion.

This should be a great match. It's the first time Somerville have made it to the final, so they are chasing their first-ever series title. Imperial have already won twice before, so they could become the first institution in the programme's history to take the trophy for a third time. The bottom line, however, is that both teams deserve to go away with a decent score, but at this rate it's a foregone conclusion. We may as well hand the trophy over straight away and let viewers turn over to *EastEnders*.

How has it happened? Imperial had a couple of unlucky interruptions to starter questions, which quickly put them on minus 10,
and this seems to have dented their confidence. Everyone is willing
them to get back into the game, but Somerville are getting all their
interruptions right, recognizing a limerick about Clement Attlee
after hearing only the first line, and the discoverer of Macchu
Picchu after just a few words.

Everyone knows it should be a close match, because both teams
have come to it with a combined score of over 1,000 points from
their first four matches and those combined scores are only 40
points apart, in Imperial's favour. But it's not a close contest. It's a
rout.

Then Somerville stumble a couple of times. They draw blanks on
a picture round asking them to name the artists responsible for
paintings of St George and the Dragon. They are shown an Uccello,
but they think it's an Aubrey Beardsley, for heaven's sake! Jeremy
uncharacteristically refrains from telling them they're out by five
hundred years.

Imperial's bad luck continues. An almost-correct interruption
identifies the mathematical problem of squaring the cube, but not
the Delian altar which gives the problem its name, and that's what
the question goes on to ask. They lose yet another five points.

They get back on track with an interruption naming the teacher
at the centre of the Tennessee "monkey trial", and do well with a
bonus set in which they come up with the terms "catechresis", "ligature" and "dieresis". Impressive for a team of scientists.

And then Imperial get the music bonuses. Folk music probably
isn't their thing, otherwise they would have recognized Peter, Paul
and Mary's "Puff the Magic Dragon". "Bad luck," Jeremy tells them.
"Your parents would have known it." He does a quick piece of
mental arithmetic. "Or your grandparents, rather."

It's now 45 to 150. Imperial are still too far behind, surely, to have
a hope of catching up.

Up in the production gallery, the mood has changed. The
Imperial lads are at least getting back on track. They've got points
on the board, and now we want them to get over 100. Even if they
can't catch Somerville, any score in three figures is honourable, and
we want both teams to depart with honour.

Jeremy realizes with relief that it is turning into a proper contest.
He picks up pace.

Suddenly, the starter questions go Imperial's way. They are beginning to find the form they've displayed in all their previous matches. They get three in succession, and make a decent job of the bonuses. It's only taken a couple of minutes, but it's happened – they've become a threat to Somerville. Now the audience is rooting for both teams, groaning with the misses, cheering the hits.

The second picture round goes to Somerville, allowing them to romp through a set on Olympic mascots. At the end of the second picture round Jeremy tells both teams there's only about six minutes of play left. If a team really gets a move on, it can put 25 points on the board in about a minute. Looking at the scores it's now possible, just about, that Imperial could overtake Somerville.

The minutes rush past. Both teams are getting starters, but more are going Imperial's way. They are catching up.

And now, with only a minute and a half to go, it's 165 to Imperial and 190 to Somerville. Finally, the match is wide open. The Imperial team is staging the most impressive comeback any of us has ever seen. They are in sight of an historic win – one which will mean they take the trophy for the third time.

Up in the production gallery – normally quiet – the tension is evident. Encouragement is yelled at both teams, whenever it's their chance to answer.

Imperial hurtle through a starter, and get two of three bonuses on English literature right. "There's less than a minute to the gong!" says Jeremy, and incredibly, the scores stand at 185 for Imperial, Somerville only five points ahead with 190. Ten minutes ago it was unthinkable. Now both teams are within a whisker of the trophy. The audience is riveted. Jeremy begins the next starter.

"Algiceras Nasier was the anagrammatical pseudonym used by which French physician and writer…"

BUZZ

Dorjana Sirola on the Somerville team interrupts. In the second between the buzzer and her answer, everyone in the studio makes the same snap calculation. If she's wrong, Somerville lose five points and Imperial will probably take the trophy. If she's right, Somerville may *just* have done enough to become champions. There's no doubt in her voice as she answers, "François Rabelais".

"That's correct; you get three bonus questions on teeth, Somerville," says Jeremy. With only seconds remaining, Somerville need only get one bonus right. That will put the game beyond Imperial's reach within the time remaining. Either that, or they can hope to hear the final gong before Jeremy can get to another starter.

But of course Jeremy knows this, and races them through the set. So they get their bonus set on teeth, of all things. Somerville clearly know nothing at all about teeth, and Jeremy isn't going to let them dawdle.

"Hurry! *I need an answer!*" They fail the first bonus, answering "milk teeth" instead of "buds".

"*Come on!*" They fail the second bonus – it's "root canal", not "dentine".

Jeremy hurtles into the last bonus, the final question about teeth. Somerville look blank. Not a clue. But they don't need one, because...

GONG

"And at the gong ..." but Jeremy can barely be heard over the screams from the audience; "... Imperial have 185 points – *Somerville have 200!*"

Somerville lose whatever interest they may have had in the correct term for the failure of the upper and lower jaws to meet. Hands are flung over mouths in amazement, then there's a lot of flinging themselves over each other as they try to let it sink in that they've become series champions. In contrast, bitter disappointment has put Imperial into suspended animation.

Up in the production gallery, the collective exhalation of breath causes paper to waft off desks. The producer and AP slump back in their chairs and stare at each other, feeling as exhausted as the teams and muttering, "Terrific match; brilliant end to the series; thank goodness Imperial did so well; frustrating they didn't get it; Somerville great and worthy winners." All of which is deeply unprofessional, because the show is still going on, and the director is trying to concentrate on recording Jeremy's next link.

"So, Somerville; can I ask you to come down and receive the trophy?" Up until this moment, the show has been recorded in one continuous take. Now, at last, there's a pause. Everyone begins to relax. The show isn't over; there's still work to do. Still, it won't be as gruelling as the last 26 minutes.

The set is re-staged for the presentation of the trophy and the single moment in the series when we get to see anybody's legs. The philosopher and educationalist Baroness Mary Warnock is going to present the trophy. She's been watching the show from the production gallery, and is taken down to her walk-on point on the set.

We come to the final moments of the programme, the final images of the series: a team of very bright young people, modestly holding a trophy presented to them by an eminent philosopher, receiving enthusiastic applause for having shown themselves capable of answering very difficult questions on just about everything. The trophy, which they keep for a year, is their only prize.

After the recording, the habit is to retire to the Green Room for what is intended to be a calm and sober moment of reflection on the day's events. This quickly degenerates into something of a scrum, and the Green Room heaves with an extraordinary number of students, many of whom we can't actually recognize as having actually appeared on screen. Somerville are looking exhilarated, Imperial are still looking stunned, despite the production team plying them with alcohol. The occasion of the final is one on which we relax the rule about, "No guests in the Green Room after the show", which is imposed simply because the budget cannot withstand the cost of entertaining hordes of thirsty student supporters. There are parents of, girlfriends of, boyfriends of team members, and Jeremy is somewhere in a corner, signing things and delighting an audience of admirers who have discovered that his rottweiler demeanour is only put on for the cameras. And there will be some glassy-eyed and extremely tired members of the production team, whose principal emotion is connected with the fact that, on the following day, they can have a lie-in.

In every series, most matches will be good, a couple may be a bit dull, and now and again they'll be outstanding. This was a terrific match, a memorable end to a great series. One of the reasons the programme has survived so long is that it can occasionally throw up great dramas like tonight's show. And survive it has; this was the end of the 31st series in the history of *University Challenge*. Different crews, different teams, different presenters have been going through this same process, in the same studio, since 1962.

University Challenge has only a few selling points. It showcases bright young people demonstrating the benefits of a liberal education. It has a format which is probably the simplest on television, with only one basic rule: you have to answer a starter question on your own, in order to win bonus questions which you discuss with your team. The highest score wins, and that's it. It has the oldest, creakiest special effect in television, which makes it look as if one team's desk is on top of another. It is old-fashioned and formal. Players are referred to by their surname, and take part for nothing more than the fun of it, the honour of their college or university, and a long-shot chance of winning the series. Good manners prevail. Win or lose, teams applaud their opponents, and champions accept the trophy with self-deprecating smiles. Like the Boat Race, it's all very, *very* British.

Except, of course, British is one thing *University Challenge* is not. It is an American format, based on a classic American show, and the way the game is played now, the level of questions, the formality with which students are addressed, the refusal to offer large material prizes and even the programme's catch-phrases, all originate with the American version, and the particular circumstances prevailing at the time of its first incarnation – as *College Bowl*, in the America of the 1950s.

THE 1950s

In 2002 we enjoy, if that is the right word, a multi-channel television environment in which quiz shows are ubiquitous. So it is all the harder to imagine a world in which a television programme which asks general knowledge questions of members of the public would be considered an excitingly original idea.

The broadcast quiz programme has its origins in the America of the 1930s. Quiz programmes were ideally suited to radio because they relied on words, allowed audience participation, and could generate an endless succession of gripping little mini-dramas. Almost all American radio programmes in the 1930s were sponsored, and a successful quiz programme allowed a sponsor a way of connecting with the audience. Consumers made a mental association between the sponsor's product and their own sense of well-being when they heard someone just like them win large amounts of money. For the sponsors, this connection proved to be a gold-mine, but it was to result in corruption, and the downfall of almost the entire genre.

From the 1930s to the 1950s, radio quizzes dominated the airwaves and, one by one, successful radio programmes transferred to television. The years of the mid-1950s saw an extraordinary appetite for quiz programmes – a phenomenon for which there is no real equivalent today – each one competing with the other to keep their sponsor's name at the forefront of the public's mind. To do this, the on-screen stakes were raised – what had been *The $64 Dollar Question* on radio became *The $64,000 Dollar Question* on television – and producers searched for ever more compelling contestants.

The programme *Twenty-One* had a nation hooked on the long-running duel between Herbie Stempel, a Jewish blue-collar worker from Queens, New York, and the Columbia teacher Charles Van Doren, from one of America's most patrician families. The programme's sponsors, Geritol, informed the producers of *Twenty-One* that they should do anything – anything at all – to maintain the programme's popularity. They responded by providing contestants with the answers before the transmission, and given them acting lessons to help them better convey the stresses of competition. In other words, the entire show became a fix, and the defeated Herbie Stempel was the one who finally blew the cover on *Twenty-One*'s corrupt practices.

Television, as a new medium, had not previously been governed by legislation. Now it was the subject of a New York grand jury's investigation, and of the scrutiny of a Congressional Committee on legislative oversight, which accepted Stempel's claims.

It was the biggest scandal ever to hit television, then or now. The big-money quiz programmes were rapidly axed. The practice of sponsorship, which helped create programmes and keep them on the air, also speeded the demise of a genre which associated its advertisers with dishonesty, and contempt for its customers. 1959 saw American quiz programmes falling off the airwaves by the dozen.

But not all of them vanished. One survivor was a cheerful, modest quiz for college students. Entitled *College Bowl*, it posed difficult questions to some of the brightest young minds in the country. It had a studio set in which one team sat above and behind the other. Contestants answered toss-up questions for ten points, and by doing so earned their team the right to confer on bonus questions. It had cheerful catch-phrases, such as "I have a 30-point bonus waiting, here's a toss-up for ten." "No, that's not right. I can hand it over to Podunk State." Winning teams earned modest amounts of money for their scholarship funds. It was completely different from all the big-money games and, like Caesar's wife, it was above reproach. And so it survived the great game-show cull; and the qualities which allowed it to survive are roughly the same as those which have made it the UK's longest-running television quiz programme.

College Bowl, the game we now play as *University Challenge*, had been devised in the 1940s by a Canadian singer and entertainer called Don Reid who, although the possessor of a fine tenor voice, was to find his lasting monument in the creation of this one game.

The precise moment of inspiration which created the format is lost in the mists of time, made somewhat mistier by Don's penchant for imaginative retellings of showbusiness anecdotes. One version, which has a ring of truth, has him watching a 'Varsity basketball match in the 1940s, during which the thought occurred to him that the academic equivalent, in which two teams of college students answered questions instead of chasing a ball, would make a compelling radio programme. Base the rules on a format as simple as a basketball game, so that anyone listening would always know exactly what was going on, and make it a positive and attractive showcase for talented young people, and it might be a hit.

College Bowl first made the airwaves as a radio programme in 1953 on the NBC radio network. Its sponsor was *Good Housekeeping* magazine, which goes some way to indicating just how wholesome its reputation really was. It was a high-tech operation with a question master, or "moderator", in a New York studio, and the competing teams on their own campuses, connected to each other by radio and telephone.

In 1959 it made the transition to television, airing on CBS on Sunday afternoons. Now it was sponsored by the General Electric Company and so was known as *G.E. College Bowl* with the portentous tag line: "At General Electric, progress is our most important product." The programme moved to NBC in 1963, and towards the end of its run, from 1968 to 1970, moved to a prime-time slot, again on NBC, on Sunday evenings.

In Britain, we've had Bamber Gascoigne, and now Jeremy Paxman. *G.E. College Bowl* had, as its version of a Paxman or a Gascoigne figure, Allen Ludden, a suave, silver-haired M.C., who was particularly respected as a quiz show presenter. Bob Monkhouse with a Ph.D might be the nearest British equivalent. Ludden had hosted an NBC series in the mid-1950s entitled *Mind Your Manners*, in which exceptionally polite young men and women talked about various concerns of the day. On the back of this series he produced several books in the mid-1950s: *Plain Talk for Men Under 21*, followed by *Plain Talk for Young Women*, then *Plain Talk for Young Married People*, and for *Young People Going to College*, and so he was viewed as an obvious choice to present a quiz programme showcasing articulate young people. He combined a presenter's ability to drive a programme with a convincing, gentlemanly intellect.

To the dismay of many *College Bowl* viewers, he left the programme to host another of America's more intelligent game programmes, *Password*. On the set of *Password* he met Betty White, a stalwart of American television as an actress and presenter, best known to UK audiences as Rose Nylund in NBC's situation comedy *The Golden Girls*. She and Ludden married. On his retirement from quiz programmes he made guest appearances on *The Love Boat* and released an album of cover versions of his favourite songs, including *On A Clear Day You Can See Forever*, which perhaps proves that it was in the area of presenters that the British version was to differ most strongly from the American. Ludden's replacement was the actor Robert Earle, who had anticipated Ludden's departure and sent the *College Bowl* producers a show-reel in which he had spliced footage of himself into the film of a show in place of Ludden.

This rather idiosyncratic programme took a hold on America's consciousness in way which always far exceeded its viewing figures. In 2001, despite having been off the air for over 20 years, *College Bowl* was voted by readers of America's *TV Guide* as number three in its list of the all-time best game programmes, the top two being *The Price Is Right* and *Jeopardy*.

Back on this side of the Atlantic, the mid-1950s saw Sidney and Cecil Bernstein, owners of the Granada Cinemas chain, debating how to deal with the threat to their cinema business of the burgeoning television industry. Taking the view that the most effective way to deal with the competition was to be a part of it, and given that the majority of their cinemas were in the south, they acquired the independent television licence for broadcasting on weekdays in the north, and Granada's Manchester studios came into being.

With a lot of broadcast hours to fill, and a very short supply of experienced television producers in what was still a fledgling industry in the UK, the Bernsteins looked across the Atlantic both for personnel and successful formats. The deal to make a version of *College Bowl* in the UK was struck between Don Reid and Cecil Bernstein, a gentlemen's agreement which was to remain in place, and on gentlemanly terms, for several decades.

The 1960s

Having done the deal and acquired the format, Granada then had to work out how to produce it for a UK market. Although today American formats are routinely purchased for UK consumption with very little alteration to the end product – the UK version of

Survivor is virtually a clone of the American version – in 1962 it was clear that *University Challenge* had to be very different from *College Bowl* in tone. The only way was to do this was to work on a long series of dry runs before it was ready for transmission.

To make the dry runs work, local students were recruited as guinea-pig contestants. Helen Haste, now a professor of psychology, was one of them. "It was the offer of a free lunch that got us there," she admits. "We were all going to have lunch at the university, and someone said we could have a free lunch if we went down to Granada to take part in a dry run of a programme. So team selection came down to tapping people on the shoulder and asking them if they wanted a free lunch."

The Manchester guinea-pigs would become one of the two teams in the first transmissions of the series, and would return again forty years later to play in the *University Challenge Reunited* series, which perhaps goes to prove the adage that there's no such thing as a free lunch.

"There were a lot of things to be sorted out – how you sat, how you used the buzzer, the very basics of the game. And the set was a load of cardboard held together by sticky-tape. It really looked like it had been thrown together by kids in a classroom – not at all plush." (Needless to say, Granada's scenic services department has come on a long way since then.)

The most crucial element was the presenter. Cecil Bernstein had told Barry Head, the first producer, that he should look for "a new face". A group of actors and journalists was selected, among them the drama critic of *The Spectator* who, at 27, would be only a few years older than the undergraduates taking part. Bamber Gascoigne had been educated at Eton and Magdalene College, Cambridge, where he had been a member of the Footlights. As a student, he had written the libretto for the musical *Share My Lettuce*, and so had some involvement in showbusiness but not, at that point, much television experience.

At that point, no one could have foreseen how crucial the choice of presenter would turn out to be. "Had we known," say Bamber Gascoigne, "we would all have been much more nervous. I rather like adrenalin – I think it helps my performance – but none of us cared that much about it, because it was only going to be for three months during the summer. It was unthinkable that anything like that could last so long.

"There were about half a dozen of us that Barry Head had got together; half were actors, and half were journalists. I'd been the drama critic for *The Spectator*, and I think he chose me to audition simply because he liked what I wrote. I had been on television before, but not much, and I did rather like the idea of being on telly, so I did want to win. But the night before the audition Granada put me into the most appalling hotel where I was given an attic room, and in the basement there was an all-night disco, and a chimney led directly from the basement into my room, acting as a kind of amplifying funnel – I felt like the dog listening to *His Master's Voice* at the end of a loudspeaker. The disco didn't close down until three; I got no sleep until then and I thought my future was in ruins, due to the ghastly stinginess of Granada for putting me in this room.

"One thing I remember about the auditions was that none of us had seen the questions beforehand, and it was probably easier for those of us who had been journalists to deal with these strange and obscure words which kept popping up, rather than the poor actors."

Helen Haste remembers the auditionees as "a variety of rather interesting people, some of whom were *very* unsuitable. Bamber shone straight away as exactly the right person. He had the academic background, but he was also very charming and highly informed. He didn't have a high TV profile before then, but as soon as the programme went out he became a cult figure, as well as a new type of quizmaster – unashamedly erudite, and immensely likeable."

Having selected the presenter, the single most important decision made in reshaping the format was that it would go up-market. The American version had included film of the buildings of the competing campuses, a description of the tactics used by the teams' coaches (coaches? unheard-of for a British quiz team!) and, given the broader intake of the American universities, a lower level of questioning. *University Challenge* would be a quiz, pure and simple, all questions-and-answers, and would fly in the face of received television wisdom by being as erudite as the teams could manage.

These aspirations reflected those of Granada at the time: ambitious, confident and determined that its programming should be distinctive. It had already created *Coronation Street*, which invented the genre of the continuing popular television drama, and with *World In Action* would create the genre of popular television journalism. *University Challenge* was part of that era of supremely confident programme-making, and in its early years in a two-channel environment, it would be able to reach audiences of 19 million.

With its presenter in place, and the Manchester guinea-pigs

formed into a team to play the first of three matches against four students from Leeds, the first edition of *University Challenge* was broadcast on 21 September 1962, at the height of the Cuban missile crisis.

Everyone admits the early transmissions lacked polish. "This was 1962," says Bamber Gascoigne, "and Peter Mullings, the director, told me that only two years before this he had directed plays live, and in the commercial breaks the cameras would have to move round to another part of the studio and film the actors presenting the commercials. Our first scoreboard wasn't even electric – there was someone working it from behind, like a school cricket board, notching up each five or ten points. And the scoreboard was placed up to my right as I faced the students, and it was at a really oblique angle to me. It's essential to know the scores at all times when you're presenting the programme, because that's how you know when to drive it forward, and I said I really couldn't present the game unless I could see the scores. So we got a car's driving mirror and attached it to the side of my desk to reflect the score, but, of course, that reversed the numbers. So we had to have another driving mirror positioned to reflect from the first one, so I could see them properly, and I'd have to adjust them very precisely before each recording. I remember a little Plasticine structure they had to sit in. There's nothing like low-tech!"

Those first students shared the view that the programme would only have a short run. "We thought it'd only run for a few weeks! For one thing, it was quite a gamble for Granada to try and launch what could be a pretty elitist show, and yet try and get a mainstream audience for it. Although it was based on the American model of *College Bowl,* the States at the time saw a far higher proportion of the population going to college. Over here, students were much more of a rarity."

One issue was a bugbear for *University Challenge* production teams from the very first days, and has persisted for forty years – the number of women who take part. If students were a rarity, women students were rarer still, and yet the Manchester team of 1962 boasted three women to one man. It was an unusual ratio for a mixed-sex institution then, and one that still occurs very infrequently in what has turned out, over four decades, to be a very male-dominated programme.

"Only about ten per cent of boys over 18 went to university, and around four per cent of girls, so you were viewed as being a bit remote and strange, and living a very ivory-towered existence," says

Helen Haste. "Of course, you were thought to be frightfully bright, which was a nice thing to be thought, but the image of women students in particular was that of the bluestocking, dowdy and boring and not interested in men. So this was a programme which showed them as carefully-dressed, attractive and normal young people, but very bright. That was a really unusual image in those days."

"As a student at the time, there was a real sense of women coming forward and finding their voice," says Sue Hurley, née Baddeley, Helen's team-mate. "I was standing for president of the Manchester Students' Union in the first year that women were actually allowed to do so, and I lost by four votes. But three years later, Anna Ford put that right by winning. But the show did reflect the way women students were beginning to feel about things.

"We were ordinary students, we were very normal, we had regional accents, and we weren't like the Cambridge Footlights lot who came down and went straight into showbusiness. We came out of the lecture theatre, into the television studio, and then back into the lecture theatre again."

They may have been ordinary students, but the impression on viewing those early shows is of the era before 1962. The 1960s had begun only in terms of the calendar; the explosion of popular culture still lay in the future, and the first show went out before most people in the UK had heard of The Beatles. "I remember a question that was going to be asked on a show about six months into the recordings," says Bamber. "It asked, 'What are the first names of the four Beatles?' And I said to the researcher at the time, 'This is impossibly difficult! How on earth can we expect people to know something as obscure as that?' And she said, 'Trust me. They'll know.' And she was right, of course."

The extraordinary erudition Bamber displayed on the programme quickly earned him the epithet "the cleverest man on television", but he maintains it was simply down to preparation. "The public had decided rather early on that I was omniscient. This was totally fallacious, but I was rather keen on this fallacy being perpetuated, and it came about because it is incredibly easy to anticipate wrong answers. I remember a question which asked, 'Which romantic poet died young in 1821?', and of course it was Keats. But I would look it up and discover that Shelley had died in 1822. So if they answered 'Shelley,' I'd say, 'Oh bad luck, bad luck!' Shelley died just one year later,' entirely as a result of having foreseen it and having sat with my *Encyclopaedia Britannica* on my desk for a whole day, literally reading around every question."

And so the series began what nobody then realized would be an uninterrupted 25-year run. Over the years, the list of series finalists would come to be led by teams from Oxford and Cambridge, but the first series champions were the team from Leicester University. Oxford took the next two titles, with wins by New College and then Oriel, although the 1960s ended with triumphs for the red-brick university of Sussex, and Keele.

The 1970s

May 1968 had seen the height of student unrest. Paris students, armed with Molotov cocktails, fought pitched battles with police the length of the Boulevard St Germaine. Later that month a general strike, partly in support of students' demands, forced De Gaulle to broadcast to the nation his refusal to quit as president.

University Challenge's moment of student unrest, sadly, fails to make quite the same league. A full eight years after the May riots, students at Manchester University chose to vent their anger at what they saw as the programme's bias towards Oxbridge, and it is certainly true that the great majority of winning teams from this decade were from Oxbridge. This was nothing to do with supposed bias on the programme's part, simply that those teams were the best – but the Manchester lot didn't see it that way. Fuelled by drink, their supporters having gained entry to the recording with forged tickets, they decided to disrupt a recording by shouting "Marx", "Trotsky" and "Marilyn Monroe" to every question asked.

Director Peter Mullings was not impressed. "We thought it was damn stupid of them! They thought we were going to have to pull the programme, but we didn't have to. The programme controller, Julian Amis, told us to broadcast the programme anyway and show up the students. There was an awful lot of press about this." The headlines the following morning rang with the lines: "TV's Bamber Shouted Down," and "Catcalls for Gascoigne".

"We knew that there was going to be trouble, and that students were forging tickets. After this happened, we changed the ticket system so that tickets had holes in them. They wouldn't be able to forge a hole!"

Bamber remembers the incident well. "It came across that they were protesting about the elitist nature of the programme, and I think it was partly that, but it turned out they were protesting about everything. The students on that team had actually dropped out of Manchester University. The four of them were living together in a house, and by some weird accident, the letter asking the Union if Manchester would like to put a team forward had been diverted to one of these four. They decided not to forward it to the Union but just to put themselves forward as a team. So we may have been part of their protest about the whole horrible, large world."

The producer halted the programme and read the riot act to the dissenting students. "After that," says Bamber, "they calmed down and played the game properly. I think they even ended up with 40 points. And after the recording they spent the evening with us, as the students always did – we always end up in the pub – and they turned out to be very endearing. By the end of the evening, we were very fond of them."

The programme was transmitted as recorded, and legend has it that as Manchester's students watched it on a set in the Students' Union bar, glee at their own antics rapidly dwindled into cringing embarrassment. The decision to broadcast was a courageous one. Had it happened today, it is far less likely that the final show would have been aired, but then, student activism being what it currently is, it is impossible to imagine it happening today.

The 1980s

By the mid-1980s, the programme's place in the ITV schedules was looking vulnerable. The ITV network was an alignment of different broadcasters, and this made it impossible for Granada to insist that every company transmit the programme at the same time. There was increasing competition from other companies, who wanted to give valuable slots to their own programmes.

The only advantage of the programme being broadcast at differ-ent times of the day in different parts of the country was pointed out in a letter written by a travelling salesman to the programme's producer. Because he travelled for a living, he was able to watch an early transmission of the programme in one region, memorize the answers, and then drive home and impress his family as they all watched a later showing. The split transmission may have been great kudos for one travelling salesman, but it was bad news for the programme.

The problem was that the network's aspirations no longer coincided with those of the programme-makers. Viewing figures were around two million, lower than the current rating on BBC2, and extremely low by ITV's standards at the time. The channel's aspirations had changed since the programme's launch in 1962, and mainstream audiences were increasingly becoming the be-all-and-end-all for an advertising-driven channel. It was failing to attract the volume of viewers needed to justify a place on a commercial channel.

LWT was the first of the licence-holders to drop the programme; the decision was made when John Birt was its Controller of Programming. Bamber says, "The last two years of *University Challenge* were pretty miserable. We'd been shifted to the afternoon, and that resulted in LWT deciding to drop it, because they'd had it on at lunchtime on Sunday for a great many years, and they rightly felt that with only 48 hours a week at their disposal, half an hour of the same show, forever, was actually too limiting, and they dropped it.

"Then Granada only managed to get it networked in the afternoons, and we invented all sorts of new rules to make it more snazzy, which didn't seem to work."

This scheduling change demanded that *University Challenge* play stripped across the channel – in other words, every weekday at the same time. Peter Mullings and Bamber Gascoigne took the view that it would be idiotic to try and play the game in the conventional format in such a high volume of shows. They had other concerns as well. It was clear from the way the game was played that one smart starter-answerer on one team could effectively block a perhaps more balanced and more able opposing team. They took the decision to introduce specialist rounds, allowing contestants to select the topic on which they would answer, and a baton, rather like a *Star Wars* light sabre, was introduced and had to be passed from one contestant to another as questions were answered. Perhaps most radically of all, a new set was constructed in which one team really did sit on top of the other. The studio audience was arranged in a kind of amphitheatre, with Bamber asking his questions from what looked like a reinforced bunker in the middle of them.

It was not a success. The new rules were baffling to both the teams and the audience, and the fundamental reasons for the programme's disfavour had not been addressed. This was a programme in which even its target audience might understand only a fraction of what was being asked, and as other ITV companies began to compete more aggressively for air-time, it was now more vulnerable than ever. It had been launched in a world of two channels, when television audiences were potentially enormous, and even a show like *University Challenge* would be seen by 19 million people. All that had changed.

The quaint charm of the programme no longer hooked people in sufficient numbers. The make-over had been a brave attempt to rejuvenate the format, and breathing new life into a struggling format is one of the hardest jobs in television. It hadn't worked, and the death knell had been sounded. Having awarded the 1987 trophy to Keble College, Oxford, Bamber signed off the series with the words, "I'd normally say 'Goodbye until next week', or even 'Goodbye until next year' – but this time, I'm afraid it's just – goodbye."

After a quarter of a century, the programme was axed.

The 1990s

"Well, I'm sure we all remember the rules," said Jeremy Paxman seven years later, "but if anyone needs a reminder, starter questions are worth ten points, you answer them on your own with no conferring…"

The resurrection of *University Challenge*, after a seven-year interregnum, is an unusual story of cross-channel co-operation. When Granada Television first went on air in 1956, an unusual decision was taken. A major programme on its first evening of transmission was a tribute to the BBC. This did two things. It announced to viewers that Granada intended to be an upmarket, intelligent and aspirational channel. And it flattened the BBC in the ratings.

Several decades later, Michael Jackson was Controller of BBC2 and, as one of the great historians of television culture, had this evening in mind when came up with a piece of belated tit-for-tat commissioning: a themed evening on BBC2 called *Granadaland*, dedicated to Granada's output. It transmitted in 1992, produced out of BBC Manchester.

The *Granadaland* evening was a success, but one of its highlights was a special, one-off edition of *University Challenge*, again presented by Bamber Gascoigne, and produced by Peter Mullings. One team was made up of famous names who had appeared on the show as students: the restaurateur Alistair Little, the television journalist

John Simpson, the comedian and author Stephen Fry, and the editor of the *Daily Telegraph* Charles Moore. They played a team from Keble College, Oxford, who were deemed to be the reigning champions having been the last team to take the trophy beforethe show went into cold storage. The celebrities won, rather convincingly, but the programme's success prompted the question: was there still life in this decades-old format?

The nagging suspicion that there may still have been life in *University Challenge* received some bolstering from an unlikely source – the notorious spoof of the programme in an edition of *The Young Ones* in 1984. The series' four leads of Rik Mayall, Ade Edmondson, Nigel Planer and Christopher Ryan played for Scumbag College against the posh kids of Footlights College, played by Hugh Laurie, Stephen Fry, Emma Thompson and Ben Elton. Griff Rhys Jones played "Bambi" Gascoigne.

In 1994, John Whiston was Controller of Youth and Entertainment Features at BBC Manchester, and had overseen many of BBC2's themed evenings, including the *Granadaland* commission. "My generation had been fanatical about *The Young Ones*, in the same way that preceding generations had been fanatical Monty Python viewers, and later people would be into *The Fast Show*. *The Young Ones'* spoof of *University Challenge* did what an extreme or comedic view sometimes can, and that is to fix in your mind what was so special about the format in the first place."

With an appetite for a return of *University Challenge*, it is perhaps surprising the BBC did not simply acquire the rights and make the programme themselves. Why commission the show from Granada, rather than approach the American licence-holders themselves? "These days, maybe," says John Whiston, who would become the BBC's Commissioning Editor responsible for the programme, "but then it would have been viewed as sharp practice. When we came to make *Granadaland* we had been completely open about what we had in mind. At the time we were also doing *Mrs Merton Show*, and later *The Royle Family*, so there was a good relationship between BBC Manchester and Granada, and to snaffle the rights wouldn't have been the right thing. And also, traditionally, Granada make programmes as cheaply, if not more cheaply, than the BBC, so from an economic point of view it was a sensible decision as well."

With an appetite from the BBC to screen it, and a desire from Granada to make it, various practical questions emerged. How should it look when it came back on screen? Should the format be changed? For John Whiston, the format was sacrosanct. "The notion of the two *University Challenge* U.S.P.s were never in doubt. And these are that one team sits on the heads of the other, and that by answering solo questions you get the right to relaxed questions."

How great was the danger of it appearing elitist? "Well, another big debate was how universal it should be. Was it elitist to restrict it to universities? Should we call it Further Education Challenge? But the relaunch coincided with the universification of the polytechnics. It fitted the zeitgeist, because it focused on entertainment and self-betterment at a time of uncertainty. *University Challenge* is a bastion of certainty. We present incontrovertible facts, posed as questions to nice young people who want to answer them, in a world where elsewhere mobs are raging down the streets with Uzis."

The most important question remained. There was then no other programme in the history of British television which had been so closely associated with one presenter for so long. Bamber Gascoigne and *University Challenge* had always been a perfect combination. Would Bamber want to do it again? And if not him, then who?

Kieran Roberts was the producer charged with the responsibility of the relaunch. "Our first thought was to see if Bamber would come back and do it. We had a few conversations, but they never really went anywhere."

Bamber decided to decline the invitation, because by this point his interests lay elsewhere. While presenting *University Challenge*, he had also been writing several books, including his *Encyclopaedia of Britain*, which came out in 1993. By the time the relaunch was being discussed, he was totally absorbed in a project which would eventually become the *historyworld.com* website. "By the time we had these discussions I was totally hooked on the project. I've never been so hooked on anything in my life – it was dominating my life, and I loved it! At the time I could think of nothing else.

"So the decision to turn down Granada was partly that I was totally hooked on what became *historyworld.com*. But also my wife had become increasingly fed-up with my being recognized, particularly by teenagers, who are very sweet, but in a crowd can be – well…"

"And I had done it for 25 years, which seemed like an awfully long time, and it had taken me a vast amount of time. We used to do two shows a day, and we recorded one day in every fortnight and I used to spend the entire previous day going through and rewriting questions."

After amicable but fruitless discussions, Kieron Roberts was beginning to accept that Bamber would not return to present the show. "I think there was a feeling from Bamber's side that he'd done *University Challenge* but in a different era, and he didn't really want to come into the new era with it. He knew it would be done differently, he knew it would have a subtly different feel, and he knew enough about the recording process to know that the schedule would be fundamentally different. They used to make two shows a fortnight in the early days, and it was all very leisurely and wonderful. TV cannot operate like that anymore. So we very quickly realized it wasn't going to go anywhere. And so we thought: *Who the hell can we find to replace Bamber?*

"Various obvious names of people who present entertainment shows, like Clive Anderson, went into the hat, but nobody was approached. The question was: who was big enough, clever enough and charismatic enough to take on something that is a part of TV legend? When the name Jeremy Paxman came up, everyone thought – that is a *really* good idea. Would he be interested? He was the only person we approached.

"We spoke to his agent, we had a lunch and we sounded him out, and thankfully he was interested. He umm'd and ahh'd for a while, because it was a big departure for him as a distinguished and serious television journalist to take on what is essentially an entertainment format, however cerebral it is. In the end, I think he was sold on three points. First, that we believed in the integrity of the show, and we weren't going to do something cheap and tacky – we weren't going to take it to the lowest common denominator of TV. The fact that it was going on BBC2 rather than one of the two mainstream channels probably helped his thoughts in that regard. Secondly, he recognized that, as television quizzes go, it's got to be the most intelligent, bar none – it really does have that cachet. Thirdly – and this is really important – he just saw the fun of it. Apart from anything else it would just be great fun, and you can see that in the way he plays the game. I think those were the factors that persuaded him – and thankfully, he didn't turn us down. He kept us waiting for a few weeks, quite rightly; he had a very serious think about whether it was a good thing for him to do in terms of his career. We had various meetings with him when he was clearly cautious about what we'd be asking him to do. There was a moment when he asked if we expected him to perform in the way he was portrayed on *Spitting Image*. I remember him asking that and we laughed, and it was then he realized we didn't want a showbusiness performance; we wanted someone who would ask the questions in the right spirit and still be entertaining. One of the reasons we went for him in the first place was that of all the distinguished news journalists, he's the one with the biggest personality. His interviews are not only incisive; they are also oddly entertaining. You remember the famous ones, like the one with Michael Howard in which he asked the same question 14 times, and it was a great piece of entertainment as well as a piece of probing investigation. And then Jeremy realized that was what we wanted to bring to the show – this forensic mind, this lawyer's-type mind, and also that great personality."

As well as a change of direction, it would also entail a great deal of extra work for someone who already presented a current affairs programme three nights a week. "When Jeremy knew he was going to do it," says Bamber, "he rang me up and asked if I had any tips for him. I said that the only tip I had was to spend enough time reading around the question. And he went a bit quiet, and then he said, 'My God! I haven't got time for that!'" The production team now works around Jeremy's other work commitments by sending him the question material several weeks in advance, rather than the day before.

A relaunched *University Challenge* would never slip back into the schedules unnoticed. The first of the new shows got four million viewers – an astoundingly good figure for BBC2 – and an immense amount of press coverage, the great majority of it favourable. But not all, as some journalists questioned the standard of the questions and the brightness of the students answering them, compared to their own memories of the show. As John Whiston says, "It raised all those questions about whether undergraduates had become stupider than before. All I can say is that from my own experience, I couldn't get on to the Balliol team when I was a student, and the Balliol team couldn't get on *University Challenge*, so that gives you some idea of the admiration I had for the people who got on to it. But any notion that the student population has dumbed down is clearly nonsense."

The 2000s

The BBC's request that we make the programme in a widescreen format, rather than the four-by-three ratio it had been made in since 1962, meant it was necessary to redesign the title sequence and the set to take the programme into the new millennium. The new set places the teams in front of a kaleidoscope of mirrors, on to which is projected an animation of slowly morphing images taken from various academic disciplines. As one journalist said, it makes them look like they're sitting in front of a flow of molten lava.

The title music was rearranged by the Balanescu Quartet, an outfit whose work straddles both the classical and the contemporary, and whose previous output has involved taking pieces by popular musicians such as Kraftwerk and David Byrne and rearranging them for string quartet. We thought it might be amusing to ask them what they made of the jaunty, rather old-fashioned *University Challenge* theme. The result is a crisp, witty rearrangement which better reflects the programme's blend of the classical and the contemporary and, we hope, its tongue-in-cheek humour.

University Challenge Reunited

Early in 2002, the *University Challenge* production office received a call from the BBC. Could the team put together an additional series to celebrate the programme's 40th birthday? The format might want to draw on the programme's archive, they suggested. Maybe there would be some mileage in inviting back teams who had played in the past? *And could the new series be ready to transmit in five weeks?*

The answer was "Yes" to the first question. To the second, it was "we'll try". A normal series of *University Challenge* will have a six-month run-up from the start of work on it to the first recordings. Five weeks was an extremely tight turnaround, but in the current climate, no independent programme-maker will turn down a commission.

After a couple of days' research, it became clear that it would be possible to invite back some of the most memorable teams who had ever played on the series, the majority of them being series champions or runners-up. The word "Reunited" was in vogue, thanks to the *Friends Reunited* website, to which Granada's entire workforce appeared to be addicted. So *University Challenge Reunited* became the series' title. The reunited teams, instead of introducing themselves in studio, would appear in short videotapes, in which they would talk about their memories of being on the show, alongside footage and photographs of how they were when they first appeared. To give the series a structure, the top-scoring teams would return to compete in further rounds, and whoever won the final match could call themselves *University Challenge Champion of Champions*.

It sounded fine on paper, but there were problems. The archive of old programmes proved to be very far from complete. Only a few shows from the 1960s and 1970s remained. By the late 1980s, advances in technology had produced broadcast-standard videotape in small and inexpensive formats, so storage space became less of an issue, and more importantly, programme-makers were waking up to the opportunities of exploiting the archive in nostalgia-based programmes.

This was too late for the bulk of *University Challenge*'s old programmes, most of which had been wiped. The list of what had been lost made depressing reading. For every famous face who had appeared on the show, with the exception of Stephen Fry, the tapes had gone. Most infuriatingly, a Parliamentary special from 1972, which had featured Enoch Powell and David Steele as contestants, no longer existed. From the many hundreds of programmes made, the surviving tapes probably numbered no more than a few dozen. Most of the lost material had been transmitted before the advent of home recording, which meant the chances of there being off-air VHS recordings could only help shows from the late 1970s onwards.

In better shape was the photographic archive, which contained a complete record of every team who had ever taken part. The task was to try and track down teams of four people who might or might not still be in touch with each other, for whom there might be no current contact details, who might or might not still be living in the UK, and ask them whether they would like to compete again in a quiz programme.

This presented a major worry: *why would they?* It is one thing to take part in the programme as a student, when you have your career ahead of you. It is quite another to jeopardize the professional reputation you have spent the best part of your working life creating.

Such worries were unfounded. Not only were the teams, in the main, easily traced thanks to sterling work by a number of alumni officers at various universities, but the great majority of players responded to the invitation with a "Yes", or a "What fun".

Beyond a bare half-dozen names, including Clive James, Stephen Fry and John Simpson, the team had no idea what had happened to past contestants, or what kind of a cross-section of the community they might now present. There was a reasonable expectation that they would have done well for themselves, but beyond that the team could only guess.

The result was impressive. A considerable number were acade-

mics, holding lectureships or chairs in various disciplines throughout the UK, and a few now taught on the east coast of America. A
judge, an ambassador, an MP (who probably had the most reason to
feel uncomfortable at the thought of coming up against Paxman),
several people working in government circles, some Sirs and the
Head of the Inland Revenue were among the programme's former
contestants.

But here was another obstacle. Student teams are easy to organize. Give them their call-time, a map of how to get to Manchester,
put them in their Students' Union minibus and the chances are they
will arrive together and more or less on time for their recordings.
Our veteran teams had proper lives, work commitments and family
ties. Often the production office found themselves negotiating with
a team member's diary secretary. Logistically, the problems were
considerable. Could we get a judge back up to Edinburgh for 9.30
on the morning after the recording? ("I'm afraid it's imperative.
They can't start the trial without me.")

A moment of extreme embarrassment occurred when we realized
we had only allocated the series a travel budget on a par with
students' travel, and found ourselves having to explain to Sir
Nicholas Montagu, Head of the Inland Revenue, that he could not
travel to Manchester on any train he chose, because our budget
could only buy him a Saver ticket. We suspected that for some it
would have been the first time they had seen the interior of a
second-class compartment since they first came to play the game.

Other considerations sprang into our minds. Could we still offer
the veteran teams the clean, comfortable but rather basic hotel
accommodation we offered to students? Worse, what about the wine
we served in hospitality? For our student teams, we feel we can offer
a basic beer and a more-or-less serviceable wine, and they do not
complain – in fact, we have to turn a blind eye as they cram
unopened cans and bottles into their bags on departure. And the
members of the production team, who are not officially entitled to
hospitality alcohol, will drink anything. But the fear was that our
veterans would notice that the pinch in our budget is reflected in
the sharpness of Granada's house white wine, which is, the label
proudly announces, "skilfully prepared from grapes".

Comparisons with the old days of the programme were bound to
be made. We had heard stories that in Bamber's day, when having
an independent television franchise was still a licence to print
money, the teams were treated to a banquet after the recording. We

were going to have to hope that the muffins we served at tea-time would be suitably sustaining.

Over the five weeks of pre-production, the series took shape. The tantalizing part of the process would always be tracing three members of a team who were keen to play again, whilst the fourth remained elusive. Sometimes a longshot paid dividends. In tracking down one team member from 1962, we listened to her name and the subject she was studying in her introduction on the show. We typed that information into an Internet search engine, which immediately brought up her current home page.

Another contestant who had eluded us for weeks was tracked down by contacting the subscriptions manager of a specialist magazine dealing with the subject she had studied at university 30 years before. Was she by any chance a subscriber? Yes, she was – and what's more, she worked only a few hundred yards from the production office. Had we known, we could have tracked her down by opening the office window and shouting her name.

A few names escaped us entirely, and short of hiring private detectives we had to admit we had drawn a blank on them. But in the main, the exercise proved that most people keep in touch, even if only indirectly, with the friends they make at university – and most people can be found, wherever they may be.

The series would inevitably put the veteran teams up against some of the more recent champions. It was an opportunity to investigate the claim that *University Challenge* questions had got easier over the years, because students were now less bright. Two troubling possibilities presented themselves. Either the veteran teams would use their extra life experience – up to forty years of it – to put the younger teams to shame, or the younger teams would have faster reactions on the buzzer and so hammer their opponents. We could only wait until we played the matches to find out.

In the event, the matches were extraordinarily close. The senior teams admitted to being slower on the buzzer, and the younger teams confessed to being baffled by questions on Latin. We had proved absolutely nothing at all, except that *University Challenge* teams are very bright. They were then, and they are now.

Gratifyingly, the four teams with the top scores, who would progress to the semi-finals of the contest, all represented different decades: Keele University, from 1969; Sidney Sussex College, Cambridge, from 1979; the Open University team from 1985, and the reigning champions, Somerville College, Oxford, from 2002.

We knew that the final stages of the *Reunited* series were likely to give us impressive matches, and so we deliberately prepared several batches of very tough questions. To no avail – the teams made mincemeat of them. The first semi-final saw a victory for the Keele team over the Open University. In the second, the Sidney Sussex team from 1979 trounced the reigning champions, Somerville, by an amazing 300-point margin, with a performance that resembled an encounter between a steam-roller and a hedgehog. But it was a creditable performance by Somerville, the youngest team in the contest, whose opponents were a generation older. Out of forty years of matches, they had come fourth, and so retired with honour.

With both semi-finals out of the way, the final match of *University Challenge Reunited* would be between the Keele University team from 1969 and the Sidney Sussex College, Cambridge, team from 1979. The teams returned to the studio to wild applause from their supporters in the audience. They settled into their chairs, poured their glasses of water, and positioned their lucky mascots. (On Sidney Sussex's first *Reunited* appearance, Jeremy Paxman noticed that the teams' mascots looked suspiciously similar to those we'd seen in their archive footage. "Which one of you is so sad that you've held on to your mascots for over 20 years?" he asked, incredulously. "That would be me," said the team captain, David Lidington MP, somewhat shame-faced.)

The recording began. "Hello," said Jeremy. "The build-up to tonight's match has taken 40 years…" What followed was the fastest and most impressive display of general knowledge we have ever recorded. The Keele team were excellent, but the Sidney Sussex team were on top of them. Each of the four was as strong as the others, and their team-work was impeccable – on several occasions they answered questions in perfect unison.

Watching the show from the production gallery was our guest Stephen Fry, who would be presenting the trophy to the winners at the end of the recording. Before the recording began we offered him a print-out of the answers to the questions the teams were going to get. "Oh no, thank you," he said politely, "I think I'll play along." And play along he did, calling the correct answer to virtually every question, ahead of the teams in the studio.

We had hoped the *Reunited* series would prove which team was the best out of all those who had taken part since 1962, and all of us watching the match knew that it had. The Sidney Sussex College, Cambridge team, class of 1979, accepted their trophies from

Stephen Fry, and so became the *University Challenge Champion of Champions.*

Perhaps it is worth holding on to lucky mascots.

The future

It's the summer of 2002. Series 31 of *University Challenge* has finished, holding its own in a slot which means it has to compete with the urban angst of *EastEnders* on one channel and the investigative journalism of Trevor Macdonald's team on another.

The *Reunited* series is in the middle of its run of transmissions, and has earned a gratifying level of audience appreciation. We've begun recording series 32.

As far as we can tell in an increasingly volatile industry, the programme will remain on air for a few years yet, and the best way to keep it there seems to be to carry on making the programmes as they have always been made. If it ain't broke, don't fix it. If we stick to that, maybe we'll make our 50th anniversary.

2

The Players

One former Head of State, one former Foreign Secretary and another two senior Tories, a few knighthoods, a couple of ambassadors, a large number of academics, a sprinkling of writers and the voice of the bunny in the Cadbury's Caramel commercials – the *University Challenge* alumni are an accomplished lot.

They represent a decent handful out of the several thousand students who have appeared on the series since 1962, for the majority of whom it will be their only television appearance. But what of those young students destined for great things? Should we expect to be able to look back at their appearance on the programme and find that they shone brighter than their team-mates, marked out with an unmistakable star quality?

Bamber Gascoigne confesses he could not spot those future stars, with the exception of one – Miriam Margolyes, who appeared on *University Challenge* for Newnham College, Cambridge. "She was the one person I found completely intriguing, and one I knew I'd remember if I saw her again. Which of course I did, in countless films." Among those films are *Yentl*, *The Age of Innocence*, for which she received a BAFTA, and *Harry Potter and the Chamber of Secrets*. It was she, of course, who gave us the seductive bunny's voice in the Cadbury's Caramel advertisements, and in 2001 she received an OBE for her services to drama.

Stephen Fry's first television appearance of many was for Queens' College, Cambridge, before he went on to prove himself gifted as a novelist, actor, comedian and director. Nicholas Montagu – now Sir Nicholas – played for New College Oxford in 1964, and has been Head of the Inland Revenue since 1997. Alistair Little played for

Downing College, Cambridge, and later became chef-proprietor of several restaurants in London and Italy, as well as a frequent broadcaster and the author of several books on cooking. In 2002, the historian Dr David Starkey was reported to have signed a deal making him the UK's highest-paid television presenter, ahead even of Cilla Black, although his first appearance will have been for expenses only, as part of the team for Fitzwilliam College, Cambridge, in the late 1960s.

This is how a few of our distinguished alumni remember their appearances on University Challenge.

"Confidence counts for more than anything."

John Simpson is now the BBC's World Affairs editor, and has reported from many of the most significant scenes of recent history, from the liberation of Kabul and the fall of the Berlin Wall to the release of Nelson Mandela and the massacre in Tiananmen Square.

For the youthful Simpson, playing *University Challenge* for Magdalene College, Cambridge was a turning-point. "I was bewildered at first by all the lights, the cables, the shouting of the floor manager, the jargon everyone used, the make-up artists, the extraordinary attention we got. I'm slightly ashamed now to say that I rather liked it. I felt I could understand the point of it all, too; and the voice of the tempter inside my head kept saying to me, 'A job like this would suit you very nicely.' Until that point – I was 21 – I had always thought I would follow a career in newspapers; from then on I felt that television was to be the thing. So *University Challenge*, in a very real sense, started me off in the direction I was to follow."

And yet this significant moment came about in an almost accidental manner. "Magdalene, my college, was a very unworldly place in those days: worse even than the rest of Cambridge," says Simpson. "Someone just pinned up a small hand-written notice on a board, which said that anyone interested in representing the college on *University Challenge* should write their name underneath; only there weren't any names. A close friend of mine who was with me said I should put mine down, and I did. About a month later someone dropped me a line to say that since there had been only four volunteers altogether, we were all automatically selected. By chance we had most of the main areas of questioning covered between us. So that was it.

"Forty years later I have forgotten virtually everything of the preparations. I just remember the suit I wore, because I bought it for the occasion – a kind of greenish tweed affair that must have made me look as if I was up in town from the pig-farm. It was the only suit I owned, and I wore it till it fell to pieces, thus adding to the country bumpkin impression. But there was no question in my mind that I should wear a suit and tie to appear on television, and I think everyone else who took part wore a suit and tie as well. Times, I've noticed, have changed.

"I found Bamber then, as now, charming, humorous, and – for someone who was only a few years older than us, but had well and truly made it in the great world – amazingly nice to a group of callow, spotty 20-year-olds. My Magdalene colleagues and I had a particular link with him, because he had been there, too, and the don who was my supervisor, the superb and much-missed Arthur Sale, had taught him. Bamber's career was a revelation to me in another way, since it showed you could be an intellectual and still get on in television. At this time, a lot of older people still regarded television as a major element in the general mind-numbing of society, and Bamber was proof that it didn't have to be that at all."

To begin with, John Simpson seems to have been something of a quiz natural. "Something very unusual came over me in the first round: I shone. Afterwards, when I saw the recording, I found I had answered 70 per cent of all the questions in that entire edition of the programme and, I think, got them all right. In the second round I still answered most of the questions, but now it was about 55 per cent, and I got one or two of them wrong. Then reality re-established itself. The questions in the next round seemed harder, and I made more mistakes. Finally, we crashed completely, losing in the semi-finals to a small Welsh theological college. It served me right for getting ideas above my station.

"I only remember one question, which I had no idea about, but got right. That's what seems to happen when you're really on a roll. It came early on in the first round; Bamber asked what advice we would have given to the citizens of London in, I think, 1763, if we'd heard that Casanova was in town. I had my finger on the buzzer and pressed it by accident – sheer nerves. Someone said in a terrifyingly loud voice 'Magdalene, Simpson,' and I felt the camera creeping in on my face and the mocking eyes of the nation watching me. My mind was a complete blank, but my mouth seemed to be working because it said 'Lock Up Your Daughters'. I've no idea why. This was the title of quite a well-known musical in London at the time, but I hadn't seen it and didn't even know what it was about. Anyway, I was right: that was the answer. It taught me an important lesson about life: bullshit does indeed baffle brains, and confidence counts for more than almost anything else. Whether that was meant to be the purpose of *University Challenge*, though, I rather doubt."

"Boy, did we lose. And it was my fault."

Novelist, journalist, critic, television presenter – the multi-talented Clive James was president of the Footlights during his time at Cambridge, and captained the Pembroke College team. "You have to realize that in those days the whole country watched every episode of *University Challenge*. They watched it in working men's clubs. The Queen Mother watched it, knuckles white, running to the telephone to place bets. If you were on television in prime-time, the whole population of the country was looking through the same small window right into your face." His team's first appearance was against the women of St Hilda's College, Oxford. "I'm sorry to say we creamed them."

Ably supported by a "walking, shouting encyclopaedia" of an American student called Chuck Beaurepaire, James' team then faced another Oxford college – Balliol. "Boy, did we lose. And it was my fault. The Balliol blokes knew more than the St Hilda's team and they were a lot quicker at hitting the buzzer. Their captain was practically a psychic. The two teams were dead even when it came to the last question, which was about music. I heard two bars and knew it was Verdi. I heard four bars and knew it was *Otello*. I hit the button whilst the Balliol captain's overdeveloped thumb was still in the air. Beaurepaire hit the button, too, but the answer was already out of my mouth. '*Otello*,' I shouted. 'It's *Don Carlos*,' shouted Beaurepaire, louder. Louder, but too late. Bamber wrapped it up. 'It was Don Carlos... Clive James should have waited. Congratulations, though, Pembroke, on being such close losers...' I think I bore up reasonably well. I was told subsequently – I am still told today by anyone I meet over the age of 40 – that the tears which I thought were jetting from my eyes merely made them shine, and that if it had not been for my mouth, which went all square like a baby ready to howl, nobody would have known that my world had collapsed."

"We were *not* the four brightest"

Several prominent politicians went through the *Challenge* process as undergraduates. David Mellor played for Christ's College, Cambridge, and later held the Putney seat for 18 years, serving as Chief Secretary to the Treasury and Secretary of State for National Heritage. David Lidington played for Sidney Sussex, Cambridge, in 1979, and became the Member for Aylesbury in 1992. He was Parliamentary Private Secretary to William Hague from 1997 to 1999, and in May 2002, shortly after he recorded his first of three appearances on *University Challenge Reunited*, he joined the Shadow Cabinet as Shadow Minister for Agriculture and Fisheries. Mary Robinson played for Trinity College, Dublin, and was appointed Professor of Law there in 1969, the same year she was elected to the Irish Senate. She became Ireland's first woman President in 1990, and in 1997 became the second person to hold the post of UN High Commissioner for Human Rights.

Sir Malcolm Rifkind's appearance was for Edinburgh University. The Conservative member for Edinburgh Pentlands for 23 years, he was Secretary of State for Scotland, for Transport, and for Defence, and became Foreign Secretary in 1995. He was knighted in John Major's resignation honours list, and the following year was elected President of the Scottish Conservatives.

"*University Challenge* was my first appearance in a TV studio, and it turned out to be useful experience for the hundreds of times I have had to make such an appearance since. Bamber Gascoigne was charming, and able to put one at one's ease – the whole atmosphere was of a rather dotty and charming academic exchange, compared to the rather frenetic Paxman style.

"The team were certainly not the four brightest undergraduates at Edinburgh!" he confesses. "The selection process was pretty amateur: I seem to recollect that about a dozen people had applied to be considered. We all had to answer questions at a fairly public meeting in the Union hall, and the four of us deemed to be the best were chosen. I think they might have been trying to choose a wide spectrum of experience and that my own choice reflected my interest in current affairs, politics and the like.

"In the first round, we were competing against an Oxbridge ladies' college. In the practice round we lost heavily and were despondent about our prospects before the real programme began. There was a two-hour break, and we were encouraged to get some fresh air and relaxation. We went to a local pub and probably consumed a little more than was good for us. The unexpected effect, however, was that we lost our nervousness and inhibitions. This made us slightly reckless, and much quicker on the buzzer. In the event we won the match, to the ladies' consternation and our amazement.

"My own performance was unmemorable, apart from one particular question. The teams were asked with which countries Senegal shared a border. Remembering that Senegal almost entirely surrounds Gambia I asked, rather precociously, whether the question referred to internal or external borders. I then rolled out the names of the five countries that border Senegal, to the amazement of my team colleagues and the cheers of the studio audience. Unknown to them, I had been fascinated by political maps for several years and had a pretty good mental picture of what the world looked like. This was a valuable talent for a future foreign secretary, but was the full extent of my *University Challenge* triumph!"

How would Sir Malcolm expect to fare if he was on the programme now? "The questioning seemed tough at the time, but, in retrospect, the questions were easier than they appear to be now. Either that or my brain cells have deteriorated in the meantime!"

"The great thing was we could smoke."

Sebastian Faulks played for Emmanuel College, Cambridge. He has since written for the *Daily* and *Sunday Telegraph*, and has been Literary and Deputy Editor of *The Independent* and a columnist for *The Guardian*. His novels include *The Girl at the Lion d'Or*, *Birdsong* and *Charlotte Grey*, the latter being filmed in 2001 with Cate Blanchett in the title role.

"At that age – 18 or 19 – your worldly knowledge is very small, but your speed of recall – of such few data as you have captured – is phenomenal. It is like a super-broadband connection to a fairly empty site. Today, the site is full, but access is via an old hand-operated exchange where it's usually lunchtime."

Our alumni's experiences make it clear that whilst some teams are put together by a carefully-constructed selection procedure run on scientific principles, the haphazard approach is much more common. "It was very unscientific," he recalls. "My friend Ian mentioned my name to another friend, Dave, who was secretary of the JCR, and he and I were both interested in girls in the same house. Maybe Ian was too. I bought Dave a couple of pints of Double Diamond, he asked me some old questions, and I was in.

"I remember very little of the studio, although I remember being being surprised that the teams did not sit one on top of the other, as per the broadcast. I was very nervous, and had drunk three bottles of barley wine before going on. The great thing was that we were allowed to smoke! I must have got through a packet of Number Six in the course of the programme. My parents were appalled!

"We had driven to Manchester in a car belonging to John Cole, a postgraduate classical archaeologist. He was the ancient world specialist. We had a scientist called Laurie, and my friend Ian Black, who was history and politics. 'And what's your strength?' they asked me. I knew nothing. I never even read the papers. 'Er... I played golf for the college last week,' I said. The very first starter began, 'In the game of golf...' and I got it.

"The questions seemed to be mostly about science – no good for me – and Scottish geography, which was great for our opponents, Glasgow University, who won easily. I got a few answers, though, and started interrupting Bamber, trying to answer everything, even questions on chemistry, which I had failed at 'O' level. I remember a film question in which we had to guess the title from a picture. We were shown a large bowl of soft, white, gruel-like food. Ian Black buzzed in and answered '*One Day in the Life of Ivan Denisovitch.*' It was obviously mashed potato, so the answer was *M*A*S*H*.

"Bamber was the first famous person I had met and I was surprised he was so normal. He laughed and talked and smiled and drank wine just like a normal person. How cool was that? It was incredibly good fun – that's what I really remember."

What conclusions can we draw from this varied bag of achievement? It's no great surprise that veterans of the Cambridge Footlights should feature prominently – Miriam Margolyes, Clive James, Stephen Fry – nor that a few of the many who study Politics, Philosophy and Economics should wind up in Parliament, although it does seem odd that of the three who entered the House of Commons, all of them are Tories. (Is the show less popular with those to the left of centre?) Success on the show demands one be able to pull obscure pieces of information out of the back of the mind at short notice, which will suit the polymaths such as Clive James and Stephen Fry. The list does not include any scientists, which may simply be because the programme is still under-representative of the sciences, or because it's much harder to hit the headlines or get yourself a television series if you are a scientist, rather than someone who can make audiences laugh. If there are *University Challenge* alumni out there with achievements in the sciences that we should know about, please do get in touch with the production office.

We look forward with interest to seeing where some of the more recent contestants will wind up in the years to come.

The Teams

Who, after forty years, is winning *University Challenge?* The answer is that the Oxford colleges have between them notched up eleven series titles, putting them far ahead of all the others. The Cambridge colleges follow, with six victories. The University of London has won twice, with a team from Imperial College in each case. The other double winners are the Open University, Sussex and Durham.

Of course, the universities of Oxford, Cambridge, London and Wales are allowed to enter from their constituent colleges, so we might expect them to feature heavily in the list of winners. If we count the Oxbridge colleges as individual entities, then for Cambridge, Sidney Sussex College and Trinity College have taken the trophy twice. For Oxford, University College, Keble and Magdalen have all done a double, the latter being the only team ever to hang on to the trophy with a second consecutive win. The great prize which remains unclaimed, and for which we have high expectations as we go into another series, is for the team which can take the trophy for a third time.

The rule which allows Oxford and Cambridge to enter as individual colleges remains controversial for some viewers. In fact, some viewers hate it, and see it as the programme having a bias towards those institutions. The accusation of bias always puzzles the production team, among whom Oxbridge graduates are only ever an occasional minority. Why, they ask, would a team of Manchester-based people, most of whom are graduates of northern redbrick universities, want to try and arrange the programme in order to favour Oxbridge colleges? Jeremy Paxman is currently the only Oxbridge graduate on the team, and he takes no part in the selection of the competitors. There is no bias – and it seems significant that the same argument is not levelled at the Universities of London and Wales, who are also allowed to enter as individual colleges. Certainly when the series began in 1962, if those universities had not been allowed to enter their colleges on an individual basis, there would not have been enough teams to make a long-running series, so there is the practical aspect of trying to make a television series out of an archaic university system which has evolved over many centuries. We retain the rule because it seems right that these colleges, which operate as broadly autonomous teaching institutions, should continue to appear as separate entities.

A strange statistic is that only three times has the series title gone to an institution outside England, when teams from Queens' Belfast, St Andrews and Dundee won successively from 1982 to '84. Although teams from England, Scotland and Northern Ireland have taken the title, no Welsh institution has yet done so.

The gender mix of successful teams reveals a distinct male bias. When the programme started in 1962, the student population was overwhelmingly male. Now the balance has shifted, and there are slightly more women students than men. Not that you would ever think it, if you watch the programme regularly; all-male teams frequently dominate the series, and no all-women team has ever been series champion, although we very often see outstanding women players. As the only regular programme offering a window on the student population, we are uneasy about presenting it as something inherently male, an impression compounded by having a male presenter and male voice-over artist. On the occasions when the series final – which naturally attracts more attention – is a contest between two teams of four blokes, we invariably wonder what kind of message we are sending out about the people in higher education.

The programme is not going to be able to answer the question of why this should be. There are a large number of theories about this state of affairs, most of them highly unscientific. There is a suggestion that women simply have better things to do with their time than take part in anything as trivial as a general knowledge quiz; that quizzing speaks to some inherently spotty, geeky part of the male psyche; that winning, and being seen to win, is an inbred male compulsion. We have decided we will not discriminate positively on behalf of female teams; all teams get on the series because they are good at general knowledge questions, and for no other reason. But we do plead with our applying universities to try and provide a team that genuinely reflects its gender composition. Some teams have realized that women seem to make very good captains, especially if there is only one woman on a team with three men. We admit it –

the gender balance on the programme is hopelessly unrepresentative of the true number of women in higher education. We are working on it – but it will only really change when we can persuade more women to apply.

Below are the series champions so far, listed in the order in which they won, and against the year in which their winning show was transmitted.

1963	Leicester
1964	New College, Oxford
1966	Oriel College, Oxford
1968	Sussex
1969	Keele
1970	Sussex
1971	Churchill College, Cambridge
1972	Sidney Sussex College, Cambridge
1973	University College, Oxford
1974	Fitzwilliam College, Cambridge
1975	Trinity College, Cambridge
1976	Keble College, Oxford
1977	University College, Oxford
1978	Durham
1979	Sidney Sussex College, Cambridge
1980	Bradford
1981	Merton College, Oxford
1982	Queen's, Belfast
1983	St Andrews
1984	Dundee
1985	Open University
1986	Jesus College, Oxford
1987	Keble College, Oxford
1995	Trinity College, Cambridge
1996	Imperial College, London
1997	Magdalen College, Oxford
1998	Magdalen College, Oxford
1999	Open University
2000	Durham
2001	Imperial College, London
2002	Somerville College, Oxford

3

The Best Moments – and the Worst

Over forty years, we have seen some astonishingly impressive teams; young people who seem to know virtually everything, with an erudition way beyond their years, who can interrupt questions with an accuracy which borders on the psychic, and leave us breathless with their knowledge and charm. These are the teams who can tell us at the drop of a hat that the smallest number which can be expressed as the sum of two cubes in two different ways is 1,729. (The answer: $1^3 + 12^3$, and $9^3 + 10^3$, of course.)

And then there are the others. The teams who stare into the camera with the sad, blank, uncomprehending gaze of a hedgehog about to experience an articulated lorry. The teams who discover they have left all their splendid general knowledge back in the dressing room with their coats and bags. The teams who discuss bonus sets by talking themselves away from the correct answer. The teams who see their scores sink slowly into the minuses as their opponents romp into three figures. The teams who cannot remember their own names, or what they are studying, or where they are from.

It would be gratifying to report that *University Challenge* has maintained an impeccable archive of the full forty years of every teams' exploits, good or bad, with a complete list of all their names, all their scores, and tapes of all their programmes. Gratifying, but wide of the mark.

Picture instead a few mouldering, slightly damp manila box files, each one containing a seemingly random collection of papers: a few pages of contact details for students who graduated decades ago, and a very paltry number of complete programmes remaining out of the many hundreds recorded over the years.

Television archiving became big business in the mid-1980s, and archive-based programmes now dominate the schedules on several channels, but this sea-change came about too late to save hundreds of episodes of *University Challenge*, which have been wiped, taped over or have otherwise vanished into the ether. Who on earth, the argument ran, would want to see an episode of a quiz programme again? And who can afford to keep a complete archive of programmes on such an expensive and bulky medium as a videotape?

To produce any statistics on the show, we have been reliant on what scraps of the archive do remain, and the memories of those people involved in making the programme at the time.

Another factor which makes it hard to compare the students of Bamber's era with those of Jeremy's is that in former times, the rules allowed a varying number of points to be scored on bonus questions, and a team might compete on up to a dozen or so occasions, whereas under the current regime, the two teams who make it through to the final will have appeared only five times. In Bamber's era, as well, the questions tended to be shorter, so teams heard more of them in each programme' – although we feel the pace of Jeremy's delivery goes some way to compensating for that.

So with what little of the archive remains, we can announce with a reasonable degree of certainty, and a fanfare of trumpets, that the highest score ever achieved on *University Challenge* was University College, Oxford's 520 points against Reading in 1987.

The team to score most impressively under Jeremy was the Open University team in the 1996–97 series. Two of that team's scores remain the highest in the series since Jeremy took over the chair. Their score of 415 points against Charing Cross Hospital's 65 has yet to be beaten. The losing team, instead of waving goodbye at the end of the programme, mimed firing pistols into their heads. This was an endearing, but unnecessarily self-deprecating gesture, from a team of four medics who had done extremely well to get as far as the semi-final, and who found themselves up against an Open team considerably their senior. This Open team had attracted considerable press for themselves with the inclusion of Ida Staples who, at the age of 72, was the most senior person to have entered the competition under Jeremy.

The same Open team, in the same series, scored 395 against the 85 points notched up by a team from Swansea; newspaper reports the following day had some unkind fun at the expense of a Swansea student with the surname Thick. By the time the Open team reached the final, there was a rumble of grumbling from some viewers that it was unfair to allow them to compete against student teams so many years their junior. One viewer, on seeing the Open team qualify for the final, wrote to say that she refused to watch the final match because it was clearly a foregone conclusion. In the event, the Open team did not take the title, but were beaten in the final by a young, state-educated team from Magdalen College, Oxford, whose scores had been consistently impressive, but not unusually high, throughout their earlier matches. Both working on *University Challenge,* and watching it, proves that the results are never a foregone conclusion.

With the top two scores occupied by the Open University, third place goes to the team from Trinity College, Cambridge, who scored 390 against New College, Oxford's 180 in the final match of the first series under Jeremy. Even so, Trinity had only just scraped their way into the final, beating an excellent Aberdeen team on a tie-break question.

As for low scores, there are various reasons why teams do not do themselves justice on the programme. Every team qualifies to appear on the same basis, which is having done well in the test paper, so nerves and bad luck are probably higher on the list of reasons for failure than simply not knowing the answers. In the Paxman era, a score of 40 points has become a sticking-point for several teams, who can get that far and no further – much to the glee of newspaper reports the authors of which, one suspects, would be hard pressed to do any better. Birkbeck College, London, in the 1996 series, Oxford Brookes the following year, and St Andrews University in 2001 are among those who got no more than 40. In 1997, four women from New Hall, Cambridge, went one better – or worse – by getting only 35. The only consolation the programme can offer to those who don't do themselves justice is that it is the one way of generating even more media attention than you get for winning. Remember, it's only a quiz programme; take it on the chin and smile for the cameras.

In the early years of the programme, the record for the lowest score was held not by a student team but by four dons from New College, Oxford. In 1964, they took part in a special match against their own students, who were the reigning champions. The Dons' team included the distinguished philosopher AJ Ayer, but they could only manage to get 50 points on the board, whilst their students were 200 points ahead of them at the final gong. Director Peter Mullings remembers the debâcle well. "The Dons would hear the question, and they would say to themselves, 'This is what the question is asking.' Then they would think, 'This is what the answer is. Let us press a buzzer, and then we will say the answer,' not realizing that by the time they'd done this the other team had already answered and were half-way through their bonuses." Although this probably wasn't what A.J. Ayer had in mind when he wrote *The Problem of Knowledge*, his abject failure on that occasion should offer some comfort to student teams who don't do themselves justice in the current era.

The all-time lowest score? It was earned by Sussex University in 1972. In those days there was a rule, later abandoned, that a winning institution could not submit a team for the following year's contest. Sussex had won in 1968 and so rested for a year, and returned in 1970 to become series champions again – the first institution to do the double. After a further fallow year, they returned in 1972 hoping to make it a hat-trick. Their score on that occasion was a mere ten points.

The Howlers

"Here's another starter for ten," says Jeremy, picking up his next card and reading from it. "Thuma, towcher, long-man, lech-man and little-man are Old and Middle English names for…"

BUZZ

"The penis!" comes the answer.

Jeremy cracks up. "You're a medical student! How many penises do they teach you we have these days? They are old names for the *fingers*. Right, here's another starter.

"The nicknames 'Cheesemongers', 'Cherry-pickers', 'Bob's Own', 'The Emperor's Chambermaids', and 'The Immortals' are or have been used for which groups of men?"

BUZZ

"Homosexuals!" we hear in disbelief. Jeremy nearly throws his card in the air. "*No!* They are regiments in the British army, and they're going to be *very* cross with you," he tells the unfortunate student.

Lest this be taken as an indication that students have become more stupid as the years roll on, let's recall a moment from the Bamber era.

"What name is given to the Roman road that stretches from London to York?"

BUZZ

"The Yellow Brick Road," offers some unfortunate munchkin.

It is so easily done. We deliberately place our students under pressure, deny them time to think slowly and clearly, and then hoot with laughter when they come out with something unfortunate. With no time at all to think, it may have seemed reasonable that our programme would consider listing derogatory terms for homosexuals as suitable subject matter for a question, but the answer is out of your mouth before you can think, and the next day your unfortunate response is reported in *The Sun*, in all its glorious idiocy.

Regrettably, students are not the only ones who can come out with howlers on the programme, and fair play demands that the production team own up to their own. Students are forgiven their lapses – but we don't forgive ourselves those we make ourselves. After all, we are paid to be right about everything.

One of *University Challenge*'s most famous howlers started out looking like a students' blunder – but it became clear that the blunder may have been ours.

New Hall College, Cambridge, has a somewhat chequered history on the programme. As one of the few remaining all-women colleges, we are always pleased when they make it on to the series because they provide a relief from the inevitable teams of four men. But because the all-women teams are unusual, their successes or failures are all the more conspicuous. The New Hall team of 1997 was famously responsible for the worst-ever score on the programme since Jeremy took over – all of 35 points – a defeat they took with remarkable good cheer. Naturally, the four who followed them in the next season's contest were determined to make a good showing.

We arrived at a picture round, and showed them one of Britain's tourist signs. Jeremy asked, "For ten points, simply tell me what it is." Imperial College, London incorrectly identified it as the symbol for a National Park. Jeremy offered it to the New Hall team. New Hall's contestant, a young woman called Wilson, buzzed in. "It's an oak leaf." There's laughter from the audience and Jeremy snorts in disgust. "Anyone can *see* it's an oak leaf! I was asking what it *was*."

But Wilson is not deterred. She does something no one else has ever dared, something unthinkable. *She answers back.* "You asked me what it *was*. You said 'What is it?', not 'What is it for?' You said, 'What *is* it?" (The sound crew would normally have turned a contestant's microphone down after an incorrect answer. Wilson's is kept at full throttle.) Jeremy comes back at her. "Your opponent almost gave you the answer, which is The National Trust. So we'll take the picture round when someone gets a starter right…"

But Wilson has got the bit between her teeth. "You should have said 'What is it for?', not 'What is it?'!" There's more laughter from the audience. They're loving it. Jeremy replies: "It is a *sign, signifying* the National Trust. I told you it was a tourist *sign.*" Then there's brief mellowing. "Actually on a point of pedantry, you may be right. But there you are. Bad luck! We'll take another starter question, and when someone gets it right, you'll get the rest of the picture bonuses."

The game continues, there's a correct starter and we're finally back on the rest of the tourist sign questions. They've gone not to New Hall, but to their opponents Imperial College. Imperial get the symbol for a country park wrong, but get the English Heritage symbol right, "although," Jeremy can't resist adding, "to New Hall it's probably a square with bits coming off it." New Hall's microphones are turned off as their opponents are answering the questions. Imperial get the last bonus, which they identify as the sign for an exhibition farm. "No, that's not specific enough; it's the sign for an agricultural museum – or, to New Hall, it's a cart! Right, three minutes to go, another starter question…"

After the recording, Jeremy approached me in hospitality, knowing that I would be taking the show into the edit suite. "That stuff with the New Hall women – you're going to keep it all in, aren't you?" I nod. "Good. I thought they were terrific."

After the show goes out, Wilson is voted *Woman's Hours'* "Woman of the Week" for standing up to Paxman, which probably makes it one-all in their spat. The only real loser is the idiotic producer who really should have known better than to word a question with something as vague as "What is it?"

It is imperative for a quiz programme to avoid vaguely-worded questions, or questions with the slightest degree of ambiguity. Any opportunity for too literal an interpretation of the question can also cause problems. Bamber recalls a question which caught him out. "The question asked, 'What have all the following got in common?' and proceeded to give a list of names. There was a short pause, and then a contestant buzzed in and said, 'I haven't heard of any of them'. And I gave him ten points – and I didn't regret it. And we never again used the formula 'What have the following got in common', without some qualification."

In 2001, the team from St Andrews University failed to acquit themselves as well as they should have done – in fact they crashed and burned with a miserable 40-point score. This low score was extensively reported in many papers, presumably because it gave picture editors a chance to run a photo of the teams' fellow-student, Prince William. But however badly the St Andrews team felt, can it compare with the production team's realization that we had made them play under the name *St Andrew's* – with a stray apostrophe not used by the university? What compounded the error was that it was not spotted by the programme's producer, who is a graduate of – no, we'll spare his blushes, but it's a small university on the Fife coast.

The most contentious decision? It's the final of the 1999 series. The Open University are against Oriel College, Oxford. We ask a starter question, not especially difficult, about a book of the Old Testament, for which we expect to hear the name "Ecclesiastes". A contestant on the Open team buzzes and answers "Ecclesiast*icus*". Has he got the right book, and is merely slipping on the final sylla- ble, in which case we would reckon he deserves his points? Or is he really making a mistake? Earlier in the same show we gave a very harsh judgement against the same contestant for answering too circuitously. We have to look fair, as well as be fair. In the back of my head I'm vaguely aware of "Ecclesiasticus" in another context, but my ignorance is my stumbling-block. Wishing, for the only time in my life, that my parents had sent me to Sunday School, I realize an entire second has passed since we heard the answer, and it's time I made a decision. "Accept it," I tell Jeremy. "It's *Ecclesiastes*," Jeremy stresses, "but I'll accept it."

On the morning following the programme's transmission, the BBC's Duty Log reports a record 50 phone-calls of complaint. It's so unusual that I'm alerted to it first thing in the morning by the BBC. Each caller is pointing out the same thing: that "Ecclesiasticus" is the name of a book in the Apocrypha. In giving us his answer, the contestant had either got the wrong book – in which he didn't deserve his points – or he had the right book in his head, but in trying to answer had inadvertently named another book, in which case the adjudication is deeply contentious. I reflect, but stick to my guns. We reward positive achievement. As a member of the Open University team, the contestant was older than the average team member. Had he been of the average *University Challenge* age, I would have had no hesitation in giving him his points, with Jeremy correcting the error. Because he was older, and clearly an extremely well-informed player, should we have expected more from him?

I have to deal with Frazer Steele, who acts as a kind of Torquemada on the BBC's behalf to producers who stand accused of error. By a fortunate coincidence, he's also a veteran of the show, having captained the Pembroke College, Cambridge team in 1970, and he is sympathetic. It's clear the decision could not have made a difference to the outcome of the show, and the Open team did indeed take that series trophy. He regrets the decision, but accepts that we need to make split-second adjudications. We live to fight another day.

Ad-libs can also land us in hot water. One question on Queen Victoria prompted Jeremy to refer to her as "an old trout". Who would have thought she would still have so many fans out there, prepared to write outraged letters attesting to her non-troutiness?

A question on a newspaper report which claimed that Sir Winston Churchill had a penchant for buying ladies' underwear brought a mailbag which suggested the programme's producer and presenter should spend some time in the Tower.

"There were 15 of them in 1982, and now there are over 2,500. What are they?" asks Jeremy. "Wind turbines," offers a contestant, not unreasonably. "Well, only in a manner of speaking," says Jeremy. "They are actually women priests."

Foul Play

No teams ever cheat on *University Challenge*. For a start, it's virtually impossible, because you either know an answer or you don't, but more to the point, it's clearly just not in the nature of the kind of people who want to take part.

This doesn't mean that dodgy practices never occur, some of them out of the watchful sight of the production office. Although many of the teams will meet each other when they arrive at Granada for the recordings, some will have met up the night before in a local hotel. Plenty of opportunity, then, for sizing up the opposition, not only to assess whether they're good at general knowledge or not, but also to find out whether they can drink. And if, perhaps, they can't… the all-male Oriel team of 1966 remembers meeting the all-female team from St Hilda's in the hotel before the recording. "They took us out to a disco and got us *very* drunk. I have no doubt this impacted on our performance the next day."

Attitudes to drink have changed over the years. In the Bamber days, students were positively encouraged to have a couple of glasses "to loosen them up", and it was common practice for students to spend a couple of hours in the pub between the rehearsal and the recording. This is now prohibited under stringent health and safety regulations, which forbid people under the influence from entering a television studio packed full of expensive camera equipment, with a floor dense with cables waiting to be tripped over. The prohibition naturally extends to other recreational substances, although once outside the studio, such activities can be hard to monitor. One recording day, we were surprised to find that every single team member was turning up at the studio looking extremely tired, and all of them were clearly in a filthy mood. It transpired that their hotel had had to be evacuated several times during the previous night, after an excessive amount of dope fumes had repeatedly set off the fire alarm. The production office felt obliged to change hotels for the next recording.

We can also get into hot water when a students' language fails to fit in with the standards laid down by the BBC for a pre-watershed transmission. The aim is to record the programme in one continuous "take", because it then feels more like a live event, the students enjoy it more, and Jeremy is better able to pace his delivery than if we stop and start in the manner of most entertainment recordings. This creates a very genuine tension on the studio floor, and sometimes the students forget themselves, as did one on a narrowly losing team, who threw his head back and yelled, "Oh, shit!" when he heard the sound of the gong. Moments like these are very difficult to restage, and we usually won't even try. When we get to the edit, we'll take the sound off, replace it with an appropriate amount of applause, and hope no one watching can lip-read. But we have found to our cost that if there's one thing *The Sun*'s journalists are especially good at, it's lip-reading. It's always the *The Sun* – never any other newspaper, never any of our viewers – who manage to spot these slips. Do they get special training? At least we know they are watching the show and paying minute attention. Kwasi Kwarteng, who played for the Trinity College, Cambridge team in 1994, was the first in the modern era to be caught out.

"Ah! The swearing! Well, it was done very, very quietly."

Jeremy has asked his team a bonus question: "Whose description of a tour with a donkey, Modestine, in *Travels with a Donkey in the Cevennes*, was published in 1879?"

Kwasi and team captain Robin Battacharyya go into a huddle. "De Maupassant," Kwasi offers him. Robin is about to give that as the answer, but Kwasi stops suddenly stops him. He seems deep in thought. Here a *Sun* reporter with the ears of a bat detected him muttering "Oh f***, f***" under his breath. He comes up with the answer Daudet.

"Bad luck. It's Robert Louis Stevenson," says Jeremy. Further bad luck for Kwasi when his slip is reported on page three of *The Sun* under the headline "Rudiversity Challenge". "My friends thought it was very funny. But my mother *wasn't* amused."

Current technology allows such a slip to be edited out of the show in a matter of minutes. If it has been spotted during the recording of the show, the guilty party can be asked to repeat his or her moment without the offending word, if it hasn't come at a crucial stage of the recording. But in the early days of videotape, such an edit was a lengthy and extremely difficult process, involving painting the tape with oxide to reveal the magnetic track, slicing it to within a thousandth of an inch with a razor blade and patching it with non-magnetic tape. One such edit would take half a day. Much better, then, to try and disguise an expletive in studio. Peter Mullings remembers an occasion when a student, searching for the name of a German composer, leaned back in his chair and muttered, "Oh, shit!" Bamber responded, "No, it's not *Schmidt*" so blithely that every viewer thought that was what they had heard, too.

With editing so much harder and slower in the earlier days of television, it was far more imperative that shows should run smoothly in the studio. Under Bamber's regime, the programme was recorded in one take on all but a handful of occasions. "One of them was the explosion of one of the lights, a large five-kilowatt "bubble" which had been set high above one of the students' desks, which showered all four of them with hot glass, setting their pullovers alight. It was one of the very few occasions when we actually had to stop the recording," Peter Mullings reflects.

"Another was when a student took our invitation to have a couple of glasses before the recording a bit too enthusiastically, and he fell asleep during the show."

Yet another occasion, this time when Jeremy was in the chair, saw a student faint during the recording. Having pitched forward dramatically onto her desk, the recording was halted and she was helped off the set and taken to Granada's medical centre. We were left with something of a hiatus. Clearly the game could not continue with one team only having three players. We could ask that team to play their reserve and re-stage the entire game, but this would have been unfair to the other team, who had notched up an unassailable lead by the time of the faint. We could play the reserve team member only for the remaining three minutes, but this would look decidedly odd to our home audience. Or... having determined our ill team member was in no fit state to continue playing, and with her agreement, we decided we would indeed carry on the game with only three members on that team. Even by the most generous calculations, they could not have won in the couple of minutes remaining. When the show came to the edit suite we did a "cut and paste", editing the missing contestant back in by "boxing" the shot of her seated at the desk in the early stages of the show, and dropping that box on to her empty place in the later shots. It all looked fine to us – the only give-away was that in the final shot she wasn't waving but simply staring at the camera. We thought we had got away with it, except that the BBC's Press Office decided it made an amusing story, and sent a press release on it to every newspaper in the land.

Whether it counts as foul play or not, the prize for the most shameless piece of self-promotion must go to the team from Dundee, who were series champions in 1984. Team introductions have always followed the same pattern. The camera pans down the team from left to right, and each player in turn gives their name, home town, and what they are reading. Team member Graham Davidson took full advantage of this by announcing that he was "reading that delightful Christmas gift for the discerning reader, *Blairgowrie and Rattray in Old Picture Postcards*", flourishing a copy of the volume at the camera. Its author, needless to say, was one Graham Davidson of Dundee. On the second occasion he did this, Bamber pointed out that despite his shameless plugging, the book clearly had not sold a tiny edition, which was bad news for the power of advertising on ITV. The Dundee team, having been series champions, were invited to play in a special match against their own Dons, to whom Bamber wittily addressed the question: "Who is the author of that delightful volume *Blairgowrie and Rattray in Old Picture Postcards*?" Even after much discussion, the Dundee Dons could only guess at the answer: "McGonagall?"

How they look

It's stating the obvious: the whole point of *University Challenge* is that you do well by proving yourself to be brainy. So it's deeply ironic that the team which attracted the most attention in the programme's history were noticed because of their looks.

The team from St Hilda's College, Oxford became, in 1965, the first all-women team to win three consecutive matches, and so progress to the next stage of the contest. St Hilda's is now the only all-women college in Oxford – in 1965 it was one of five – and if seeing students on television was still something of a rarity, seeing four women students winning was a distinct oddity.

One member of the team was Gilly Elliot: "The newspaper coverage was along the dreadfully embarrassing lines of 'beauty and brains' – if only," she adds, modestly. Newspaper photographs had them setting off from St Hilda's on their bikes, as if going to lectures, wearing patent-leather boots and comparing their hairdos, and the column inches detailed the various proposals of marriage they received as a result of their appearances. The assumption appeared to be that these "girls" were especially lucky, because being so brainy might make it easier for them to get a husband.

Granada realized the value of the media attention they brought to the programme, and invited them back on several occasions to play in Christmas specials, black-tie affairs for which the programme purchased ball-gowns for them to wear. Bamber allowed himself the luxury of extraordinarily flowery introductions to the team, full of the kind of gallantries one might expect from a rake in a Restoration comedy. "We're delighted to welcome back the team who most impressively combined beauty with brains, so much so that most of the country fell in love with them, as did the production team, and indeed," (at which point he appears to lose the thread), "as did the producer, in *his entirety*." With these chivalries out of the way, the games begin, with Bamber referring to "the girls" throughout.

The St Hilda's team members see their place in history differently. "We were the first generation of women who could have it all. We had the best education, and we were able to combine our careers [with] having families."

It would be gratifying to believe that this media attention was merely a product of the chauvinism of the 1960s, but over 30 years later, the same thing happened again.

The Magdalen College, Oxford, team in the 1998 series consisted of three men and one woman, Sarah Fitzpatrick, who was their captain. This was clearly a very able team, with an impressive array of knowledge between them, including a particularly gifted scientist in Phil Jones. Sarah handled the captain's role of listening to her team-mates and then making an informed decision with great aplomb. The team were articulate, charming and well-groomed. But the production team started to notice a particular media buzz following each of the team's appearances as they went through the rounds, all of them focusing on Sarah's appearance rather than the team's ability to answer general knowledge questions. One journal-ist offered the opinion that "she can make the words 'We don't know' sound like an invitation to a MENSA pyjama party". Even the impartial and impervious Jeremy, who can normally be dismissive of student teams when they fail to answer, responded differently. "I'm afraid we don't understand," said Sarah, after her team had left Phil, their only scientist, to struggle alone with a particularly tough set on differential equations. "Don't worry," said Jeremy, dreamily. "Neither do I. Neither does anyone in the entire studio."

As the Magdalen team approached the finals, the attention on Sarah increased, culminating in an offer from *The Sun* newspaper, which we had not hitherto identified as a fan of the programme, asking her to be photographed for its Page Three. On top of this were piles of letters, "some extremely strange, and even schoolboys coming to my door. Partly very nice and flattering, and partly really weird and slightly scary. It came while I was doing my Finals, and so ended up being quite stressful when people wouldn't go away. In a way it *was* very flattering – it'll be something to tell my children – but I hope it *never* happens again."

If we're honest, the men on the *University Challenge* teams have sometimes been described as tending towards the geeky and nerdy. This is no longer the case, we should stress – anyone watching the programme now would have to accept that the vast majority look perfectly normal. But the first twenty-five years fixed the programme in many people's minds as featuring men who thought the sharp centre parting was quite the thing, with their hair looking sleekly groomed after its weekly wash.

Granada's make-up department used to complain bitterly about the personal hygiene of the male contestants, or the lack of it, and if nothing else the programme has demonstrated a revolution in the grooming of young men. The make-up team routinely referred to the programme as *The Spot Show* in the earlier days, on account of the crepuscular young men they had to make look presentable. But working on the programme did have its compensations, such as taking some liberties with the appearance of their charges. On one occasion, when three shows were being recorded in one day, they attached an ever-increasing amount of false whiskers to the young Frank Booth, playing on the University College, Oxford team in 1972, so that from one show to the next he went from being merely bearded to sporting a luxuriant growth. For his final appearance, they really went to town and left him looking positively Amish.

But not all men appeared on the programme without a thought about their appearance. The prize for the most eccentrically-dressed team goes to Sidney Sussex, Cambridge, the series champions in 1979, who deliberately dressed so that they would appear in decreasing order of formality when the camera panned across them from left to right for their introductions. The first wore full evening dress; the player next to him wore jacket and tie. The next wore an open-necked shirt, and the fourth, a caftan and beads. When they returned to play again in the *Reunited* series in 2002 they were, alas, rather more conservatively dressed.

The Prizes

In its modern incarnation, no prize other than the trophy is awarded to the teams. The trophy is a piece of sculpture by the Manchester artist Adrian Moakes and represents an open book, on the pages of which are inscribed various symbols taken from different academic disciplines, the initial letters of which will spell out the words *University Challenge* for anyone who takes the trouble to decipher them. On winning a series, the team's name is engraved at the foot of the page, along with those of the other team champions.

The only other material incentive to take part is a rugby shirt which has Jeremy's catch-phrase "Come on!' embroidered discreetly across the chest, and these are given to each team member if the programme has not gone over budget, and if the production team actually remembers to order them.

The decision not to award a prize is not out of meanness, or at least not entirely. As budgets shrink, it becomes harder to find the kind of prizes that have a genuine meaning for the recipients. And anyway, do they get a prize each? Is it something that should go to the university or college? Clearly teams enter because they think it will be fun and they want to win. We've never believed that offering a prize will make a difference to that. One team member made it to the final, only to be defeated. He later went on *Who Wants To Be A Millionaire* and earned himself £64,000. Even so, he confided that would have exchanged his cash win for having won *University Challenge*. Whilst not everyone would make the same swap, it's a flattering reflection on the way the programme is regarded, and on the people who take part.

Past years have seen prizes awarded, the first, to the champions of Leicester, being a first edition of *Johnson's Dictionary*. Other have included prints of Hogarth's engravings of the *Idle and Industrious Apprentice*, and a punt, which the winners named "Bamber".

Other prizes have tried to reflect the times. One winning team was awarded a peculiar device which apparently allowed one to type with only the fingers of one hand and which has now, one suspects, gone the way of the Sinclair C5. Keele University won themselves a groovy multicoloured Plexiglas sculpture installed on the campus so that, no doubt, there is a small corner of Keele University where it will always be 1969.

Tie-breaks

The best moments on *University Challenge* must be the tie-breaks. On average, they will occur only around once a series. They generate the most tension, and place everyone in the studio on a knife-edge. It is the one point in your life when you can make really good use of an otherwise useless piece of information.

The rules say that if both teams are tied on the same score at the end of a match, the presenter will continue to ask starter questions until one team gets one right and so wins. But the rule of the five-point penalty for an incorrect interruption still applies. So teams have to try and get to the buzzer first, but the risk of interrupting and getting it wrong is not just five points away, it's handing the victory to your opponents without them having to open their mouths.

In the previous chapter, Clive James described the sensation of being the person who blurts out the wrong answer and so loses the match for his team. Close scores in the final seconds are what we always want to see, and one of the best, closest matches staged in recent years was the semi-final of the 1994–95 series, between Aberdeen and Trinity College, Cambridge. At the final gong, both teams were on 235 – a very high double score which meant that throughout the match, both teams had been getting virtually all the questions right.

Eric Grey, now a Professor of English at Harvard, then a member of the Trinity team, remembers the moment vividly. "At the very end of our semi-final match we answered a question to tie it, and Robin (Battacharyya, the team's captain) actually collapsed by the side of me." And indeed, on screen we saw Robin lurch forward over his desk.

"It's a sensational result!" says Jeremy, shouting to be heard over the feverish applause. "Each of you on 235!" Cromer, the Aberdeen captain, is so stunned he actually gets up out of his chair and starts to wander around. His team appear to be sitting on top of Trinity, so the effect is rather surreal. "Sit down!" Jeremy explains to him.

Eric continues: "What was running through my mind was that there are two possibilities. Either Robin is dead, or he is alive. If he is alive, I want him to answer the next question. If he is dead, maybe I can hold him up for long enough so that we can finish the game before anyone notices."

Sean Blanchflower was another member of that Trinity team. "The funny thing was, before the match, we'd gone through all the subjects that we could possibly cover. Robin had said that he'd cover sport, but didn't know anything about chess or bridge. I said 'Don't worry, I'll handle that.' And Jeremy read out the starter: 'In conventional chess notation…' – and I thought, 'Oh my goodness, the responsibility lies with me. I've got to get this, or it'll be my fault.'"

"…which letter represents the knight?" asks Jeremy.

"My mind was alert; I'd even managed to work out that it was going to be the knight, because it's the only one which has a letter that's not the initial letter of the name of the piece. And so just before Jeremy was going to say it, I buzzed in, heard him say it, and in what seemed like an eternity I heard my name and I knew that I'd done it."

BUZZ

"N!"

"N is correct," Jeremy confirms, "so Trinity – you win!" On screen, Sean Blanchflower's body seems to go into spasm. Arms flail as the team tries to hug and applaud itself at the same time. Trinity College, Cambridge, go through to the series final. And they win that, too.

4

Are the Questions Getting Easier?

The planet is getting warmer, policemen are getting younger, and the questions on *University Challenge* are getting easier as an inevitable response to the total collapse of standards in higher education over the past forty years.

Or at least, this is the view some newspaper reports would have had us believe when the show returned in 1994, suggesting we were reflecting a society which has dumbed down – one which values Homer Simpson as highly as Homer.

In the seven-year gap between Bamber's last show and Jeremy's first, the programme seemed to have crystallized in many people's minds as a strange, black-and-white production in which the effortlessly intellectual Bamber asked the most recondite questions of two teams, invariably male, whose heads were full of dandruff and an unlimited fund of obscure information.

Of course, it was never actually like that, but when the programme returned in 1994, with T-shirted teams representing institutions which had, until a couple of years previously, been classed as polytechnics, answering a range of questions which included some on popular culture – as the show had always done – those journalists who wanted to do so were able to propound the theory that there was something rotten in the state of higher education.

The programme-makers have always taken the view that the questions were difficult "back then", and they are certainly just as difficult now. Kieran Roberts, who produced the re-launch in 1994, had the task of deciding the level of difficulty for the questions under

Jeremy. "As an exercise, I sat down in a room with the core group of question-setters from the original series, and we watched tapes of the old shows, to get a sense of where to pitch the questions. The question-setters all said the same thing – that, actually, these aren't *very* difficult questions, but there's something about the presentation that makes them *sound* very difficult. Everyone had been looking at *University Challenge* as if through the wrong end of a telescope, as something slightly mystical and shrouded in old age, and our memories of it were of something incredibly difficult. When the programme aired, we did weather the storm of the accusations that the questions were easier, and that students had become stupid. But it's clear from the *Reunited* series that the newer teams are just as good as the older ones."

The questions are not easier, but they are different. We include much more material on the sciences, which is a reflection both of an increased emphasis on the sciences in our universities, and of the popularity of books on the sciences in the bestsellers' lists. The "two nations" debate may still rage, but the programme takes the view that an acquaintance with the sciences is no longer an optional extra. We do cover popular culture and trivia, because it's amusing to see teams who can answer on quantum theory and the life of Eleanor of Aquitaine blushing deeply and admitting that they also know about Pokemon characters and Postman Pat. As we tell the teams, it's not just *what* you know – it's what you're prepared to *admit* you know, in front of the gaze of millions of viewers.

Our two presenters have very different styles of asking the questions. Bamber Gascoigne read the questions at some speed, but was more likely to enter into a discussion with an answering student, perhaps coaxing them out of English into the Latin he wanted to hear, or nudging them towards a more complete answer if they were most of the way there. Jeremy Paxman will, if the teams can take the pace, go at an even greater speed, and his trademark cries of "Come on," "I'm going to have to hurry you," and "We can't hang around" will push the final minutes of the programme into a very fast gear. He is also more brutal when it comes to accepting answers. If a team member interrupts and answers in English before hearing that the question goes on to ask for a response in Latin, that's their bad luck – and their five-point fine. Answers have to been given promptly and in full. He is fair – and *very* firm. But this allows a trailing team a better chance to stage a comeback or qualify as one of the highest-scoring losing teams, and we also reckon it's simply very entertaining to see teams playing at such a speed, and with such strict adjudication.

Another change in the playing of the game over the years is that currently, all bonus questions are worth 15 points, almost always in a three-part structure with five points for each one. In 1962, bonuses were of varying length and different score values were placed on them, depending on how difficult they were judged to be.

In the end, a difficult question is simply one to which we don't know the answer, but in an attempt to nail, once and for all, the accusation that our questions have dumbed down, what follows is a reconstruction of some questions exactly as they were asked on the programme, but forty years apart. The first set is from 1962, transcribed as Bamber asked them on the earliest extant tape, which is of the third show ever transmitted.

The 1962 Questions

Starter 1:   Q.   Thursday is named after the god Thor; for whom is Wednesday named?

Bonus 1:   Q.   Five men were chiefly responsible for the revolution by which the modern view of the solar system replaced that of Ptolemy and Aristotle. Ten points each for any four you can name.

Starter 2:   Q.   Give the sentence which immediately precedes these lines of Shakespeare: "It is twice blessed, / It blesseth him that gives / And him that takes."

Bonus 2:   Q.   By what names are the following Beethoven symphonies known?
a) The Third?
b) The Sixth?
c) The Ninth?

Starter 3:   Q.   Identify the man who may be described as organ builder, organist, architect, philosopher, author, minister, theologian, number man and doctor?

Bonus 3:   Q.   Four answers, five points each. We call George Washington "the Father of his Country". Other men have played similar parts in other countries, and for five points each, I want you to tell me who was the

similar man in each of these countries:
a) Modern Turkey?
b) Colombia?
c) Post-Imperial China?
d) Haiti?

Starter 4: Q. 1776 was the date of a revolution in the science of economics. Who produced this revolution?

Bonus 4: Q. Two answers for ten points each.
   a) How many people were found guilty of offences of all kinds in England and Wales in 1961, and I'll accept anything to the nearest 100,000?
   b) What proportion of these were traffic offences, and I'll accept five per cent either way?

Starter 5: Q. "At last democracy is no longer a series of isolated units. It has become a cohesive organism, determined to fulfil its great purpose." These were the words of Ernest Bevin speaking in Washington in 1948. An important political alliance had just been formed. What was it?

Bonus 5: Q. The following exchange of dialogue takes place in a famous play: "That passed the time." "It would have passed in any case." "Yes, but not so rapidly." For ten points, what is the name of the play, and for a further five points each, who are the two characters with those lines?

Starter 6: Q. Who was the last Tsar of Russia?

Bonus 6: Q. For ten points, *The Witches' Sabbath* in Gogol's story *St John's Eve* was the inspiration for which of Mussorgsky's works?

Starter 7: Q. Solomon Grundy was born on Monday. When did he die?

Bonus 7: Q. For five points in each case, in which wars did the following battles take place?
   a) Edgehill?
   b) Cape Matapan?
   c) Bunker Hill?
   d) Zama?

Starter 8: Q. In which modern country would you be, if you visited the city that Wordsworth described as "the eldest child of liberty"?

Bonus 8: Q. The basic equation of the physical universe is said to be $E=mc^2$. For an easy ten points, who propounded it, and for 20 more, what do the symbols mean?

Starter 9: Q. According to the Bible, who were Reuben, Simeon, Judah, Zebulon, Issachar, Dan, Gad, Asher, Naphtali and Benjamin?

Bonus 9: Q. For 40 points: according to Greek mythology, Zeus had not only a very full sex life, but an extremely imaginative one. For ten points each, I want you to tell me in what form he seduced the following ladies:
    a) Leda?
    b) Danäe?
    c) Io?
    d) Alcmena?

Starter 10: Q. In 1834, six Dorset labourers were sentenced to seven years transportation for administering unlawful oaths in forming a trades' union. What collective name were they given?

Bonus 10: Q. For 40 points in all, ten for each one; dying speeches are often apocryphal, but the following are genuine. I want to know who said them.
    a) "Thy necessity is yet greater than mine."
    b) "Let not poor Nellie starve."
    c) "Now God be praised, I will die in peace."
    d) "All my possessions for a moment of time."

That was what those earliest teams were up against. Some of these questions are of a type we would not ask now. Asking how many people in Great Britain were convicted annually of offences would, we guess, draw blank looks from today's teams, who don't need to carry such information around in their heads when it can be accessed quickly on the Internet. A question asking for the name of the scientist who gave us the formula $E=mc^2$ is now so easy that we could not include it; it's interesting that the 1962 team hesitate over giving their answer. Questions on the names of Beethoven's symphonies, the forms adopted by Zeus for his seductions, and the names of those who shaped our ideas about the cosmos are all standard quiz-programme material, whatever the decade. They could easily have appeared in the following questions, which were given to the teams who met in the final of the 2002 series.

The 2002 Questions

Starter 1: Q. Described as having bones as strong as pieces of brass or bars of iron, and believed by some to be a reference to a hippopotamus, which creature in the Book of Job has a name which is now used to indicate the extreme size of any thing or animal?

Bonus 1: Q. Three questions on students in literature:
a) In a work of 1818, which fictional character was educated in Geneva and at the University of Ingolstadt as a student of natural philosophy, where Professor Krempe dismisses his outdated study of Paracelsus and Albertus Magnus?
b) Which tragic hero is a student at the German University of Wittenberg, although his studies are interrupted by his father's death and his mother's remarriage to his uncle?
c) In a novel of 1945, which Oxford aesthete startles his fellow-students by reciting sections of T.S. Eliot's "The Waste Land" through a megaphone?

Starter 2: Q. Which phrase, taken from John's Gospel, is the title of an oratorio by Sir Arthur Sullivan, a poem by Sir Edwin Arnold, and an allegorical painting by Holman Hunt depicting Christ carrying a lantern and knocking at the door of the soul?

Bonus 2: Q. Three questions on crowns:
a) Saint Edward's Crown, first used in the coronation of Charles II in 1661, is now generally substituted for another crown after ten minutes of the coronation ceremony; for what reason?
b) Which Holy Roman Emperor, crowned on Christmas Day 800, is buried at Aix-la-Chapelle and, according to legend, waits, crowned and

armed in Oldenburgh for the day when the Antichrist appears?

c) The 11th century St Stephen's Crown is a symbol of the nationhood of which east European country? Given to the US troops after the Second World War to prevent it from falling into enemy hands, it was returned in 1978.

Starter 3: Q. In physics, what name is given to the hollow hemispheres of brass or copper, used by Otto von Guericke in his experiment of 1654, in which they were placed together to form a sphere, out of which air was pumped to demonstrate atmospheric pressure? The name is that of von Guericke's home town, of which he was also burgomeister.

Bonus 3: Q. Three questions on cinema:

a) The 1932 film *Das Blaue Licht* or *The Blue Light* was the work of which film director, much admired by Hitler and later responsible for the filming of the Nuremberg rallies?

b) The 1950 film *The Blue Lamp* features Dirk Bogarde as a small-time criminal who kills a policeman played by Jack Warner, who was later resurrected in which long-running television series?

c) Which director's film of 1993 was made as he was losing his eyesight, and consists of an unchanging plain blue screen, *Blue* being the film's title?

Starter 4: Q. What name was given to the series of agreements formulated in Switzerland in October 1925, which attempted to guarantee the post-Versailles treaty frontiers between Germany, France and Belgium?

Bonus 4: Q. Three questions on physics:

a) The innermost electron shell of an atom is normally denoted by which letter?

b) The K-shell is full when it contains how many electrons?

c) Three of the four quantum numbers of the two electrons in a full K-shell are the same; what are the two values of the remaining magnetic spin quantum numbers of these electrons?

Starter 5: Q. Which British statesman described his own career in this self-penned limerick: "Few thought he was even a starter, / There were many who thought themselves smarter, / But he ended P.M., / C.H. and O.M., / An Earl and a Knight of the Garter"?

Bonus 5: Q. Three questions on biblical dances:

a) Who, according to Mark's Gospel, was so pleased by his daughter's dancing at his birthday feast that he allowed her to name her reward, and was asked for the head of John the Baptist?

b) According to Exodus, who fashioned the golden calf before which, during the absence of Moses on Mount Sinai, the people of Israel danced naked?

c) Who, in the Second Book of Samuel, brought the Ark of the Covenant to Jerusalem, dancing "with all his might before the Lord", "girded with a linen ephod"?

Starter 6: Q. Escaping detection by the Spanish Conquistadors and "discovered" in 1911 by the Yale University Professor Hiram Bingham, which archaeologically important fortified Inca town lies on a steep-sided ridge in the Peruvian Andes, beneath the mountain peak which gives it its name?

Bonus 6: Q. Three questions on 19th-century thoughts about education. In each case, identify the writer:

a) Firstly, lines from 1895: "The whole theory of modern education is radically unsound. Fortunately, in England at any rate, education produces no effect whatsoever."

b) Which American wrote, in *A Curious Dream* in 1872: "Soap and education are not as sudden as a massacre, but they are more deadly in the long run."

c) Which novelist, in a work of 1818, has her heroine Anne Elliot say: "Men have had every advantage of us in telling their own story. Education has been theirs in so much higher a degree; the pen has been in their hands"?

Starter 7: Q.   What word, from the Spanish meaning a rogue or adventurer, is applied to episodic novels relating the histories of characters often in low social circumstances who live on their wits, some English examples being *Tom Jones* and *Moll Flanders*?

Bonus 7: Q.   Three questions on units in science:

    a) What is the fundamental S.I. unit of luminous intensity?

    b) Which derived unit for luminous flux can be expressed in fundamental S.I. units as candela steradians?

    c) What unit of luminance can be expressed as lumens per metre squared?

Starter 8: Q.   What name is given to the branch of science which deals with the emission of electrons from heated surfaces?

Bonus 8: Q.   Three questions on composers who suffered from blindness:

    a) Which composer was blind for seven years before his death in London in 1759, but continued to conduct oratorios and revise scores with the assistance of his devoted friend J.S. Schmidt?

    b) Which German-born British composer went blind in the mid-1920s but carried on writing, his works from that period including *A Song of Summer, Songs of Farewell* and *Fantastic Dance*?

    c) Which composer, who died in Madrid in 1999, was blind from the age of three and was widely regarded as the leading post-Civil War Spanish composer, coming to prominence after the first performance of his *Concierto de Aranjuez* for guitar and orchestra in 1940?

Starter 9: Q.   Chrystabel Leighton-Porter, who died in December 2000, appeared on stage and in films as the heroine of which newspaper cartoon strip, described by Winston Churchill as Britain's secret weapon in boosting Allied morale during the Second World War?

Bonus 9:   a) Derived from the Latin for "to bind", what name is given to a single character formed by two or more letters, such as the "oe" in the French term "hors d'œuvres"?

b) What name is given to the mark placed over a vowel, especially the second of two adjacent ones, to show that it is to be pronounced separately; an example is the mark placed over the "i" in the word naïve?

c) Which word, derived from the Latin for "to strike out", is used for the suppression of a vowel or syllable, an example being of the "e" in the French word "le" when it precedes a noun beginning with a vowel?

Starter 10: Q. Which animal phylum, characterized by pentamerous symmetry, includes starfish, sea urchins and sea cucumbers?

Bonus 10: a) What name is given to the collection of seven prominent galaxies, of which Andromeda and the Milky Way are the most dominant, along with around two dozen less conspicuous members?

b) Which 19th-century Norwegian mathematician gives his name to the most intensively studied of the topological groups, in which the topology of each point is like that of an "n"-dimensional Euclidean space for some fixed "n"?

c) Which organization, founded in 1935 by Robert Holbrook Smith and William Griffith Wilson, is arranged in a large number of local groups whose members attempt to follow the so-called "12 steps"?

These questions were from the 2002 series final between two young teams from Somerville College, Oxford and Imperial College, London. The answers are at the end of this chapter, but if you wish to compare your answers directly with today's students, you'll want to know that the teams failed to answer the starters about Otto von Guericke's experiment, and the treaty signed in 1925. They also failed to identify the artists of a series of depictions of George and Dragon – one of them by Raphael – which prompted Jeremy's remark: "Well, I was told they were all *first-year* fine art questions, but there we are."

The Imperial team of four scientists could not name the branch of science which deals with the emission of electrons from heated surfaces, or the S.I. unit of luminous intensity. The Somerville team, which included an English undergraduate, failed to recognize a quotation from Oscar Wilde, attributing it to Bernard Shaw. In a later stage of the program, they could not identify which of Jane Austen's novels has Anne Elliot as its heroine, and couldn't give the name given by George Eliot to the fictional county which she used as the setting for *Middlemarch* – this latter failure was much to the dismay of Dame Mary Warnock, who had been invited to present the trophy to the champions and so was watching the show from the back of the recording gallery. Otherwise impressed, she was staggered by this lapse. "How could they not know *Loamshire?* Astonishing!"

Before we get carried away with listing the failings of these teams in this one show, it has to be recorded that they answered the majority of their questions correctly and quickly in the pressurized environment of a television studio, and both gave extremely creditable performances, worthy of any series final. And all students seem to dislike answering on their own subjects – the risk of failure is, of course, the humiliation of having to apologize to one's tutor the morning after the show transmits.

The answers: 1962

Starter 1:   Woden
Bonus 1:   Copernicus/Galileo/Kepler/Newton/Brahe

Starter 2:   "The quality of mercy is not strain'd. It droppeth as the gentle rain from Heaven upon the place beneath."
Bonus 2:   a) Eroica
            b) Pastoral
            c) Choral

Starter 3:   Albert Schweitzer
Bonus 3:   a) Atatuk
            b) Bolivar
            c) Sun Yat Sen
            d) Toussaint l'Ouverture

Starter 4:   Adam Smith

Bonus 4: a) 1,152,397
b) 61 per cent

Starter 5: North Atlantic Pact
Bonus 5: a) *Waiting For Godot*
b) Vladimir
c) Estragon

Starter 6: Nicholas II
Bonus 6: *Night on Bare Mountain*

Starter 7: Saturday
Bonus 7: a) English Civil War
b) Second World War
c) American War of Independence
d) Second Punic War

Starter 8: Italy (Venice) (from his poem "On The Extinction of the Venetian Republic")
Bonus 8: a) Albert Einstein
b) Energy = mass times speed of light squared

Starter 9: The sons of Jacob
Bonus 9: a) As a swan
b) As a shower of gold
c) As a cloud
d) In the shape of her husband, Amphitryon

Starter 10: The Tolpuddle Martyrs
Bonus 10: a) Sir Philip Sidney (offering water to a wounded soldier of the field of Zutphen)
b) King Charles II (talking about Nell Gwynn)
c) General Wolfe (on the heights of Abraham)
d) Queen Elizabeth I

The answers: 2002

Starter 1: Behemoth (*Job*: 40,18. Possibly from the Egyptian 'p-ehe-man' [water-ox], hence the identification with the hippopotamus)
Bonus 1: a) Victor Frankenstein

　　　 b) Hamlet
　　　 c) Anthony Blanche (in Waugh's *Brideshead Revisited*)

Starter 2:　"The light of the world" ("Then spake Jesus unto them, saying, I am the light of the world: he that followeth me shall not walk in darkness," *John*: 8, 12. The works of 1873, 1891 and 1954, respectively)
Bonus 2:　a) It is too heavy
　　　 b) Charlemagne
　　　 c) Hungary

Starter 3:　Magdeburg (hemispheres)
Bonus 3:　a) Leni Riefenstahl
　　　 b) *Dixon of Dock Green*
　　　 c) Derek Jarman

Starter 4　The Locarno Pacts (initialled in Locarno on 16 October 1925)
Bonus 4:　a) K
　　　 b) Two
　　　 c) ½ and –½ (plus and minus ½)

Starter 5:　Clement Attlee (in a letter of 1956, quoted in Kenneth Harris' *Attlee*, 1982)
Bonus 5:　a) Herod (Antipas) (his daughter is unnamed in Mark's gospel, but identified by Josephus as Salome)
　　　 b) Aaron
　　　 c) David (an ephod being a priest's vestment)

Starter 6:　Machu Picchu
Bonus 6:　a) Oscar Wilde (in *The Importance of Being Ernest*)
　　　 b) Mark Twain/Samuel Langhorn Clemens
　　　 c) Jane Austen (in *Persuasion*; Anne Elliot is speaking to Captain Harville)

Starter 7:　Picaresque (from the Spanish: picaro)
Bonus 7:　a) Candela
　　　 b) Lumen
　　　 c) Lux

Starter 8:　Thermionics

Bonus 8:   a) (George Friederic) Handel
            b) (Frederick) Delius
            c) (Joaquin) Rodrigo

Starter 9: Jane (appeared in the *Daily Mirror*)
Bonus 9:   a) Ligature (from *ligare*)
            b) Dieresis (from the Greek meaning separation)
            c) Elision (from the Latin *elisio*)

Starter 10: Echinodermata (accept Ecinoderms)
Bonus 10:   a) The Local Group
            b) (Marius Sophus) Lie
            c) Alcoholics Anonymous

5

How the Series Gets Made

While the first-round matches of one series are transmitting, work begins on the next, and by each new year the production team will have started to come on board.

The first task is to redesign the poster which, we hope, will go up in every students' union throughout the UK to advertise the series and convince students of the fun of taking part. It's the moment for the team to take some liberties with Jeremy's person. The current poster has him as Jack Nicholson in *The Shining*, with his diabolical face on one side of a door which is being smashed by an axe. On the other side of the door is a terrified student in place of Shelley Duvall – although in fact it is our director, Tracey Rooney, standing in for her. The legend underneath reads "Here's… JEREMY!" This replaces the previous poster, which was a pastiche of the famous *Trainspotting* image of Ewan Macgregor standing in a drenched T-shirt. Jeremy's face was superimposed over Macgregor's, in a fair reproduction of the original artwork, with the title changed to "Brainspotting".

Contact is made with every students' union and JCR. With they take our posters? Will they advertise taking part in the programme? Will they get a team together? So begins a five-month process of cajoling, pleading and begging students to return our applications form to us. They will, of course. The vast majority of forms will arrive within two days of our final deadline, and some a few days later, along with the kind of excuses of which their lecturers and tutors must tire: I was ill, we couldn't quite manage to, left it on the bus, well, here it is anyway.

Here lies one of the admitted inequalities of the programme. It is so much harder to organize a student team from an urban campus of perhaps 15,000 people, spread over many locations, than it is to find four willing volunteers from a small Oxbridge college, the members of whom will all know each other at least by sight, and most of whom will pass the same noticeboard every day. No wonder, then, that the Oxbridge entries will be the first to arrive, leaving the production team to wonder if the red-bricks and newer universities will ever get their acts together. Fortunately, they always do.

The application form is the easy part of the process. Each team member's contact details are recorded, and we also ask for a photograph of the team, which makes them a great deal easier for the researchers to recall after the interview process. The photograph tells us other things about a team as well – a single shot of all four together lets us know that at least they all know each other; four individual passport photographs suggest the opposite. The team who posed as four derelicts in sleeping bags outside their college doorway clearly have a sense of humour; as have the team who think they can get away with sending us a photo of the four stars of *Dawson's Creek*.

The application form also includes a straightforward test paper, which we ask the team to attempt together, without using reference books, allowing themselves around 15 minutes. These are the questions the teams on the 2002–03 series were asked:

1. For the closing ceremony of the Sydney Olympics, which Australian singer performed a version of Abba's "Dancing Queen"?
2. Which food has a name deriving from the Chinese for "rotten beans", and is a curd made from mashed soya beans?
3. Sven-Göran Eriksson's first game in charge of the England football team was a friendly against which European country?
4. Which part of you would be inflamed if you suffered from quinsy?
5. "*Es vinculum invalissimum, vale!*" is a Latin translation of which TV catchphrase?
6. The chemical symbols of the metallic elements potassium, nickel and iron, when placed in that order, spell the name of which kitchen utensil?
7. Give the more familiar name for *hypericum perforatum*, a flowering plant increasingly used as a herbal treatment for mild depression.
8. In February 2001, Jamie Bell took the BAFTA for Best Actor for his first film role – in which film?

9. How many nanograms make up a milligram?

10. Discovered by the American astronomer Gerard Kuiper in 1949, the satellite Nereid is one of the eight known satellites of which planet?

11. Which comedian and author wrote the words for *The Beautiful Game*, a musical set in Belfast about a football team, with music by Andrew Lloyd Webber?

12. Gruoch, Queen of Scots from 1040 to 1057, is better remembered by which title, familiarized by her depiction in a play by Shakespeare?

13. Which country voted a decisive "nej" or "no" to joining the Euro in a referendum held in September 2000?

14. Following the assassination of Spencer Percival, under what name did Robert Banks Jenkinson become Prime Minister in 1812?

15. What was declared to be out of danger in January 2001, after a correction to its vertical axis restored it to the position it occupied in 1810?

16. What name is used for the person, often a mayor or sheriff, who is responsible for the conduct of a parliamentary election?

17. "The schoolmaster was leaving the village and everybody seemed sorry" is the opening line of which novel by Thomas Hardy?

18. Which Japanese word means "harbour wave", and refers to a long, high sea wave caused by an underwater earthquake or other major disturbance?

19. Edward Borough, John Neville (Baron Latimer) and Sir Thomas Seymour were all married to which of Henry VIII's wives?

20. Which Frenchman vacated his post in January 2001, less than a year after his appointment as chief executive of the Millennium Dome?

21. The 20th-century opera *Gloriana*, describing the relationship between Elizabeth I and the Earl of Essex, is the work of which English composer?

22. What word comes from the Latin meaning "under penalty", and refers to a writ ordering a person to attend a law court?

23. According to classical mythology, the three-headed dog Cerberus was lulled to sleep by Orpheus' playing of which instrument?

24. "I think it was a sympathy Damehood, because I didn't get the Booker last year." Which British writer described her new title thus in November 2000, after failing to win the Booker for a fifth time?

25. What is the English name for the island with an area of only a square kilometre, known to the French as Aurigny?

26. Which two words complete the maxim derived from Aristotle: "Probable Impossibilities are to be preferred to…"?

27. "Things can only get better" were the last words of which TV character, in the broadcast which killed him off on 20 November 2000?

28. The central keep of the Tower of London, containing part of the Royal Armouries Collection, is better known by what name?

29. Who was the author of *Die Traumdeutung*, or *The Interpretation of Dreams*, published in 1900?

30. What is the name of the American photographer, born in 1890 as Emmanuel Rubnitsky, whose best known work featured the back of a female nude resembling a violin?

This test is part of a softening-up process. We reckon these are reasonably easy questions – deliberately so, because we are trying to reassure students that they will manage the level of difficulty they'd get on a show. The harder test comes later, but on this one we would expect a team of four students between them to get most of the answers right; a score of 25 or over, out of 30, is an encouraging sign.

We also want this test to give us a simple indication of the rough general knowledge level all the teams are happy with, and to tell us whether one year's intake will be up to the mark of the previous year's. Invariably they are; every year we make the questions harder, and the teams have never failed us yet.

When the teams come to meet the researchers, they face a much tougher written test. For this they answer on their own, with no conferring – just to get them into the habit should they make it to studio – and they have to complete the entire test in 15 minutes. This is the test paper for the 2002–03 series:

1. How were the phrases "bad hair day", "Full Monty" and "boy band" linked on Thursday 14 June 2001, along with the term "docusoap" and Homer Simpson's expression "Doh!"?

2. Nicknamed "The Red" on account of the colour of her hair as well as her politics, which MP led the march to London by two hundred men from Jarrow in November 1936?

3. In what context is 83 "Farfetch'd", if 37 is "Vulpix", 57 is "Primeape", 101 is "Electrode" and 142 is "Aerodactyl"?

4. Which of Shakespeare's plays begins with four characters

dressed in mourning: Bertram, his mother the Countess of Roussillon, an old lord called Lafeu, and Helena?

5. From the Greek for "without colour", which adjective describes a combination of lenses that transmits light without separating it into its constituent colours?

6. In October 2000, a former sheet metal worker became the 156th person, and the first Catholic since the Reformation, to be elected to which parliamentary office?

7. The BBC radio version of the word game *Just a Minute* contains three possible grounds for a challenge, namely hesitation, repetition and which other?

8. Which word derives from the Corsican Italian meaning "thicket", and came to be applied to the French resistance movement during the German occupation of the Second World War?

9. During the 2000 season, only two teams won Formula One races. Ferrari was one. What was the other?

10. In 1897, Rudyard Kipling's poem *Recessional* was published in *The Times* to commemorate which royal event?

11. In a piano or similar instrument, what is the name for the felted block that rests on a string to keep it from sounding, and is lifted by means of a pedal?

12. Which politician served as Italy's Prime Minister from 1996 to 1998, and in 1999 was appointed President of the EU commission?

13. Which islands have an area of about 540 square miles, are also known as the Sheep Islands, and were granted home rule in 1948 by Denmark, of which they remain an overseas administrative division?

14. Iqaluit is the capital of the Nunavut territory of Canada, and is situated on which island, named after the British pilot who explored the area in 1616?

15. Which theory was established in 1948 by Claude E. Shannon as a statistical analysis of the factors pertaining to the transmission of messages through communication channels?

16. What collective name is given to the Mishnah, or oral law, and the Gemara, consisting of commentaries on the Mishnah, which are the fundamental code of Jewish religious law?

17. Which animal phylum is generally classified into eight major groups, including tryblidia, scaphopoda, cephalopoda, bivalvia and gastropoda?

18. Set running for the first time in over a decade to mark the 2002 National Science Week, the marine chronometer designated "H4" was built by which 18th century engineer?

19. On a computer spreadsheet, what term is applied to the spaces formed by the intersections of rows and columns?

20. Which of the Lake Poets was appointed Poet Laureate in 1813 and, despite writing a number of long narrative works, is perhaps better known for his shorter pieces such as *The Battle of Blenheim*, and his biography of Lord Nelson?

21. Whose term as President of the Democratic Republic of the Congo came to a premature end when he was shot by one of his bodyguards in January 2001?

22. In which opera by Verdi is the title character a hunchbacked court jester, cursed by the Count of Monterone?

23. What, in terms of cos theta, is the value of cos (180 degrees minus theta)?

24. Which Saint's feast day is 11 November, and is recognized in Scottish common law as a Quarter Day?

25. Which European country was occupied by the French from 1795 until 1806, and known by them as the Batavian Republic?

26. The English scientist Sir James Chadwick was awarded the 1935 Nobel Prize for Physics for his discovery three years earlier of which particle, after analysing the radiation emitted by beryllium when bombarded with alpha particles?

27. The struggle between two families for control of the region of Kurukshetra is told in which epic poem, a sacred text in Hinduism dating back to the oral traditions of the first millennium BC?

28. During the 2000 US Presidential campaign, which Democrat senator was Al Gore's running-mate?

29. In medicine, what noun describes the spontaneous rapid and irregular contraction of the individual muscle fibres in the walls of the chambers of the heart?

30. In the classification of burgundy wines, as with champagnes, which term indicates a superior grade to Premier Cru?

31. To keep in line with the natural year, in which calendar were years organized into groups of four called "Franciades", each year having five intercalary days called the "Sans-culottides"?

32. Also called the malar, what is the common name for the zygomatic bone which adjoins both the frontal bone at the outer edge of the orbit or eye socket, and the sphenoid and maxilla within the orbit?

33. What popular name is given to Shostakovich's "Symphony Number Seven", because it portrays a siege by German forces during the Second World War?
34. What collective title is given to the trilogy of plays entitled *Agamemnon, The Libation Bearers* and *Eumenides*?
35. Which phrase is the title of a Victorian painting by W.F. Yeames, now in Liverpool's Walker Art Gallery, depicting a Roundhead officer questioning the child of a Cavalier family?
36. The name of which ancient city has served as a colloquial expression for London in reference to its supposed wealth, luxury and dissipation, and occurs in Benjamin Disraeli's novel of 1847, *Tancred, or, The Modern Crusade*?
37. In June 2000, the English National Ballet announced that its retiring chairperson, Pamela, Lady Harlech, would be replaced by which former BBC newsreader?
38. Lead shows two valences in its compounds; one is +2, what is the other?
39. The obelisks known as Cleopatra's Needles originally came from which ancient city, near present-day Cairo and dedicated to the cult of Ra, the Sun God?
40. Which river rises in the Cottian Alps of Piedmont, flows east through Turin and drains into the Adriatic, making it the longest river in Italy?

What we look for in this test paper, apart from the right answers, is a good spread of knowledge among all the team members. The test is marked as a team effort, which means that if only one team member answers correctly, it still counts as a point for that team. This means that a team of four, who might score only ten out of 40 each, would, if they all answered a different ten questions correctly, give themselves a more or less completely correct set of answers, and so beat a team where one player scored very highly but the other three did not.

The test is conducted under exam conditions, invigilated by the *University Challenge* researchers, who will visit a large number of the UK's universities to meet up with the applying teams. When they meet them, they will also try and assess how each would come over on screen. Would they be nervous? Would they be over-confident? Have they selected the right person to be captain? These and other points are noted down as soon as the teams leave the interview room. They will prove invaluable in gauging how to deal with those teams if they make it on to the show.

The Recording Day

I've never had a ready answer to the question "What does a producer *actually do?*" There is no training other than what one learns on the job in junior roles, and the leap into the role is made because of a coincidence of one's wanting to do it, coupled with one's bosses thinking that, perhaps, you might be able to do it. Each studio recording day is different. But most follow an increasingly familiar pattern.

08.25

Arrive at the Granada Television studios. Earlier than normal, because it's a studio day, and the chances are all of the production team will have lain awake with a knotted stomach since 05.00. Walk to work with that tense sense of how much has to be done before we can all go back to bed.

The Granada building is a prime example of early 1960s architecture, a rectangular slab lying off Quay Street in the centre of Manchester. The guide book to Manchester's architecture praises "the sculptural expressiveness of the cantilevered entrance canopy, heroic roof-top spiral stair tower, and the confident use of typography on the entrance and roof-top signage". All very lovely, no doubt, but this morning we're all preoccupied.

Lift to the fourth floor, and the large open-plan office which houses the Entertainment department. The *University Challenge* team occupied one small corner of it, referred to as "Dictionary Corner" by the young glamour-pusses who occupy the same floor and work on *Stars in their Eyes* and *You've Been Framed!*. Somewhat strange bedfellows for a show such as ours. There's the familiar, wearying feeling of arriving for work before the cleaners have left. Kettle goes on. Log on. Read e-mails.

08.30

The rest of the team arrive. Television is a very young industry. Only two of us on the production team – myself and the programme's associate producer Irene Daniels – can remember pre-decimal coinage. For the others, the Falklands War is something their parents told them about. There's a different atmosphere on a studio day. We forget the usual pleasantries about the night before.

Conversations start with words like, "Something that's been worrying me is…" We've got the morning to sort ourselves out.

Make list entitled "Tasks, in order". Add nothing else, but stare at it with a worried expression.

It's the producer's job to ensure that, by the end of the day, we have recorded four half-hour shows – two hours of peak-time entertainment – to the highest standard, on time and on budget.

It's television, but there's also a sense of theatre about a studio day. We are staging a show. There will be a performance, an audience, and applause – we hope.

08.45

We divide up according to our work priorities. The researchers' jobs are to meet and greet the teams, and get them though wardrobe and make-up in a manner that appears relaxed, but is actually timed to the minute. They have to make sure that they are all and watered, they must calm the nerves of those too frightened to eat, speak or smile, and brief them about their performance ("Remember, it's only a quiz programme. *It's not important!*") They also have to ensure they arrive in studio in perfect time to march on to the set to rapturous applause from their supporters.

For Irene and I, our jobs this morning involve looking again through the questions allocated for today's shows, looking for anything that shouldn't be there. Facts which niggle away at us and need another check, any questions which duplicate material in another show, anything that sounds too much like a question the teams will hear in their rehearsal. I have long since recognized this constant revisiting of questions as a nervous compulsion, but it does serve a purpose. The imminence of studio focuses the mind, and it's amazing what mistakes can be spotted at the last minute, even on material you've looked over so often before. It's at times like this you realize you were going to allow through a set of bonus questions on 19th-century literature, which included one on Mary Shelley's *Frankenstein*. Let's NOT do that, shall we?

Tracey Rooney, our director, arrives and makes herself a cup of tea. Directors are a separate breed in television because they have a tangible and highly marketable skill, unlike the rest of us who claim little more than that we've done the job before and we still haven't been fired. Tracy is in the lucky position of having little preparation to do – but then she has spent all week directing

Coronation Street. We beg her for Street gossip, but she's being tight-lipped.

The questions for the picture round are re-read, and compared with print-outs of what the students will see on screen. Is the wording absolutely correct? This is another great opportunity for howlers to creep in. We tell our students they're going to see a map of Britain, but what they see on screen shows only England and Wales, bringing a furious postbag from north of the border. Or, perhaps even worse, we realize we were going to show a photograph of Seamus Heaney in a set asking them to identify British poets.

09.30

The researchers are squabbling over which teams they will look after in the course of the day. Each has a preference, based on a rapport they've developed since they first met the teams or, less professionally, on whichever team has players whom they fancy. Each researcher will, with the aid of the studio runners, look after two teams in the course of the studio day. There'll be ferocious competition between them for whoever has looked after the most winning teams. Researchers tend to view a team's success as being down to the subtle and tender nurturing they've lavished on them during the course of the day, whereas the teams tend to view their success as having something to do with their ability to answer general knowledge questions.

10.45

Jeremy Paxman rings from his hotel. When he arrived last night, he'll have picked up an envelope with the question-cards for the day's shows and copies of his introductions to each team. He looks over them for one final time over breakfast and phones through his notes. Irene answers the phone to him, as always. "Hello Jeremy! Good morning! Did you sleep well?" I can't hear Jeremy's reply, but note that whatever it is, Irene is laughing very heartily and blushing crimson. *And* I notice she's had her hair done. Make mental note to tease her later. Jeremy's presence in the building is always warmly anticipated by many of the female staff. Some quite senior executives are reduced to gibbering wrecks by his presence. Others who would never normally wear lipstick arrive for work having discreetly applied it. Jeremy remains completely oblivious.

Some several minutes later, the conversation gets on to a professional footing, and Irene scribbles down Jeremy's queries on the questions. How should he pronounce "Corca Dhuibhe", which is the Gaelic term for the Dingle peninsula? Isn't the Teletubbies question a bit trivial even for our show? And he suggests we ditch a question about a current cabinet minister, because there's a very good chance he'll no longer be a cabinet minister by the time the show airs.

The phone call over, we get to work on the points he's raised. All must be sorted within an hour, by which time he'll arrive in the building. Pronunciation queries go straight to the BBC's Pronunciation Unit who, with a dedication above and beyond the call of duty, allow us to call them at home on a weekend morning. Factual queries send us back to the reference books or onto reliable sources on the Internet. Questions are checked. Either we're satisfied with them and they stay in the show, or we add a qualifying footnote, or they get ripped in half and put in the bin.

11.30

The Reception desk calls up to say the first teams have arrived. On one memorable occasion, a team from a venerable Oxford college was announced with the words, "I've got Jesus in Reception".

Up in the office, the researchers exchange glances. It has begun. They pick up their clipboards, compose their features into an expression of pleasant efficiency and head for the lifts to meet their teams. (The clipboard is to the television researcher what the whistle is to a football referee, or the plastic shield to a police officer on riot control. It is a symbol of authority, a comfort blanket, a defence mechanism. Some researchers sport state-of-the-art clipboards with textured coverings, their names embossed on the front and the whole thing covered with scores of pen-holders and strange clip mechanisms. They look down on their poor relations who make do with something from the stationery cupboard. They will go far. Soon it will be me asking them for a job.)

11.45

"Hello, old fruit!" booms a voice from behind my shoulder. Jeremy has arrived and settles into the office. There's some fussing over him, offers of tea, re-introductions of the team members he met last series, exclamations of surprise that, yes, it *does* always seem to be raining whenever he's in Manchester, how strange, reassurances that this is just an amazing coincidence, but he's increasingly disinclined to believe it after travelling here several times a year for eight years.

12.00

Another call from Reception. "I've got Neville Cohen and Stan Shaw in Reception." We ask for them to be sent up to our floor. We meet and greet them at the lift doors. Neville and Stan are the question-setters who provide the bulk of the science questions we use on the show. Neville is a lean, grizzled Scouser, a veteran of *Mastermind* and one of the country's leading question-setters. He's able to set questions in maths and physics, which is beyond the ability of most question-setters. Stan's areas of expertise are the life sciences. They're here because, unlike the arts-based questions, Jeremy, Irene and I need to have the science material explained to us, in terms which would not upset a 12-year-old. The production team can boast a modest collection of arts degrees, but have a thundering ignorance of the sciences. We are well aware that if a student offers us an almost-right answer to a science question, or an acceptable alternative to what might appear on Jeremy's card, we need to know immediately whether they deserve their points or not. It's a practical demonstration of C.P. Snow's "two cultures" debate: a group of people who consider themselves moderately well-educated, who will at the drop of a hat talk about art and literature, but who could not between them summon up a satisfactory explanation of the scientific term "mass".

Jeremy, Irene, Neville, Stan and I retire to the Oval Office, so named because it features a large oval table, and also in honour of Monica Lewinsky, who serves as a role model to an industry full of ambitious young people. The table is spread with photocopies of the science questions, and some largesse representing Granada's hospitality: sandwiches with orange fillings; a bowl of fruit, in which impenetrably hard pears feature prominently; a bottle of wine, which no one dares touch. We settle down to work.

14.00

We leave the Oval Office. I have in my head, and in my notes, enough information to be able to make an adjudication on any of the science

questions which might come up. I hope. My head is full, and yet some-
how feels utterly empty. I work through the science questions once
again, to check I'm confident I can deal with any point that seems
ambiguous. We say goodbye to Neville and Stan. We'll see them again
for a drink in hospitality after the final show has gone out.

Irene goes back to her desk. All the notes arising from the science
session need to go on the question cards. Other points need to be
checked. At this point I leave her to it.

I grab my clipboard (it's a hard habit to break) and head down-
stairs, first to the canteen, not because I want anything to eat – pre-
studio nerves put paid to that – but to look in on the researchers
sitting at the canteen tables, having lunch with their respective teams.
It's an opportunity for me to see the teams for the first time, and for
the researchers to catch my eye if they need to tell me anything: such-
and-such a student is petrified; this team is very confident, so let's tact-
fully keep them away from the less confident ones. That team is badly
hungover, another team can't understand why we won't let them leave
so they can go to the pub, promising to be back five minutes before
they are due to record. We explain television doesn't work like that, at
least not any more. Others sit silently at their canteen table, leafing
though encyclopaedias. Others test each other.

How a team prepares for a match varies enormously. Firstly, we try
to keep them in ignorance of which team they've been drawn
against until they arrive at Granada. This is to avoid them feeling the
psychological disadvantage of coming up against the team representing the reigning champions, or any of the other giants who have
a strong history with the show. Even so, some of them manage to
work out our entire recording schedule weeks in advance by e-mail-
ing amongst themselves once they know their call-times at Granada.
On one impressive occasion, we found the entire fixture list for the
first-round matches posted on the Internet within a couple of hours
of the teams being informed they were on the series.

In the same way, we never tell the teams what they scored in their
test paper, or how their opponents scored. There tends to be only a
very narrow range of points between them, but we don't want one
team to feel dismayed at having been drawn against a team who
scored higher than them in the preliminary test.

The idea is that teams will only get a chance to size up the opposition when they arrive at Granada on the day, unless they've arrived
the previous day and spent the night trying to get each other drunk
in the hotel.

This is also the point at which they learn which desk they'll be sitting at. This turns out to be extremely important to them. On the one hand, they want to sit on the left-hand desk, because that will appear at the top of the screen. But they also want to sit on the right-hand desk, because that's a yard or two nearer Jeremy. We refrain from telling them about an unnerving moment on an earlier series, when it was discovered that one team desk appeared to be "luckier" than the other. Week after week, the team seating at that desk would win. This was a disturbing moment for the production team – was there some subtle but fundamental flaw in the studio design that gave one team an advantage? Had the unlucky desk been cursed by a losing team in the past? Did we need an exorcist? Fortunately the situation resolved itself and the series reverted to a statistically acceptable pattern of results. But we now monitor which desk has been occupied by each of the winning teams, in case the curse strikes again. We never let on which desk it was.

14.15

I go into the studio for the first time today. The director, Tracy, is in the gallery looking at shots. She sits in front of a bank of monitors, each one of which gives the picture coming from one of the cameras. It's the first time in this recording block she's seen the set on camera. Is it lit correctly? Is the split-shot set up accurately? Are the cameras able to offer her the shots she wants, framed as she wants them? It's a slow, painstaking process. We have very little time to do this. In a few short years, television has shifted from being one of the most profligate industries to one of the most careful with money. Budgets are scrutinized endlessly to find savings, calculated not by thousands or hundred but by tens. If we can shave ten minutes off the rehearsal time, we have to make every effort to do it.

I do my rounds. This involves saying hello to members of the crew I may not have seen for months, asking if they have problems – if they have, there's little chance I can do anything about them – and offering my own irritating comments. There's a light spill from under one of the desks. Part of the backing to Jeremy's position isn't meeting properly – and isn't Jeremy's chair usually on a plinth? Where's the plinth we had last time? Some of the woodwork on the teams' desks is chipped and needs a repaint. All of which is met with a cheerful "Yes, we're sorting it", and an unspoken but deafening "Now *please* bugger off and let us get on with it".

Back up to the gallery. The gallery is a series of three connected rooms from which the production is controlled: lighting and record machines to the left, sound to the right, and in the centre the director's position with, on her left, the vision mixer, who will actually cut the pictures together from the shots offered by the cameras on the director's instructions, and on her right the PA, who will keep the entire production informed of timings.

Behind them, at a raised desk so we can see over their heads, sits the editorial team; myself as producer, Irene keeping an extra eye on the questions, Tricia double-checking the scoring.

14.20

By now the audience is in the studio. There's a combination of regulars who come to lots of the shows, and the students who have travelled up to support their teams, most of whom will have come up on the students' union minibus that morning complete, no doubt, with a plentiful supply of lager. We scan the audience discreetly. Anybody carrying or wearing anything like scarves, placards, anything at all offering the teams support, will be placed right in front of the cameras. (The winning team from Magdalen College, Oxford, in 1997 was supported from the audience by a lifesize, naked effigy of the captain, complete with flashing nipples. One can't help but be touched by the care that goes into such tokens.) We are also on the look-out for T-shirts bearing untransmittable advertising slogans. Anyone wearing these has to sit at the back.

Denny Hodge is beginning his warm-up. Even a show as staid as *University Challenge* will have a warm-up man. It is his job to shift the mood of the audience from the collective gloom of a group of people who have had to stand outside Granada in the rain for 15 minutes – and who had other things to be doing on a Saturday afternoon anyway – into a group of happy and enthusiastic people ready to applaud our modest little quiz programme. Audience enthusiasm has to be judged just right. Screaming, whooping and hollering, of the type that might suit *Blind Date*, is out of place for us – and too much audience noise means the teams can't hear the questions.

Roger Tilling climbs into his perch. Roger is the man who announces the team name and which player has buzzed in for each starter question. It's an essential piece of the grammar of the show, and also actually confirms to the contestant concerned that he or she really is the one who got to the buzzer first. Roger's perch is a small scaffolding tower which allows him to see the team desks from over the heads of the cameramen. In these few moments before the show begins, he can look at the names on the still-unoccupied team desks, and begin practising any he thinks he might find difficult. We'll catch him muttering "Battacharyya, Battacharyya" under his breath, or "Ng, Ng".

14.25

Jeremy enters the studio. No grand entrance; he'll sidle through the cyc, the curtain which runs the parameter of the studio, and make his way over to Pat, whose autocue contains his introduction to each show. One last quick read through. Are the intros too long? Are they sufficiently rude about the teams? The script for each team's intro-duction will already have been shown to the student teams, to check they are happy with what's going to be said. The only time they ask for a correction is when the introduction is not quite condescend-ing enough. "Can't Jeremy be ruder about us? Timmy Mallett went to the same place as us; why don't you mention that?"

14.30

Lynn, the floor manager, wanders over. "Any reason," she asks politely, "why we can't *get started?*" We glance over to the far side of the studio. The teams are there, waiting nervously in a television studio's equivalent of the wings. Now is the time for their last-minute warm-up rituals: the group hug, commonplace among mixed-sex teams; a Maori haka, which frightens the audience; a quick burst of disco-dancing to Abba tracks – can that *really* help? Another team's final good-luck ritual was to kiss a photograph of the late Queen Mother, who was their college's patron.

Each team has the researcher allocated to it at the front, like a general leading a tiny army. We all look ready to go. Lynn signals to Denny, who queues the applause for the teams. They get applause for simply walking on to the set and sitting down behind their own names. Each team is introduced in turn, and the sound team will play a suitable piece of music for their walk-on – the theme from *Rocky II*, or "*We Are the Champions*," something cheery and good-natured. Jeremy and I view the teams from behind his desk. "Four blokes *again*," he sighs. "Don't they know *any* women?" Jeremy walks over the set to meet them (to the shower-stabbing music from

Psycho, although he doesn't seem to notice). He says hello, poses for photographs with each of them and reminds them it's only a quiz.

14.35

I leave the studio floor and jog up the iron stairs which lead to the gallery. The PA, director and vision mixer sit on the front row of chairs, and in front of them is a desk of knobs, switches, dimmers, faders and God-knows-what-ery which could put the bridge of the Starship Enterprise to shame. But having said that, I've only ever seen half a dozen of these buttons actually get pushed in the course of a recording, and deep down suspect that it's a con to convince those of us not in the know that it's all hideously complicated.

Behind them, in our raised area so we can see over their heads, sit Irene, Tricia and I. Tricia gives us a back-up score throughout the show, so if a team queries whether the scores went wrong five minutes ago, we can tell them that they didn't. Irene and I each have a copy of the questions in front of us.

We are ready. Irene, Tricia and I exchange glances. How often have we been in this situation before? The three of us have worked together for many years. This is unusual in an industry where the workforce is in such a state of flux. We have produced hundreds of editions of quiz programmes together. Still the same knot in the stomach, still the same quiet tension.

On my desk in front of me is a small box which connects me by voice to Jeremy, to floor manager Lynn, to the autocue and to the scorers. We check Jeremy can hear us. "I can hear you, old man, but you're very faint. Not that I care," says the presenter laconically. His little joke. I boost my sound level to something considerably more audible for him. He sniffs in acknowledgement.

Jeremy addresses the teams. "OK, we're about to go. We'll try and do it in one take, but we probably won't manage it – the director's on work experience. Or I'll make a mess of it or something."

"Good luck everybody," calls Tracey. "Roll VT," is Sandra's next line. Up in the gallery, the title sequence rolls. Jeremy can be heard down in studio, calling across to the teams again: "And remember it's only a quiz, it's not important. Just enjoy yourselves."

"Cue Roger," calls Tracey, and we hear Roger saying "University Challenge!" at the exact moment the words form on screen. Audience applause. The picture cuts to the high, wide shot of the studio. "Asking the questions... Jeremy Paxman!" Now we're on

Jeremy at his desk. The camera pulls in and settles on him. "Hello! Tonight, we meet two more teams of students..."

Intro over. The teams introduce themselves in turn. For many, this is the biggest ordeal. The shock and shame of forgetting your home town, the degree you are studying for or, indeed, your own name which is written in large letters on the desk in front of you, prompts many students to write all three facts down on a crib sheet. For them, the worst part is now over. You can coast through *University Challenge* not saying a word if you have to, just nod and agree with your colleagues. At least you didn't forget your own name.

"I'll remind you of the rules," says Jeremy. Irene and I adjust our question sheets. It's our job to follow the questions throughout the show: make sure no words are missed, that each question has been delivered correctly. In particular, if there's any point of adjudication it's up to me as the producer to make it. "Accept," or "No". Occasionally Jeremy and I will disagree. He'll give the team the benefit of the doubt and award points, and I'll have to pull up the show and make him take them off a team. Sometimes it's the other way around.

Our job is to make the show in one continuous take, so the half-hour you see on screen is the exact half hour we recorded in studio, nothing added and nothing taken away. This helps Jeremy present the show, building up speed towards the end, and we believe it helps the teams give it their best. The last thing we want to do is to inter-rupt the competition because we missed a camera shot, or because something falls over. If we have to, then we have to. But the trick is to get it in one take. This is rare now for a prime-time television show, except for a live broadcast. Old-fashioned? Us?

We're five minutes into the show. It's going fine, but we can speed things up a little. One team is being too leisurely in its discussion of a bonus set. "You can hurry them," I tell Jeremy through his ear-piece. This is translated into pure Paxmanspeak, his trademarked, weary, haven't-we-all-got-something-better-to-be-doing bark of a "*Come on!*" It's the show's catchphrase. It's what's embroidered on the rugby shirts we give the teams as a souvenir. We're going to hear it a lot more this show.

Halfway through. One team is lagging behind. They need to get a move on if we're going to have a close match. The leaders are coming to the end of a bonus set. "Worth encouraging the losers," I tell Jeremy through his ear-piece. "There's plenty of time to catch up," he tells them. "Maybe you'll get going with this starter."

We don't want the trailing team to lose their nerve. You can put 100 points on your score in five minutes if you really go for it. Often scores which are far apart at the halfway mark are extremely close at the finish.

Five minutes to go. Point of adjudication. Jeremy's hesitating. He's asked for the hereditary condition believed to have caused the madness of George III. We want to hear "porphyria". The contestant has said something that sounds closer to "porphyry", which is a form of igneous rock. *Decide.* I decide it's a case of a slight mispronunciation of a word that is not in everyday conversational use, and we should reward positive achievement. "Accept," I tell Jeremy. "Porph*yria*," he corrects, "I'll accept it."

Two minutes to go. The teams are 20 points apart, which means there's time for it to go either way, and whichever team gets a bonus set is going to be hurried on because they can't simply waste time to stop their opponents getting a crack at more questions. "*Come on!*"

"*One minute to the gong,*" announces Sandra. "And with only a minute to go, here's another starter question," says Jeremy, now going at a speed which has a red shift.

One team is in there with a correct answer. They get the bonuses. It's probably all over. Even at Jeremy's speed, a starter and bonus set take a minute to get through. Jeremy hurtles the team through it in the hope we can get another starter in and give their opponents a crack at a comeback. Not this time, though.

"Cue the gong," calls Sandra, who has had her eye on her stop-watch for the precise second we need to hear it.

BOOM.

"And at the gong," says Jeremy, leaning back, as do the teams, and he tells them their scores. One team is patting each other on the back, the others are hunching their shoulders – but at least they didn't disgrace themselves.

"Well, bad luck," he tells the losers, finding a few words of cold comfort before turning to the winners. "Terrific score; we look forward to seeing you in the next round. I hope you'll join me next time," he says straight down the camera lens, "but until then," and he invites goodbyes from the teams. "And it's goodnight from me. Goodnight." Credits roll.

It's over. Quick glances all round the gallery. Good match, we tell ourselves. "Thank you, Jeremy. Good match." "Yes, it was, wasn't it? Am I clear?" Tracey tells him he's clear, and he rushes off to get changed.

Now everyone is moving. The teams are collected from their

desks by the researchers, who'll take them to hospitality and give them drinks. The stagehands move in and peel the teams' names off their desks and start putting up the names for the next match. The old names are kept by the production team if the team won, because we'll need them when they play again in the next round. If a team lose, they take their names with them, and they leave the studio with them draped over their shoulders, like the sashes of the runners-up in the Miss World contest.

The audience is allowed out for a pee. The camera crew get a quick coffee in a plastic cup. Two minutes to stretch our legs in the car park at the back of the Granada building, in the little space between the crew vans and the pig-bins. It's surprising how welcome this unpromising outlook can be after a long stint in studio. Then back inside.

The audience are shepherded back in. The next teams are waiting in the wings, two more tiny armies. Jeremy is back; new shirt, jacket, tie, and he's looking through the autocue for the next show.

I run back to the gallery. "Good luck everybody," calls Tracey again. The music plays, and on screen the titles roll. "Remember," Jeremy calls to the two new teams, "it's only a quiz."

And we do it all again.

Then we have dinner. After dinner, we do it again.

And then we do it once more.

"… and at the gong," says Jeremy, recapping the final scores and moving the fourth show of the day towards its end; the production team slump back in their chairs and try to follow his final link. The credits roll.

Thank you to the crew, well done, see you tomorrow. Who's going through to hospitality? See you there.

We grab our question-scripts and clip-boards. Any unasked questions can go back into the pile.

21.30

Hospitality is always well under way by the time we arrive. The teams will have gone through straight from the studio, and will have had wine or beer poured for them by the researchers. Now they are reviewing their performances, laughing at their mistakes, congratulating themselves on pulling obscure pieces of trivia out of the recesses of their minds at the last minute, under pressure. Jeremy is surrounded by a small gaggle. He's being gently indiscreet, telling them who out of the current crop of cabinet ministers is certifiably bonkers. It's not always the ones you'd think.

We wander around saying "Well done" to any team member who needs to have it said to them. I hardly ever see the teams to speak to until this moment. Occasionally Jeremy will point me out with the words, "Why don't you ask him? He's the producer?" when I'm going to be taken to task for a strict adjudication.

The teams seem to have enjoyed it – and this is important, because the winners have to come back to us again, and maybe again after that.

Irene gives Jeremy his homework: the questions for tomorrow's shows, copies of the scripts. He takes a taxi back to his hotel.

22.00

Irene and I grab some drink and a bowl of peanuts and head back up to the office.

Time for a final look through the questions for the next day's shows. Check facts yet again; look through pronunciations.

22.50

The researchers make it back up to the office. The last teams have left the building, back to their hotel and whichever of Manchester's Saturday night delights they chose to sample. Quick review of the day's events. Which teams were more nervous? Did they all leave happy? Have the winners got their recording dates for the next round? What's our call time for tomorrow? We agree on 8.30. "Thanks for all your hard work." They leave.

23.30

Irene and I call it a day. Log off, and as we head home, we have a quick chat about the days to come. Tomorrow, it's another four shows. The day after that, another four, and then another four after that. Then, it's customary to have a bit of a "do" for the production team. Have we booked a table at Dimitri's? It's a local Greek restaurant, and it's been a second home to the *University Challenge* team for over a decade. Can't wait. Studio days are fun, but they do take it out of you.

6

How to Answer the Questions

Each series of *University Challenge* is played over five rounds. The questions get tougher with each round, not only because the brighter teams will be the ones qualifying for the next stages, but also because increased exposure to the questions makes them easier to answer. Just as anyone who regularly tackles a crossword will become familiar with how the compiler's mind works, so our teams become accustomed to how our questions are structured. Often starter questions will give a series of clues to the answer, the last one of which may be relatively simple, so daring to hang on until the end can pay dividends – assuming your opponents don't get the answer before you.

Often questions are designed to make use of scraps of knowledge at the back of the mind, or to allow for a reasonable, educated guess at an answer. If the question is asking about a German composer, it's probably always worth guessing "Beethoven" even if you really haven't got a clue. As long as you don't interrupt a starter question, there are no penalties for guessing, other than the risk of provoking an incredulous presenter to repeat your error back to you, for the benefit of the entire nation. "*Aristotle?* You seriously think *Aristotle* lived in a tub? Good heavens no. The answer I wanted was Diogenes."

The questions are designed to be hard, or at least, to sound hard – they often sound harder than they really are – and we try to aim for questions which prompt correct answers, or reasonable attempts, for about 70 per cent of them. On a set of three bonuses, the aim is to have one question which any team should be able to answer, even if none of them is studying that particular area. Two right answers is a good average, while a clean sweep of three tells us that a team really knows its stuff.

The number of questions asked in each programme varies. The brighter, faster teams will get through more questions – and the brighter the teams, the higher the proportion of bonuses to starters, so a bright team will get even more of an opportunity to confer on bonus questions. Weaker teams will reveal themselves by needing to hear a higher proportion of starters.

For each programme, we allocate a batch of 35 starters and 25 sets of bonuses to each match, with an additional emergency stack for Jeremy to grab in the event – unlikely, but not unheard-of – of us running out before the end of the recording. A contest between two well-matched teams in an average programme will probably hear about 30 starters and 20 sets of bonuses asked, so there are roughly 600 points up for grabs for both teams. Our rule of thumb is that if a team can get a score in three figures, that is at least respectable. Anything over 200 is impressive, and anything over 300 tells us that team should try to get out more.

The most important points a player should bear in mind are: don't be put off because a question sounds hard – the obvious answer is often also the right one; you can add a lot to your score by some inspired guess-work – if you don't interrupt starters too often; if the question reminds you to think of the answer *before* buzzing in, you must do just that. On these questions you'll be allowed even less time than usual for prevaricating.

Teams who are playing first-round matches should remember that highest-scoring losers will also get a chance to play again, so it's in *both* teams' interest to get through as many questions as possible.

On bonuses, if you are the captain, make sure you know every-one's strengths and weaknesses before the match. During it, listen to everyone's opinion. Encourage quick discussions – don't let the team sit in silence. If you want another team member to answer a bonus question – which can be a good idea if it's a difficult foreign pronunciation which they know and you don't – make it clear that is what is happening.

If you're not the captain, remember not to blurt out an answer directly to the presenter. You should go through the captain, follow-ing a discussion with the team. If anyone addresses an answer clearly to the presenter it will be taken as the offered response, whether it comes through the captain or not.

How to Ask the Questions

What follows should help anyone who fancies the view from the presenter's chair. If you want to test yourself, or test anyone else, you might want to bear in mind the way we play the game in studio.

We have, perhaps, the most famous rules in quiz show history. Even people who never watch the programme will probably be aware of the "starter for ten, no conferring".

So yes, starter questions are worth ten points, and whoever answers must answer on their own, without conferring with their team-mates. Once you've indicated that you can answer, you must answer promptly and in full. You may not signal that you want to answer and then spend time thinking about it, just as in studio, once a contestant has buzzed in, the answer must be given immediately.

If the answer is incorrect, or the contestant fails to answer, the question is handed over to the opposing team, one of whom must answer it on their own.

If a starter question has been interrupted and answered incorrectly, that team is fined five points and the question is offered to the opposition, with the unasked portion of the question being completed. Should that team also interrupt incorrectly, there is no five-point fine.

If a starter question is answered promptly and more information is given than necessary, then as long as the required information has been given, the points should be awarded. However, contestants cannot simply circumlocute in the hope that they will eventually say the words the questioner wants to hear. If they ramble on, give them a "No" and carry on.

Each starter question answered correctly means that team can confer on a set of bonus questions worth 15 points, and these will nearly always ask three questions for five points each. We strongly recommend that all answers to bonuses are given through the team captain. This discipline encourages a proper discussion, and prevents one team member from blurting out an answer. But if an answer is given clearly and directly to the questioner, whether it comes from the captain or not, it should be taken as the answer that is being offered.

Incorrect or failed answers to bonuses are not handed over to the opposing team.

A sound will be given to indicate "time up". The rules state that an answer must have been given clearly before the gong is heard for it to earn points.

If, at the final gong, two teams are tied on the same score, the questioner will ask a tie-break question, which will be the next starter question. A correct answer wins the game for that team. An incorrect or failed answer from both teams will lead to another tie-break question, until the match is resolved. An incorrect interruption to a tie-break question will lead to a five-point fine and will automatically give the match to the opposition.

The great majority of questions are designed to be answered very simply, often by one word. If there are acceptable alternative ways of saying the answer, these will be listed either alongside the answer, or underneath as a footnote. A footnote may also occasionally give a little more information which does not need to be heard when giving the answer, but allows questioners some extra information to help them decide whether an answer which sounds close is actually correct or not. Other footnotes may remind the questioner of the dates of a person's lifespan, to facilitate those astonished responses: "Good grief, no; you're out by a *century!*"

The shortest way of saying the answer is usually the best. For example, asking a question which needs a person's name as the answer, we will award points for the surname only. We do not expect to hear a full name or title, even though that will often be, for the sake of accuracy and completion, how it will be recorded as the answer. The only instance in which we will press for additional information would be when two or more people share the same name or title. An answer such as "King George" would not be acceptable without the correct regnal number.

One team may answer a question and get it wrong, but do so in such a way that the right answer becomes clear to the opposition, without them having to do any work. In this instance, it is down to the questioner's discretion whether or not the question is handed over. Generally speaking, on the programme we would usually decide not to hand it over, on the basis that some work has to be done for points to be earned.

To anyone using this book to create their own team competition and who finds themselves in the position of adjudicating, we offer the advice – *never* be lenient! *Never* award points out of sympathy to a team which is trailing badly! Awarding unearned or undeserved points can seem like a nice gesture to people who are doing badly in the early stages of the contest, but the questioner will come to regret it if that team catches up and comes within striking distance of its opponents. What looks like a trouncing in the early stages may turn into a tie-break in the final moments, in which case one overly lenient decision will have wrecked the game. When the final whistle, or gong, or alarm clock sounds, you will want to know that all your judgements have been fair.

If teams are conferring on bonuses, you will need to allow them a reasonable amount of time to discuss the answer, but not too much. How much is too much? For us, it depends on the type of question. If a set of mathematical equations need to be worked out, it seems reasonable to allow a decent length of time – and anyway, it's fun to watch someone sweating over something which sounds incomprehensible, especially if they can then provide the correct answers. To those bonuses which one either knows or one doesn't, less time needs to be allocated, especially if the team are staring at each other blankly.

It is also necessary to watch out for a team which has a lead in the final minutes, but prevaricates over answering its bonuses in order to stop more questions being asked which might allow its trailing opponents to catch up. The time-wasting request "Can you repeat the question, please?" from a leading team usually gets short shrift from Jeremy. When we record the programmes, we foil such games-manship by adding on to the running time of the game the same amount of seconds we feel have been wasted. Then, when we come to edit the show, we cut the same number of seconds out of an earlier, slower stage of the programme. But for anyone playing the role of presenter without an editing suite as back-up, you will have to rely on a stern sense of fair play.

If you are testing yourself, we suggest two particular rules. First, give yourself a severe time limit. On screen, teams get only a few seconds to buzz in for starters, and not much longer to confer on bonuses. You can have a few seconds longer on bonuses because you are on your own, but not too long, because you haven't got the pres-sures of studio lights, cameras, an audience of millions and a scary presenter.

Secondly, *write your answers down* before you check the answers. It's extremely easy to flick to the back of the book, look at the answer and tell yourself, "Oh yes, I knew that. Ten points to me."

Five rounds of questions follow. Good luck.

7

What Are We Asking?

What, exactly, do we claim to be testing on *University Challenge*? Bamber Gascoigne retains a very clear idea. "From my experience on *University Challenge*, I came passionately to believe that there is a *real* territory called general knowledge. It is a definable area. It varies from generation to generation, and from country to country, but even between countries and generations there is a core of knowledge, a core of information, which for most of us should ring a bell. And quiz games can perpetuate that."

Dr Richard Dawkins, Professor for the Public Understanding of the Sciences at Oxford, was only half-joking when, as our trophy presenter in 1998, he suggested that 'A' levels be scrapped in favour of school-children sitting *University Challenge*-type tests. His point was that the ability to retain a very wide range of information, and to be able to access it at speed, are very necessary skills. Time after time on the programme, we will see our teams doing well on subjects they thought they knew little about, simply because they're good at retaining an eclectic mix of facts, often from the most outlandish sources.

Alison Reeves, a member of the Magdalen College, Oxford, team which won the series in 1997, remembers surprising herself by answering a question she would have supposed to be beyond her. A starter for ten asked, "Derived from the Swedish for 'field stone', which group of aluminosilicate minerals containing calcium, sodium or potassium constitute the major component in most igneous rocks, and are the most common minerals in the earth's crust?" Being a student of modern languages, the aluminosilicate minerals belonged in a book she was happy not to have opened, but she still buzzed in and answered, correctly, "Feldspar". "I know nothing at all about geology," she confesses, "but I'd been looking through the IKEA catalogue just before we went on, and there were some rather pretty plates in it called *Feldspar*. It just stuck in my mind." So having encountered the word feldspar, and having heard the question refer to the Swedish for 'field stone', the question becomes gettable for a non-geologist, if she has the ability to cram her head with diverse scraps of knowledge.

Even so, it is difficult to define the parameters of Bamber's idea of the world of general knowledge. How much can we reasonably expect of our students, some of whom are still teenagers when they appear on the show? Recent programmes have found them unaware that Stanley Baldwin was a Conservative, confusing him with Ramsey MacDonald, to Jeremy Paxman's naked disgust. Another team was asked for the title of the Henry James story which concerns the governess in charge of the two children Miles and Flora, and offered the answer *Mary Poppins*. At this point, the programme almost ground to a halt, because Paxman was rendered close to speechlessness. "You really think Henry James wrote *Mary Poppins*?" he eventually managed to splutter. If he had had a piece of chalk handy, he'd have thrown it at them, but his disdain was enough to turn the screw on the unfortunate team. Stanley Baldwin's political allegiance will surely lie within the concept of a reasonable general knowledge, and even someone who has never read a word of Henry James might be expected to know enough to work out that *Mary Poppins* wasn't quite his style. As Paxman often tells the teams, "You really should know this stuff." Well, if they didn't then, they certainly do now!

In the end, you either know it, or you don't. On one of the later *University Challenge Reunited* matches, Jeremy read out as a starter question a quotation from a letter written in 1867: "We are told we ought to ask for £30,000 at least...not a large sum, considering that there is but one college of this sort...", at which point John Gilmore, playing for the Sidney Sussex team of 1979, buzzed in and answered, correctly, that the quotation referred to Girton College, Cambridge. Again, Paxman was amazed; "How *on earth* did you work that out from what you heard?" he asked. "It's an easy question," Gilmore replied, "if you happen to know the answer."

In this chapter, you'll encounter some questions of the level of difficulty we'd use in Round One. Easy, if you know the answers.

ROUND ONE QUESTIONS

STARTER 1

"Sunrise, Sunset" and "Tradition" are songs from which musical set in Tsarist Russia?

BONUS 1

Three questions on valleys:

A. In which American state is the winter sports area of Squaw Valley, north-west of Lake Tahoe, and the venue for the Winter Olympics of 1960?
B. Inland from Causeway Bay and a famous home to horse-racing, Happy Valley race course is in the middle of which island?
C. Which Philadelphia-born actress turned her hand to writing with enormous commercial success when, in 1966, she published *Valley Of the Dolls*?

STARTER 2

In criminal law, what name is given to a voluntary statement made by a person charged with a crime in which that person acknowledges that they are guilty of the crime?

BONUS 2

Three questions on punishment:

A. Which novel of 1866 has the impoverished student Raskolnikov as its protagonist, who commits a murder to prove he was "beyond good and evil"?
B. "To let the punishment fit the crime" is the objective of the title character in which Gilbert and Sullivan opera?
C. The punishment of *bastinado* involves caning which specific part of the body?

STARTER 3

What name is given to the charge made by a restaurant for allowing customers to bring their own wine into a restaurant?

BONUS 3

Three questions on islands:

A. Bathurst and Melville islands are home to the Tiwi people who belong to which indigenous group, having preserved their homeland more successfully than their mainland counterparts?
B. The Kiriwina or Trobriand Islands are coral formations in the Solomon Sea of the southwestern Pacific, lying some 90 miles north of the southeastern tip of which large island country?
C. Torshavn, on Stromo Island, is the capital of which group of islands, a self-governing region within the kingdom of Denmark?

STARTER 4

Which musical, set in "No Name City", starred Lee Marvin and Clint Eastwood in the 1969 film version?

BONUS 4

Three questions on popular music:

A. Which single reached Number One in Britain in July 1979, and took as its title the reply Brenda Spencer gave when asked why she had run amok with a gun in San Diego?
B. Who wrote the song "Manic Monday", which was a hit for The Bangles in 1986?
C. "Blue Monday" entered the British singles chart four times in the 1980s for which group?

STARTER 5

In the nursery rhyme "Oranges and Lemons", which bells sing "I owe you five farthings"?

BONUS 5

Three questions on initials relating to matters of health:

A. What is represented by the initials FHSA, which in Britain has replaced the family practitioner committees as the body responsible for running general medical services ?
B. What is the OHS, a voluntary scheme by which employers provide a mainly preventative approach for their workers?
C. In occupational health, what is represented by the letters COSHH, which requires everyone in a workplace to ensure that, for example, toxic chemicals do not have adverse effects ?

STARTER 6

Which fictional hero's adventures were first published in 1876? He lives with his priggish brother, Sid, and his good-hearted Aunt Polly in the town of St Petersburg, Missouri.

BONUS 6

Three questions on soils:

A. What word describes a distinctive layer within a soil, that differs chemically or physically from the layers below or above ?
B. If the "A", "B" or "C" horizon is appended by lower case "g", it indicates that which process has occurred as a result of intermittent waterlogging ?
C. What does the "L" represent when the layer of plant material on the soil surface is classified as the "L" horizon ?

STARTER 7

The dancer Jane Avril was immortalized in posters for the Moulin Rouge painted by which French artist?

BONUS 7

Three questions on the Soviet secret police forces:

A. Which four letters referred to the Soviet secret police force which operated from 1934 to 1946, and had the abbreviated Russian name for "People's Commissariat for Internal Affairs"?
B. What name was given to the period of the 1930s when the NKVD helped organise the arrest, trial and often execution of millions of people perceived as dangerous to Stalin?
C. The assassination of which Communist Party leader in 1934 is generally held to mark the beginning of The Great Purges?

STARTER 8

Which broadcaster, who began her career in South Africa, presented *Woman's Hour* for many years before joining the *Today* programme as one of its regular presenters?

BONUS 8

A. In Harry Enfield's television comedy series, which actress played Waynetta Slob?

B. Kathy Burke starred with Ray Winstone in the 1997 film *Nil By Mouth*, which marked the directorial debut of which British actor?

C. Gary Oldman's first major screen role came in 1986 when he portrayed the punk star Sid Vicious in which film, directed by Alex Cox?

STARTER 9

At the instigation of the Italian-American civil rights league, which term is never used in the film *The Godfather*?

BONUS 9

Three questions on Ancient History:

A. Marduk was the supreme god in the mythology of which region of Mesopotamia, which lay along the lower reaches of the river Euphrates?

B. The extensive ruins of Babylon lie near the modern town of Al-Hillah in which country?

C. In 331 BC, Babylon surrendered to which conqueror, who intended to make the city his imperial capital but who died in Nebuchadnezzar's palace in 323 BC?

STARTER 10

Members of the new Welsh Assembly have which two letters after their names?

BONUS 10

Three questions on men's names:

A. Although "Joe" was his name, how was Clint Eastwood's character known in the 1964 film *A Fistful of Dollars*?

B. *The Man Who Was Thursday* and *The Man Who Knew Too Much* are works by which English writer, born in 1874, who converted to Roman Catholicism in 1922?

C. "Any man who goes to a psychiatrist should have his head examined" is a quote attributed to which film producer, who died in 1974?

STARTER 11

In 1999, which club's Nationwide League status was dramatically preserved when goalkeeper Jimmy Glass, on loan from Swindon Town, scored the winning goal after four minutes of injury time?

BONUS 11

Three questions on flyers and flying:

A. The French airman and writer Antoine de Saint-Exupéry, who was declared missing after a flight to North Africa during World War Two, is particularly remembered for which story, first published in 1943?
B. In 1996, which Dutch footballer informed his club and country of a phobia about flying which threatened to cost him his international place?
C. Which American author published *Fear of Flying* in 1974?

STARTER 12

Which sports arena, opened in its present incarnation in 1968 and renovated in 1991, was originally a converted New York railway station?

BONUS 12

Three questions on literature and music:

A. In Tolkein's *The Lord Of The Rings*, what is the name of the swift, tireless horse tamed and ridden by Gandalf?
B. To what is Macbeth referring when he says, "Hence, horrible shadow! Unreal mockery, hence!"?
C. Which Canadian performer worked with the veteran producer Owen Bradley on the 1988 album *Shadowland*?

STARTER 13

Aurigny is the French name for which of the Channel Islands?

BONUS 13

Three questions on musical instruments:

A. First described in the late 15th century, the sackbut was developed from the medieval trumpet probably in Burgundy, and was an early form of which instrument?

B. Born in Scotland in 1732, John Broadwood trained as a cabinet maker before becoming one of the greatest early manufacturers of which instrument, his early square models in the mid-1770s being based on those by Zumpe?

C. Also associated with clarinets and oboes, Theobald Boehm made several improvements to which instrument in the mid-19th century, changing the conical bore to the one now in general use, making fingering easier and so producing a more even tone?

STARTER 14

If you subtract the number of the Just Men from the number of Pillars of Wisdom, what number are you left with?

BONUS 14

Three questions on woods and their uses:

A. What name is usually given to the wood of any of several tropical hardwood timber trees, including the family *meliaceae*, which is of a reddish-brown colour when mature, much used in making furniture?

B. Which American timber, the true form of which is produced by four species of carya, has been used in the manufacture of lacrosse sticks because it can withstand the strain of hard play?

C. Which European species of maple, especially those with a wavy grain, provides the traditional wood for violins?

STARTER 15

The Sally Lunn Museum, where Sally Lunn's buns are baked daily, is a tourist attraction in which city?

BONUS 15

Three questions on dates and events:

A. In *Romeo and Juliet*, Juliet's birthday is described as being "on Lammas-eve" and therefore fell on which date?

B. On 31 July 1996 African leaders met in Tanzania to impose a total economic blockade on which country, following the previous week's military coup?

C. On 31 July 1997, the Conservatives won the first parliamentary by-election since the May general election; in which constituency was it held?

STARTER 16

"Simba" is the Swahili word for which large member of the cat family?

BONUS 16

Three questions on proverbs:

A. According to the proverb, what "is a dish that tastes better cold"?
B. Revenge is described as "the dish which people of taste prefer to eat cold" in which Ealing film comedy of 1949, involving the serial killing of an aristocratic family?
C. Which English poet wrote: "Sweet is revenge – especially to women", in his work *Don Juan*, published between 1819 and 1824?

STARTER 17

In North America, the season lasts from four to six weeks, beginning in January in southern areas and ending in April in the northern regions, for tapping the sap of which tree, for the purposes of making syrup?

BONUS 17

Three questions on British men:

A. Which Scottish composer was born in Edinburgh in 1928, studied in Paris under Nadia Boulanger and wrote the operas *Mary, Queen of Scots* and *A Christmas Carol*, and the ballets *Beauty and the Beast* and *A Tale of Thieves*?
B. In which country are the Musgrave Ranges, a series of granite hills sighted in 1873 by the English explorer William Gosse?
C. First performed in 1959, which English dramatist wrote the play *Sergeant Musgrave's Dance*, in which the title character displays an oddly violent pacifism?

STARTER 18

If you had one coin of each of the five lowest values which are legal tender in this country, how much are they collectively worth?

BONUS 18

Three questions on the 19th-century aesthetic movement:

A. Walter Pater, one of the leading influences on the English aesthetic movement of the 1880s, is associated with which four-word phrase, which claims to sum up the aesthetic doctrine and implies that art is self-sufficient?

B. What was the name of the literary and art periodical, which ran from 1894 to 1897 and provided a forum for writers of the aesthetic movement, its name coming from the art editor Aubrey Beardsley's distinctively coloured covers?

C. According to W.S. Gilbert's satirical attack on the aesthetic movement in *Patience*, "You will rank as an apostle in the high aesthetic band / If you walk down Piccadilly with a poppy or..." – which flower – "in your medieval hand"?

STARTER 19

Which island is connected to Brooklyn by the Varranzano Narrows bridge, completed in 1964?

BONUS 19

Three questions on battles:

A. Which British monarch became, at the Battle of Dettingen in 1743, the last British sovereign to command his troops in battle?

B. "Probably the Battle of Waterloo was won on the playing-fields of Eton, but the opening battles of all subsequent wars have been lost there." Which English writer wrote these lines in *The Lion and the Unicorn* in 1941?

C. Published in 1956, *The Last Battle* is the final volume in which sequence of novels for children?

STARTER 20

Which eponymous hero is found as a baby in Mr Allworthy's bed, is later thrown out of Allworthy's house and after traversing the country finally marries his love Sophia Western?

BONUS 20

Three questions on sequels to novels not written by the original author:

A. Emma Tennant's novel *Pemberley* is a sequel to which classic, published in 1813?

B. Which British female writer, whose works include *I'm the King of the Castle* and *The Woman in Black*, produced a 1993 sequel to Daphne du Maurier's *Rebecca* entitled *Mrs de Winter*?

C. In 1998, Jill Paton Walsh published *Thrones, Dominations*, based on surviving drafts by Dorothy L. Sayers, and featuring which detective hero?

STARTER 21

Barani, turntable, seat drop, crash-dive and free-bounce are movements in which sport?

BONUS 21

Three questions on acronyms used in computing:

A. A measure of computing speed and power which became increasingly common during the 1980s, what does the acronym MIPS represent?
B. Which expression, often abbreviated to a four-letter acronym, originated as computer jargon to imply that what emerges from a system is dependent on the quality of material entering it?
C. What words are represented by the acronym MIDI, being an electronic device enabling equipment such as synthesizers to be connected to computers and used simultaneously?

STARTER 22

The opening words of *The Wind in the Willows* tell us that "Mole had been working hard all the morning…" – doing what?

BONUS 22

Three questions on monuments:

A. Which monument on a hill outside Pretoria commemorates the Battle of Blood River and the achievements of the first Dutch farmers in leaving the British Cape Colony in Southern Africa and moving to the interior during the 1830s?
B. The 500th anniversary of the death of which Portuguese prince is commemorated by the "Monument to the Discoveries" in Lisbon, erected in 1960?
C. "The Memorial to the Disappeared" bears the names of those who went missing in detention at one end of its 180-foot length, whilst those executed for political beliefs are at the other end; it was erected in which South American city, in remembrance of the coup of 1973?

STARTER 23

"Andy in the Garden", depicting a Warhol-like figure, was one of the works in an exhibition which opened on 1 May 1999, at a gallery in the small town of Siegen near Cologne. Who was the artist?

BONUS 23

Three questions on figures in Greek literature:

A. In Aeschylus' play *Seven Against Thebes*, the rival claimants to the throne are the sons of whom?
B. Tiresias, the Seer of Thebes who plays a prominent part in the Oedipus cycle of legends, suffers from which physical handicap?
C. Who was the faithful daughter of Oedipus, who accompanied her blinded father into exile and took care of him in Colonus?

STARTER 24

Which organization, often referred to simply as the World Bank, is represented by the initials IBRD?

BONUS 24

A. Also known as Inchcape Rock, what is the alternative name for the reef off the north-east coast of Scotland with a lighthouse designed by Robert Louis Stevenson's grandfather?
B. Completed in 1503, "Bell Harry" is the great central tower of which English cathedral?
C. Which American-born poet was a Fulbright scholar and received her MA from Cambridge in 1957, and was the author of the partly-autobiographical novel *The Bell-Jar*, published in 1963, the year she died?

STARTER 25

What is the alternative two-word term for a depth-finder, used to determine water depth by measuring the time it takes a sonic pulse to return from the bottom?

BONUS 25

A. Journalists Nicci Gerrard and Sean French write crime fiction novels such as *Killing Me Softly* under what name?
B. Mary J. Latsis and Martha Henissart write a series of novels featuring the Wall Street banker detective John Puttnam Thatcher under what pseudonym?
C. Which former England football coach created the private eye Hazell with Gordon Williams under the pseudonym PB Yuill?

STARTER 26

In the spring of 1999, who followed in the footsteps of Elizabeth Taylor, Lana Turner and Rita Hayworth to become the face of cosmetics firm Max Factor?

BONUS 26

Three questions on breeds of hound:

A. Also called the lion hound, which dog originated in southern Africa and takes part of its name from a section of hair on its back which grows in a direction opposite to the rest of its coat?
B. Also used to hunt bear and game birds, the elkhound is said to be able to detect an elk's scent over a distance of three miles, and originated in which Scandinavian country about 6,000 years ago?
C. The Saluki is one of the oldest pure-bred dogs, and is said to have been used with hawks for hunting which type of antelope, thus giving the dog its alternative name ?

STARTER 27

Factoring the answer to its lowest term, what is five-sixths of two-thirds?

BONUS 27

A. Which cartoon character was created by Leo Baxendale, made her first appearance in *The Beano* in 1953, and is known for her trademark pigtails and tam o'shanter?
B. "Percival Proudfoot" are the forenames of which character, also created by Baxendale, and known by an abbreviation of his surname? He acquired his own short-lived comic in 1977, after over 30 years as part of a famous gang.
C. Which character was originally devised as a Native American version of Dennis the Menace, and was Baxendale's first major character for *The Beano?*

STARTER 28

Which form of transport reappeared on the streets of Paris in April 1999 with a version designed by the Leonhart brothers? It consisted of a fibreglass cabin mounted on a 21-gear tricycle, and was inspired by their travels in Asia.

BONUS 28

Three questions on 20th-century artifacts:

A. Which Spanish porcelain factory is named after the three brothers who founded it in 1952, and is famous for its stylized, long-
   limbed figures?
B. In the late 1930s, Paul Ysart developed new techniques for the
   making of which highly-collectable objects, taking his skills to
   Caithness Glass in 1963 before starting his own business?
C. Which Italian design company was founded in 1921, is known by
   the surname of its founder, Giovanni, and is particularly associated with the design of household objects?

STARTER 29

What would be eaten by a person described as a geophagist?

BONUS 29

Three questions on emancipation:

A. Which of the Tsars issued the "Emancipation Manifesto" of 1861,
   which freed the serfs of the Russian Empire?
B. Abraham Lincoln's "Emancipation Proclamation" of 1863 freed
   slaves in the rebellious southern states of the USA, its provisions
   being extended and confirmed by which amendment to the
   Constitution?
C. The Australian Emancipists were former convicts who campaigned
   from the late 18th century for equal civil rights with the free
   settlers. What collective name was given to those free settlers who
   opposed the campaign?

STARTER 30

Particularly associated with period pieces, which actress
commented, "I am glad... there is not a corset involved" when
discussing her role in *Women Talking Dirty*, the first feature from
Sir Elton John's film production company?

BONUS 30

Three questions linked by an ordinal number:

A. According to John Milton, which year of his life, quote: "Hath
   time, the subtle thief of youth, stolen on its wing"?
B. Which is the 23rd and penultimate letter of the Greek alphabet?
C. In the King James Bible, the 23rd psalm opens: "The Lord is my
   shepherd; I shall not want. He maketh me to lie down in green
   pastures. He leadeth me beside the still waters." What immediately
   follows?

STARTER 31

What nationality was Vladimir Remek who, in March 1978, became the first non-American and non-Soviet in space?

BONUS 31

Three questions on an English town:

A. Dubris was the Roman name for which town on the south coast of England?
B. The flight to Dover, and a sojourn with his eccentric aunt Betsey Trotwood, form part of the adventures of which of Dickens' eponymous heroes?
C. "Many's the Jack of Dover you have sold/That has been twice warmed up and twice left cold." These are translated lines from the prologue to which of Chaucer's Canterbury Tales?

STARTER 32

With reference to royalty, what is represented by the abbreviation TRH?

BONUS 32

Three questions on archaeology:

A. About 3,000 prehistoric standing stones, some bearing images of Roman deities while the addition of crosses and other symbols indicates the arrival of Christianity, are to be found near which village in the Bretagne region of western France?
B. In the news during 2000, what name has been given to the arrangement of circular wooden posts surrounding an inverted tree stump, over 4,000 years old and located on the sands at Holme-next-the-Sea in Norfolk?
C. The recent excavation of Roman remains in Greenwich Park in south-east London was a joint project between the Museum of London, Birkbeck College and which Channel Four programme?

STARTER 33

What number is the square of 18?

BONUS 33

Three questions linked by a surname:

A. Born Walker Smith Junior in 1921, which boxer held the welterweight title from 1946 to 1951, and then defeated Jake LaMotta to win the first of his five middleweight championships?

B. The former Irish President Mary Robinson took up which office with the United Nations High Commission in 1997?

C. In February 2001, which British actress followed Kathleen Turner and Jerry Hall in the role of Mrs Robinson in Terry Johnson's West End stage production of *The Graduate*?

STARTER 34

Which chess piece is known in German as *springer*, meaning "jumper", and in French as *cavalier*?

BONUS 34

Three questions on the human heart:

A. What name is given to the thin-walled chambers serving as collecting stations for blood flowing into the heart, which form the upper and smaller part of the organ?

B. The valve between the right atrium and right ventricle has three flaps and is called the tricuspid. Also known as the bicuspid, what name, deriving from the Latin for "girdle", is given to the valve on the left side that has two flaps?

C. Diastole is that period of heart activity when the ventricles relax; what word means the period when they contract?

STARTER 35

In April 1999, a first-floor suite at the Hotel de la Grotte in Lourdes was the setting for the ordination as a Latin Tridentine priest of Mother Bernadette Marie, better known by what name?

BONUS 35

Three questions on classical music:

A. Who is being described? An Italian-born French composer, he was also a dancer and instrumentalist. His operas include *Alceste* and *Armide*, and he died in 1687 after hitting his toe with the cane he used to beat time, resulting in gangrene.

B. From the 1660s onwards, Lully collaborated with which dramatist on several works, including *Le Bourgeois Gentilhomme* in 1670?

C. Which 17th-century French composer also wrote incidental music for Molière's productions, as well as sacred music such as the harmonization of carol tunes in *Messe de Minuit pour Noël*?

STARTER 36

Native to south-east Asia, "hamadryad" is the alternative name for which animal, which can measure up to five-and-a-half metres in length, and is the world's largest venomous snake?

BONUS 36

Three questions on wood and wood substitutes:

A. What type of wood is made from an odd number of constructional veneers, bonded face-to-face with the grain running in alternate directions?
B. What type of material results from spreading resin-coated particles of soft wood on a flat plate, and bonding them under high pressure and heat?
C. To which three words do the initials MDF refer, in the context of the material much favoured by television DIY programmes?

STARTER 37

In physics, a positively-charged ion is known by what name because it moves towards the cathode during electrolysis?

BONUS 37

Three questions on librarians who went on to other things:

A. After graduating from teacher-training school in 1918, who worked as a librarian's assistant at Peking University in the months leading up to the anti-Japanese "May the Fourth" movement in 1919?
B. Which playwright and novelist worked at the Royal Library in his native Stockholm in 1874, five years before the publication of his first novel *The Red Room*?
C. Which Scottish historian and philosopher was, in 1752, made keeper of the Advocates' Library in Edinburgh, during which time he produced his multi-volumed *History of England*?

STARTER 38

Which organization, with its headquarters in London's Stephen Street, was founded in 1933 to encourage "the use and development of the cinematograph as a means of entertainment and instruction"; the organization also runs the London Film Festival?

BONUS 38

Three questions on notable achievements:

A. In 1999, Eileen Collins became the first American woman to take command of what, describing her achievement as a "huge milestone" for women and one that was "long overdue"?

B. In February 2001, who finished second in the Vendée Globe Yacht Race to become the fastest woman and youngest person to circumnavigate the globe in a single-handed event?

C. Describing herself as, quote: "just a simple human being who gets annoyed when there's no toilet roll in the bathroom," which athlete won the women's 400 metres gold medal at the Sydney Olympics?

STARTER 39

What name is given to the honey-like substance, released from the tamarisk tree of the Arabian desert by the action of feeding insects, or secreted by the insects themselves, and was regarded by the wandering Israelites in *Exodus* as God's gift of bread from heaven?

BONUS 39

Three questions on censorship:

A. The rigid censorship of literature deemed to be corrupting or salacious was advocated by the New York Society for the Suppression of Vice, led by which moral crusade who died in 1915?

B. "Comstockery" was a term coined by which writer, when he heard that the New York Public Library, under Anthony Comstock's influence, had banned the play *Man and Superman*?

C. Which English editor produced the expurgated *Family Shakespeare* of 1818? Among his many deletions was the complete removal of the prostitute Doll Tearsheet from *Henry IV Part Two*.

STARTER 40

What French term refers to the technique used by some painters, notably Max Ernst, whereby paper is placed over a textured surface and rubbed with pencil or crayon to produce an impression?

BONUS 40

A. What Latin name did the ancient Romans give to the Mediterranean Sea, suggesting that they viewed it as their territorial waters?

B. The Cosa Nostra, or Mafia, operates by a moral code known by what name, from the Italian meaning "conspiracy of silence"?

C. *Euroleon nostras* is a species of ant-lion fly, resembling the damsel-fly and also known by the name of which English county, it having been first observed in 1994 on the RSPB's nature reserve at Minsmere?

STARTER 41

What, in theatrical slang, is Kensington Gore?

BONUS 41

Three questions on John Grisham novels adapted for the cinema:

A. Which actor appeared in *The Firm* as Avery Tolar, mentor to the Harvard Law School graduate Mitch McDeere, and also in *The Chamber* as white supremacist Sam Cayhall?

B. Having previously directed *Klute* and *All The President's Men*, who directed the 1993 adaptation of Grisham's novel *The Pelican Brief*?

C. Which film of 1997 stars Matt Damon as an inexperienced lawyer taking on the case of a leukaemia victim in dispute with his insurance company?

STARTER 42

The comedy writer John O'Farrell's account of, quote, "Eighteen miserable years in the life of a Labour supporter," was published in 1998 under which title, shared with a song by the group D:Ream?

BONUS 42

Three questions on a herb:

A. Which herb has a name said to derive from a Norse word meaning 'to lull', as at one time it was thought to induce sleep? It is often used in the process of pickling salmon.

B. "Pennyroyal", "apple" and "ginger" are all varieties of which herb?

C. Which herb has dull, grey-green leaves and a name deriving ultimately from the Latin meaning "safe", in reference to its healing properties?

STARTER 43

Born in St Joseph, Missouri in 1904, with which instrument was the jazz musician Coleman Hawkins particularly associated?

BONUS 43

Three questions on 1990s popular culture:

A. Which two-word logo, evoking the extreme sports ethos, was introduced in 1990 by the brothers who had created the "Life's A Beach" surf clothes of the previous decade?

B. In the animated television show *Ren and Stimpy*, the slow-witted character of Stimpson is a cat; what breed of dog is the "asthma-hound" Ren Höek?

C. The culture surrounding rap music, which also embraces graffiti and break-dancing, is given what name, first heard as word-play in the record "Rapper's Delight" by The Sugarhill Gang?

STARTER 44

Originally the name for a single gun-decked, three-masted, square-rigged sailing vessel of French design, adopted by the British, which class of small, single-screw warship was devised for convoy escort duties during the Second World War?

BONUS 44

A. In brass musical instruments, what name is given to the detachable piece of metal tubing, usually inserted between the mouthpiece and main body, to allow the player to reach notes not included in the harmonic series of the original air column?

B. The 19th-century British scientist Sir William Crookes is noted for his discovery of which bluish-grey metallic element, resembling lead and found in iron pyrites, which is toxic to humans and has the atomic number 81?

C. According to Greek mythology, in addition to pastoral or idyllic poetry, of what was Thalia the muse?

STARTER 45

Kiritimati, one of the islands of the west central Pacific Ocean, is the largest island made entirely of what substance?

BONUS 45

Three questions on settlements:

A. Called Edenglassie when it was a convict settlement in the 1820s, which city is Australia's third largest in terms of population, and changed its name to honour a former governor of New South Wales when it was declared a town in 1834?
B. Nakuru, a settlement near the Mau escarpment of the African Rift Valley, is the third largest settlement in which country?
C. Belo Horizonte has a population of over 2,000,000, making it the third largest city in which South American country?

STARTER 46

"Lodovico's Technique" is an experimental form of mind control to which Alex is subjected during a term of imprisonment in which novel of 1962?

BONUS 46

Three questions on the human skeleton:

A. Rachis (pr: ray'kiss) is the anatomical name for which section of the human skeleton?
B. The first cervical vertebra in the neck region of the backbone is called the atlas. What name is given to the second cervical vertebra, because it forms a pivot on which the atlas can rotate?
C. What collective term is applied to the 12 bones of the vertebral column to which the ribs are attached?

STARTER 47

The Rhymney, Ely and Taff rivers flow through which British city?

BONUS 47

A. Which fruit plant of the genus *fragaria* and family *rosaceae* is low-growing and has hairy leaves with a saw-tooth edge, while the fruit itself contains partially embedded achenes or seeds?
B. "Gardenia perfume lingering on a pillow,/Wild strawberries only seven francs a kilo" are the opening words of a verse of which

song, written in the 1930s and performed by many artists including Frank Sinatra and Bryan Ferry?

C. Who wrote "If you are foolish enough to be contented, don't
show it, but grumble with the rest" in his book of 1886, entitled
Idle Thoughts of An Idle Fellow?

STARTER 48

What name was given to the area of Manhattan's Central Park
which lies opposite the Dakota Building on West 72nd Street, in
memory of John Lennon and recalling the title of a Beatles song
of 1967?

BONUS 48

Three questions on American dentists:

A. In 1846, the American dentist William Morton made the first
successful public demonstration of which volatile liquid as an
anaesthetic?

B. Graduating from the Pennsylvania College of Dental Surgery in
1872, which dentist, also a gambler and gunman, assisted the
Earp brothers at the celebrated gunfight at the OK Corral?

C. Which American actor and comedian played Orin Scrivello, the
pain-inflicting dentist in the 1986 film *Little Shop of Horrors?*

STARTER 49

Called Milou when Hergé's cartoon strip first appeared in
Belgium's *Le Petit Vingtième*, Tin Tin's dog is more familiarly
known to English readers by which name?

BONUS 49

Three questions on famous tombs:

A. Which landmark in Rome was constructed as a tomb for the
Emperor Hadrian and his successors, and because of its strategic
position became the city's most impregnable fortress?

B. Which king of England was buried at Saint Stephen's in Caen,
although his corpulent body proved too large for the stone
sarcophagus that had been prepared?

C. In which Andalusian city is the Gothic cathedral of Santa Maria
de la Encarnacion, containing the Royal Chapel with its tomb of
Ferdinand and Isabella?

STARTER 50

Who was Superior General of the Roman Catholic Order of the Missionaries from 1950 until March 1997 when her Indian-born successor, Sister Nirmala, was finally named to continue her work with the poor and needy?

BONUS 50

Three questions on literary dedications:

A. In which book of 1923 did Winifred Holtby write "To David and Alice is dedicated this imaginary story of imaginary events in an imaginary farm"?
B. Agatha Christie dedicated *The Mirror Crack'd From Side to Side* 'in admiration' of which actress, who had achieved popularity in the film role of Miss Marple?
C. Which author dedicated his children's book of 1863, "To my youngest son, Grenville Arthur, and to all other good little boys"?

8

Who writes the questions?

Our question-setters are the unsung heroes of *University Challenge* – a dedicated band of obsessive individuals compelled for ever to carry notebooks with them wherever they go, constantly jotting down any fact, any scrap of information which could be turned into a question.

It sounds an easy job, and it is easy to write a few questions, or even a few dozen. The great skill lies in providing hundreds, perhaps thousands, year in, year out, without repeating material, and without getting too obscure.

We look for two things in our question-setters. One is that they should have an academic background; most will be former teachers or lecturers. And the other is that if possible, they should have gone through the quiz-show process as a contestant; there's nothing quite like having to sit in the spotlight on the receiving end of a few tough questions for really focusing the mind on what is a fair thing to be asked, and how a clearly-worded question should sound.

Century Quiz is the Liverpool-based firm of Neville Cohen and Janet Barker, both of whom are ex-*Mastermind* contestants, and who now provide a large amount of questions for *University Challenge*, as well as for other television quizzes. Neville and Dr Stan Shaw, a retired lecturer from Salford University, between them supply most of our science questions. David Elias is a former *Krypton Factor* contestant; he, along with Janet Crompton, Christine Ansell and Saira Dunnakey, a former *Mastermind* question-checker, supply the bulk of our question material.

Because our questions are harder to answer, they're also harder to write. We won't ask which actor plays which role on *Emmerdale* – although some of our teams might wish that we did – and the areas other programmes rely heavily on, such as pop music, film, television in general and soap operas in particular, we include only rarely. When we do allow questions on popular culture, it is usually for one of two reasons: there are those areas of popular culture worthy of anyone's attention (the American sit-com *Frasier* crops up frequently), and there is the fun of luring contestants into abandoning all their street-cred by admitting that they know more than any adult should about Bananarama or Barbie.

There are several tricks to writing *University Challenge* questions. The first is to make them sound harder than they actually are. We use academic terminology to ask about a subject some of our teams will have studied at 'O' level. We enjoy hearing Jeremy say, "So, Warwick, your bonuses are on quantum theory," or "Your bonuses are on the Cathars" because it sounds as if what follows will be extremely difficult but, again, questions will be pitched in such a way that our teams will have a reasonable chance of answering at least one. Another trick is to include the inevitable. If a team is answering a set on Flemish painters and they've only ever heard of Breughel, they should stick to their guns and keep saying Breughel throughout the set, because there's a very good chance they'll get five points on the last question. The hardest of the three bonuses usually goes in the middle, and the easiest will be at the end so that teams will, hopefully, get applause from the audience for at least one right answer.

To be fair to our students, they do seem to get brighter, year on year. When the programme relaunched in 1994, the production team used a couple of devices to try and ensure teams acquitted themselves reasonably well or, as Jeremy likes to put it, "To reassure the taxpayer their money is being well-spent." Every third starter would be one that we considered any team should be able to answer. Failing that, if both teams were struggling with starter questions, Jeremy would have a pile of easy questions hidden to one side of his desk which he could grab to get them back on track. We're happy to report the easy pile now goes largely untouched..

And what follows are the kind of questions we would allocate to a second-round match – none from the 'easy' pile.

ROUND TWO QUESTIONS

STARTER 51

Since 1986 all federal offices, schools, banks and post offices have closed across America on the third Monday of January, to celebrate the birth, the life and the dream of which famous person?

BONUS 51
A. Convicted of treason in the US in 1949, but pardoned in 1977, Iva Toguri D'Aquino was one of about a dozen women broadcasters collectively given which nickname by American troops serving in the Pacific during the Second World War?
B. Mildred Gillars was an American woman convicted of treason in 1949 for her broadcast to American forces shortly before the Allied invasion of Normandy. What was her nickname?
C. What alliterative nickname was given by American troops to the North Vietnamese broadcaster Trinh Thi Hgo, whose propaganda broadcasts were heard on *Voice of Vietnam*?

STARTER 52

In recognition of the fact that, at the time, Britain's secret services were headed by a woman, Stella Rimmington, which role in the Bond film *Goldeneye* was played by Dame Judi Dench?

BONUS 52
Three questions on film:
A. The film *Gladiator*, directed by Ridley Scott, contains scenes completed with computer animation, following the death of which actor during the filming schedule?
B. Which horror film actor's death resulted in him being replaced by the director's wife's chiropractor, in the cult classic *Plan 9 From Outer Space*?
C. Which actor was killed during the making of the thriller *The Crow*, with some of his scenes being finished by computer animation?

STARTER 53

Invented by Russian-born electronics engineer Vladimir Zworikin, the iconoscope, patented in 1923, and the kinescope, patented the following year, formed the first all-electronic system of what?

BONUS 53

Three questions on Elizabeth I:

A. The 20th-century opera *Gloriana*, describing the relationship between Elizabeth and the Earl of Essex, is the work of which English composer?

B. In which film of 1978, directed by Derek Jarman, is Elizabeth I transported to the 20th century, being largely appalled by what she sees?

C. In which novel by Virginia Woolf is the eponymous hero a favourite of Elizabeth who lives live for 400 years, surviving into the 20th century and changing gender on the way?

STARTER 54

What nickname was given to the Boeing 747 which, when it came into service in 1970, had twice the carrying capacity of any previous jet passenger airliner?

BONUS 54

A. Which word describes a mudflow of volcanic material, such as that formed by rain on ash material, or the mixing of debris with river water, an example being that which enveloped Herculaneum following the eruption of Vesuvius in 79 AD?

B. Lahore is the second largest city by population in Pakistan, and is the capital of which province?

C. Lahina was the 16th-century originator of the Punjabi script called Gurmukhi. It is notably used in sections of the sacred *Adi Granth*, which forms the basis of which religion?

STARTER 55

Which sport has a playing area whose maximum dimensions are 62 feet 10 and $^{11}/_{16}$ ths inches by 42 inches?

BONUS 55

Three questions on popular music:

A. Which popular music group was formed in 1964 by Scott Engel,

John Maus and Gary Leeds?

B. Taking their name from a term used for them by their black fans, which duo was formed in 1962 by Bobby Hatfield and Bill Medley?

C. Taking their name from a then-current slang term for a marijuana cigarette, which group was formed in 1970 by John Hartman, Tom Johnson, John Shogren and Patrick Simmons?

STARTER 56

The Red Arrow train runs from Moscow to which city?

BONUS 56

Three questions on industrial management theory:

A. Born in 1856, which American inventor and engineer introduced the concept of scientific management, a forerunner of time and motion studies based on the breakdown of tasks?

B. "Theory X" views workers as fundamentally lazy and in need of carrot-and-stick management. Which American psychologist suggested "Theory Y" which, in contrast, argues that there is a psychological need to work and achieve responsibility?

C. Which New York-born psychologist, after working on McGregor's "Theory Y", produced a theory of "Hierarchy of Needs" in motivation, based on the urge to satisfy basic needs such as food, as well as more abstract needs such as self-actualization?

STARTER 57

Which four-letter word can mean a unit of mass equal to 32.174 pounds, a bullet, a gulp, especially of liquor, or a garden pest?

BONUS 57

Three questions on "good men":

A. Which writer was described by Lenin as, "a good man fallen among Fabians"?

B. Described in Luke's gospel as "a good man, and a just", which Biblical figure begged Pilate for the body of Christ after the Crucifixion?

C. Which American president said, in a speech of 1903: "A man who is good enough to shed his blood for his country is good enough to be given a square deal afterward"?

STARTER 58

In the Second World War, what term was used by the Germans for a prisoner-of-war camp for officers, the term "Stalag" referring to a camp for non-commissioned officers and men?

BONUS 58

Three questions on autobiographies:

A. Opening with his childhood as a white, Jewish South African with the nickname "Little Ant", which actor and novelist produced his autobiography in May 2000 under the title *Beside Myself*?
B. *All of Me*, written with Robin McGibbon and published in 2000, is the autobiography of which actress, and includes her description of herself as, quote "A right little goer"?
C. Posters advertising which author's autobiography were removed by London Underground in 2001 because they depicted him as a child with a cigarette in his mouth?

STARTER 59

What name is given to the young of a beaver or a squirrel, although it is more usually applied to the young of another animal?

BONUS 59

Three questions designed to test how much time you spend in Internet chat rooms:

A. Acronyms are frequently used in Internet chat rooms to speed up communication. Suggesting that the recipient's amateur attempts are not quite up to the mark, which six-word phrase is represented by the acronym DGUYDJ?
B. Suggesting that the writer is describing a first, or uninformed response, which six-word phrase is represented by acronym: OTTOMH?
C. Suggesting that the reader should try to be alert to the current situation, which six-word phrase is represented by the acronym: WUASTC?

STARTER 60

Traditionally the work of the semi-legendary Queen Sammuramat or of King Nebuchadrezzar II who may have built them to console his Median wife, Amytis, who missed the mountains and greenery of her homeland, which wonders of the ancient world were situated within the walls of the ancient palace at Babylon?

BONUS 60

Three questions on television presenters:

A. Which television presenter was born in London in 1944? At the age of five he moved to New York; after graduating from law school he worked for Robert Kennedy, later becoming the youngest ever Mayor of Cincinnati.

B. Which television presenter won a court battle in 1998 against Texas cattle ranchers, who claimed she had defamed the beef industry in a programme about BSE? She was obliged to move her show from Chicago to Amarillo during the trial.

C. Which television presenter has also been a successful actress, having starred in the cult films *Last Exit to Brooklyn, Serial Mom* and *Hairspray*?

STARTER 61

Envied by her beautiful but cruel stepmother, which daughter of a king is known in the original story by the Brothers Grimm as "Sneewitchen"?

BONUS 61

Three questions on traditional pub games:

A. Which game is played with a pack of cards and a peg-board, and is the only card game allowed to be played in pubs, for "small stakes only"?

B. Popular in Kent, which game requires a batsman to strike a small rubber ball between two posts at the other end of a 21-yard pitch, the bowling side trying to knock over a wicket which the batsman is not allowed to defend?

C. Invented in France in 1910, and imported into the UK by holidaymakers, which variant of the game boules takes its name from Marseilles slang meaning "feet tied together"?

STARTER 62

Beginning in 1955 with *The Quatermass Experiment*, which film production company, named after one of its co-founders, gained fame and fortune from its cycle of horror films?

BONUS 62

Three questions on electronic circuit analysis:

A. Which Russian scientist gives his name to laws of current and voltage, the latter stating that the algebraic sum of all voltage sources and voltage drops in a closed loop equals zero?

B. Whose theorem suggests that any linear circuit, consisting of a resistance and one or more sources of voltage and having two output terminals, can be replaced by a single voltage source and a single series resistance for the purpose of circuit analysis?

C. Whose theorem states that any linear circuit, consisting of resistances and one or more voltage sources and having two output terminals, can be replaced with a single constant-current source and a single parallel resistance for the purpose of circuit analysis?

STARTER 63

Of what are the following all types: "Betweens", "Sharps", "Bodkins" and "Darners"?

BONUS 63

Three questions on 18th-century personalities:

A. In what context did Jack Sheppard, James Maclaine and John Rann achieve notoriety in the 18th century?

B. Known as "The Gentleman Highwayman", James Maclaine, executed in 1750, was assisted in much of his crime by a failed apothecary. What was his name?

C. Which two actors played Plunkett and Maclaine in a recent film adaptation of their story, under the tag-line: "They rob the rich, and that's it"?

STARTER 64

What name has been used in English law to mean an anonymous party in a legal action, and has come to be used in the USA to mean an ordinary or typical citizen roughly the equivalent of the English "Joe Bloggs"?

BONUS 64

Three questions on things black:

A. *The Black Tulip* is a novel of 1850, set in 17th-century Holland, by which French author?

B. "Black Rod" is the chief usher of whose department of the Royal household?
C. "Black Agnes" was a palfrey horse, named after the 14th-century Countess of Dunbar, and owned by which 16th-century monarch?

STARTER 65

Augustine Aloysius were the middle names of which Irish writer, born in 1882?

BONUS 65

Three questions on chain stores:

A. Which chain of stores was founded by brothers Clemens and August Brenninkmeijer in the Netherlands in 1841, and announced the closure of all its British branches in June 2000?
B. Which chain of British stores was founded by Richard Block and David Quayle in Portswood Road, Southampton, in 1969?
C. Which travel company takes its name from the initials of the son of its founder, the company originally being named after the founder himself?

STARTER 66

Only just visible to the naked eye and evident as clumps on the underside of fern leaves, which reproductive structures derive their name from the Greek for "sow", and are produced by bacteria, algae, protozoa, fungi and some plants?

BONUS 66

Three questions on modern journeys using old technology:

A. In June 2000, Adrian Nicholas made a 7,000-foot parachute descent over South Africa using a parachute based on a design produced around 500 years earlier by whom?
B. Funded in 2000 with £100,000 of National Lottery money, the Millennium Stone project aimed to move a four-tonne bluestone from the Preseli Hills in Pembrokeshire to which site in England?
C. What was the name of the reed boat in which Thor Heyerdahl crossed the Atlantic to within 600 miles of Central America in 1969, proving it may have been possible for Ancient Egyptians to influence pre-Columbian culture?

STARTER 67

Which word can mean all of the following: the spawn or larvae of shellfish, especially oysters; a petty quarrel; and a short cloth gaiter covering the instep and ankle?

BONUS 67

Three questions on the Internet:

A. As an integral part of an Internet website address, what do the initials TLD stand for?
B. What TLD should designate an international non-profit-making body?
C. In Internet terms, what does the acronym URL stand for?

STARTER 68

In the play by Shakespeare, what are the final four words of the dying Hamlet?

BONUS 68

Under the terms of the Gaming Act 1968, it is permissible to play certain games in a British public house, for small stakes, without a licence. There are seven such games.

Q. Name three for five points, five for ten points and all seven for fifteen.

STARTER 69

What word derives from the name of the form in which Krishna's image was carried through the streets of Puri in a heavy chariot, devotees reputedly throwing themselves under its wheels? The word has come to mean any overwhelming force, or a large and heavy motor vehicle.

BONUS 69

In mathematics, if the term J is used to describe the square root of -1, what are the values of the following?

A. J^2
B. J^3
C. J^4

STARTER 70

Which is the oldest infantry regiment in the British Army, their ceremonial outfit consisting of tunic, tartan trousers and Glengarry cap?

BONUS 70
Three questions on human biology:

A. Which gland of the body is divided into anterior and posterior sections, is situated just below the brain and is also known as the hypophysis?
B. Released by the posterior or neuro-hypophysis of the pituitary, ADH is responsible for the control of what in the body?
C. What type of diabetes is caused by the under-secretion of ADH causing patients to produce copious quantities of urine, resulting in thirst and dehydration and characterized by excessive drinking?

STARTER 71

"Mori Cambo", the old Celtic name for the Lune Estuary which was referred to by the Greek geographer Ptolemy in the second century, is the origin of the name of which inlet of the Irish Sea?

BONUS 71
Three questions on quotations about war:

A. "War is peace, freedom is slavery, ignorance is strength" is a quotation from which 20th-century novel?
B. Which American soldier and politician addressed the American Congress in 1790 with the words: "To be prepared for war is one of the most effectual means of preserving peace"?
C. Which Roman soldier and poet, born in 65 BC, wrote in his satires: "In peace, as a wise man, he should make suitable preparation for war"?

STARTER 72

What name is given in the book of Isiah for a sea serpent, and has come to mean both a large and powerful ship and an autocratic monarch or state, in allusion to the book by Thomas Hobbes?

BONUS 72
Three questions on the common names of upland birds in Scotland:

A. What name is given to *lapogus mutus*, the white grouse of high mountains in Scotland?
B. What name is given to *Tetrao Urogallus*, the largest of the grouse family inhabiting pine woods in Scotland?
C. What name is given to *Tetrao tetrix*, well known for its communal mating displays or "leks" in Spring?

STARTER 73

When asked to stand to the right of Lady Thatcher at a photocall marking the 20th anniversary of her first election triumph, the reply "That would be difficult" reputedly came from which former British Prime Minister?

BONUS 73

Three questions on parents and children in science:
A. Which female scientist had a daughter who made the first artificial radio-isotopes, work for which she and her husband were awarded the Nobel Prize in chemistry in 1935?
B. What was the surname of Francis, who with his father Charles reported their experimental work on plant movements in 1880?
C. What is the surname of William who, with his son Lawrence, founded the science of X-ray crystallography?

STARTER 74

What is the chief feature of the medical condition bradycardia, sometimes found in healthy individuals, especially athletes, but also seen in some patients with reduced thyroid activity or hypothermia?

BONUS 74

Three questions on coniferous trees in the British Isles. What is the common name for the following?
A. First, trees of the genus *abies* (pronounced abees)?
B. What is the common name for trees of the genus *picea*?
C. And finally, the species *pinus sylvestris*?

STARTER 75

Assuming that there are no jokers, if the two of diamonds is removed from a pack of playing cards, what is the probability, expressed as a fraction, that the next card pulled from the pack will be a diamond?

BONUS 75

Three questions on slang terms for sums of money:
A. Represented by a small horse less than 14.2 hands high, what is the slang term for £25?

B. How much money is represented by a 2,240-pound weight, or 20 hundredweight?

C. What animal of the order primates is slang for £500?

STARTER 76

Easter Sunday 1999 saw the first use of *The New Methodist Worship Book*, which replaces the 1975 text and significantly includes a reference to God as what?

BONUS 76

Three questions on winds:

A. Which word means a mild or gentle breeze, and derives from the name of the Greek god of the west wind?

B. The seven sons and three daughters of which Old Testament figure were killed when a violent wind came from the desert and destroyed the house where they were eating and drinking?

C. Since 1970, Belmopan has served as the capital of which Central American country, its original administrative centre having been destroyed by a hurricane in 1961?

STARTER 77

What animal would be classified as follows: kingdom *animalia*, phylum *chordata*, class *mammalia*, order *carnivora*, family *canidae*, genus *canis*, species *canis familiaris*?

BONUS 77

Three questions on telephone services:

A. One of the most frequently dialled lines in Britain, with a record number of calls taken during 2000, 08457 484950 is the telephone number of which enquiry service?

B. What is the name of the organization which can be contacted on the number 0800 555111?

C. What service is called with the number 0845 4647?

STARTER 78

Which word, from the Greek for "grace", can be used in a religious sense for a divinely-bestowed talent or power, and can also describe a strong ability to attract people and inspire loyalty and admiration?

BONUS 78

Three questions on an outlaw:

A. *The True History of the Kelly Gang*, presenting a sympathetic portrait of the 19th-century outlaw Ned Kelly and published in 2000, is by which Australian author, a former winner of the Booker Prize?
B. Knighted in 1981, which Melbourne-born artist made his name with a series of paintings of Ned Kelly, begun in 1946?
C. The 1970 film *Ned Kelly*, directed by Tony Richardson, featured which performer in the title role?

STARTER 79

Although now little used, an important contribution to the industrial revolution was the "puddling process" for the manufacture of what?

BONUS 79

Three bonus questions:

A. Which word is said to have been coined by Richard Owen, the first director of London's Natural History Museum, after he prepared a public exhibition of fossils in 1842?
B. Walter Alvarez, the physicist born in San Francisco in 1911, was the first to argue which theory to explain the extinction of the dinosaurs around 70 million years ago?
C. Which actor provided the narration for the BBC television series *Walking With Dinosaurs*?

STARTER 80

Which writer and naval administrator was appointed Secretary of the Admiralty in 1672, and was deprived of his post in 1679 and imprisoned in the Tower of London for his alleged complicity in the Popish Plot; he was reappointed in 1684?

BONUS 80

Three questions on medicine:

A. Which acute, highly contagious infection, now rare in most western countries, takes its name from the Greek for "leather", probably because of its tendency to form a soft, grey membrane across the throat?
B. What name is given to the emergency surgical operation, some-

times necessary in cases of diphtheria, in which an artificial opening is made through the front of the neck into the windpipe?

C. Which Hungarian-born American paediatrician lends his name
to the test he developed in 1913 to determine susceptibility to
diphtheria in humans?

STARTER 81

Who said "About time too" on hearing that he was to receive an
honorary fellowship from the Royal Photographic Society, the
presentation in April 1999 coinciding with the launch of an exhibition of his work at the Barbican Centre entitled "Birth of the
Cool"?

BONUS 81

Three questions on writing about dreams:

A. Who was the author of *Die Traumdeutung*, or *The Interpretation Of
Dreams*, published in 1900?

B. Who was the author of 1816 of *The Dream*, a poem in which he
described his love for his cousin Mary Chaworth, and the disaster
of his marriage to Annabella Milbanke?

C. Who was the author in 1866 of *The Dream of Gerontius*, a poem later
set to music by Edward Elgar?

STARTER 82

The signatures of Casanova and the Marquis de Sade have been
found close together on the wall of which notorious emperor's
subterranean golden palace in Rome?

BONUS 82

Three questions on gases:

A. Developed in Germany during the Second World War, what name
is given to the deadly nerve gas which was used in 1995 during an
attack by the Aum Supreme Truth terrorist group on the Tokyo
Underground?

B. The chlorinated compound 1-O-chloro-phenyl-2, 2-di-cyano-
ethylene is more commonly known by which name, derived from
the initials of the chemists who devised it?

C. Which gas is a powerful vesicant attacking the skin, eyes and
lungs, and was first used by the German army on the battlefield of
Ypres in 1917?

STARTER 83

With Alexei Sayle as its first M.C., what was founded in May 1979 by Don Ward above a Soho strip club?

BONUS 83

Three questions on battles:

A. Now used colloquially to refer to the struggle to lose weight, the "Battle of the Bulge" was originally a German counter-offensive of the Second World War to gain control of which city on the *Schelde* River?
B. A satire in which ancient and modern tomes attack each other in St James' Library, *The Battle of the Books* is a prose work of 1704 by which writer?
C. Originally staged to mark the coronation of Edward VII and Queen Alexandra, the "Battle of the Flowers" is now held annually on which island?

STARTER 84

Who said, after being named Footballer of the Century, "It's a pleasure to be standing up here. It's a pleasure to be standing up"?

BONUS 84

Three questions on survival techniques:

In 1999, Joshua Piven and David Borgenicht produced *The Worst-Case Scenario Survival Handbook*. For your bonuses, identify the survival advice they give for each scenario:

A. First, in advising on how to wrestle free from an alligator, assuming the attack takes place on land, into what position should you try and manoeuvre yourself?
B. In advising on how to escape from a sinking car, what advice is offered first, for the moment your car hits the water?
C. If you are completely buried by an avalanche of snow, what suggestion is offered for determining which way is up?

STARTER 85

Which event, held on 30 May 1999 and won by Sweden, closed with the contestants joining in a song for peace in the Balkans?

BONUS 85

Three questions on proverbs in Shakespeare:

A. In which of Shakespeare's comedies does Lysander observe, as he is preparing to elope with Hermia: "The course of true love never did run smooth"?
B. Which of Shakespeare's characters has the lines: "Since brevity is the soul of wit and tediousness the limbs and outward flourishes, I will be brief"? He holds the position of Lord Chamberlain at the court of Elsinore.
C. In which of Shakespeare's plays is it written on a scroll, "All that glisters is not gold"?

STARTER 86

What is the English term used to describe roads such as the Parisian Boulevards Exterieurs and Boulevard Péripherique?

BONUS 86

A. In Italian cuisine, what are taleggio, fontina, provolone and cacio-cavallo?
B. Which Persian mystic of about the 6th century BC is reputed to have lived on nothing but cheese for many years?
C. Hervé and the strong-smelling Limburger are cheeses most closely associated with which European country?

STARTER 87

The upper valley of the River Elan, a tributary of the Wye, has been dammed to provide water for which city in the English Midlands?

BONUS 87

Three questions on eternal life:

A. In Greek mythology, who was the lover of the goddess Eos? He was granted the gift of eternal life but not eternal youth, and grew weaker, older and smaller until he ended his days as a cicada.
B. Becoming decrepit and simple-minded as they aged, requiring the care and support of the young for ever, the Struldbrugs are an immortal race in which 18th-century satire?
C. Which author created the everlasting Buddhist paradise of Shangri-La, in a novel in 1933?

STARTER 88

Stephanie Maria are the forenames of which German sports-woman?

BONUS 88

Three questions on political exile:

A. Exiled from South Africa for her political views, which Johannesburg-born singer married the radical black activist Stokely Carmichael in the USA, moving with him to Guinea in 1969?
B. The Dalai Lama Tenzin Gyatso was forced into permanent exile from Tibet in 1959, afterwards establishing a democratic alternative government from a base in which hill station of Himachal Pradesh?
C. Which politician was a founder of the National League for Democracy, and rejected an offer from the Burmese government in 1994 to free her from house arrest on condition that she exile herself abroad?

STARTER 89

Which American city, built on the site of Fort Duquesne in what is now Pennsylvania, was laid out in 1764 to a design by John Campbell and named after a British Prime Minister?

BONUS 89

Three questions on eponymous characters:

A. How is Anne Catherick described in the title of Wilkie Collin's novel of 1860?
B. What name does John Fowles give to the French Lieutenant's Woman in his novel of that name, published in 1969?
C. What names does DH Lawrence give to the *Women In Love* in his novel of 1921?

STARTER 90

"Born" Edna Beasley, who was created a Dame on TV in the 1970s in a spontaneous gesture by Australian Prime Minister Gough Whitlam?

BONUS 90

Three questions on schools in Dickens:

A. Which girl at Miss Twinkleton's Nuns' House School at Cloisterham

is persuaded by her father to become the fiancée of Edwin Drood?
B. Who was sent from London by his Uncle Ralph as assistant to the Yorkshire schoolteacher Wackford Squeers?
C. The words "Take care of him; he bites" are written on a placard and worn by which of Dicken's eponymous heroes as he first attends school at Salem House?

STARTER 91

Which drummer, when inadvertently shown with Freddie Mercury, became the first living non-royal person to appear on a British postage stamp?

BONUS 91

Three questions on BBC personnel:

A. Quote: "I only ever applied for two jobs at the BBC: the first, in 1970, as a reporter on Radio Teeside – which I failed to get – and the second, nearly 30 years later, as Director General." Who made this admission during his MacTaggart lecture in 2000?
B. A former producer of *File on Four*, which broadcaster was appointed controller of BBC Radio 4 in 2000?
C. Which Los Angeles-born musical conductor succeeded Andrew Davis in September 2000 as chief conductor of the BBC Symphony Orchestra?

STARTER 92

In the world of popular music, Jim and Vic have topped the charts, and Martha reached No.4; what surname do they share?

BONUS 92

Three questions on comedy:

A. The American comedians Steve Harvey, D.L. Hughley, Cedric "The Entertainer" and Bernie Mac are featured in *The Original Kings of Comedy*, a stand-up concert film made by which American director?
B. *Car Wash, Uptown Saturday Night* and *California Suite* are among the films to star which American comedian, described in his early years as "The Black Lenny Bruce"?
C. Which American comedian, best known for his parodies of black attitudes in the USA, co-wrote, produced and starred as a middle-class rapper in the spoof *CB4*?

STARTER 93

Supposedly Ian Fleming's own choice to play James Bond, which actor played Sir James Bond in the 1967 spoof Bond movie *Casino Royale*?

BONUS 93

Three questions on dictators:

A. In power in Uganda from 1971 to 1979, Idi Amin subsequently became a resident of which Middle Eastern country, granted asylum there on condition that he make no political statements?
B. Zimbabwe's Robert Mugabe offered a safe haven to which Ethiopian dictator, deposed from power in 1991?
C. Granted asylum by the Brazilian authorities, Alfred Stroesner had led an oppressive military regime in which South American country until he was deposed by a coup in 1989?

STARTER 94

Pongo pygmaeus is the Latin name for which primate, an endangered species found in the wild mainly in Indonesia and Malaysia?

BONUS 94

Three questions on the EU:

A. Two years before the Treaty of Rome was signed in 1957, plans for a European Economic Community had been formally discussed at a conference of ministers in which city of north-eastern Sicily?
B. In which EU member state did Margaret Thatcher sign the Single European Act in February 1986?
C. Marking the first involvement by a Labour government in Europe for 18 years, Britain signed up to the EU Social Chapter at a conference staged in 1997 in which capital city?

STARTER 95

Which four-letter word can be a garden flower, a part of the eye or the Greek goddess of the rainbow?

BONUS 95

Three questions on medical conditions:

A. Which medical term describes an abnormally low level of sugar in the blood, most common in diabetes melitus, which, in very severe cases, may lead to coma?

B. Syncope is a medical term for a loss of consciousness more commonly known by which name?

C. Halothane, the potent general anaesthetic used to induce unconsciousness in a patient undergoing a surgical operation, is generally administered by which method?

STARTER 96

The Far Corporation, a studio group put together in Germany in 1985, had a hit with which Led Zeppelin classic, also a hit for Rolf Harris in 1993?

BONUS 96

Three questions on appointments:

A. Formerly the director of Australian Ballet, who was appointed to succeed Sir Anthony Dowells as Director of the Royal Ballet at Covent Garden from 2001?

B. A former head of the New York subway, which 63-year old American was appointed by Ken Livingstone in October 2000 as Chief Executive of London Transport?

C. What is the nationality of Duncan Fletcher, appointed in 1999 to coach the England cricket team?

STARTER 97

In law, which word is used in a statute to mean "immediately" or "within a reasonable time"?

BONUS 97

Three questions on the names of London Bridges:

A. Which bridge crosses the Thames to the west of Southwark Bridge, and takes its name from the religious community which, from 1276, occupied the site on its north bank?

B. The name of which bridge is believed to derive from a term meaning "Muddy Landing Place", and is shared with a palace on its south bank?

C. Which 19th-century public figure lends his name to the bridge which links Chelsea to the north with Battersea Park to the south?

STARTER 98

In its broadest definition, what word refers to that part of the total repertoire of human action which is socially, as opposed to genetically, transmitted?

BONUS 98

Three questions on footballing firsts:

A. In the second match ever played between England and Scotland, England's captain, Kenyon-Slaney, became the first player to do what?
B. Charles Wreford-Brown, in the 1860s, is credited with being the first person to use what term for Association Football?
C. The first international match to be played between non-British nations took place in 1902 between which two countries, then at the centre of a European empire?

STARTER 99

In the United Kingdom, the rate of interest used by commercial banks as a basis for the rates they charge their customers is called the base rate; by what name is it known in the United States?

BONUS 99

Three questions about brothers:

A. In a traditional song, which French monk is roused from sleep to ring the Mattins Bell?
B. *Brother of the More Famous Jack* was which South African-born novelist's first work, published in 1982, and was followed by *Temples of Delight* and *Juggling*?
C. In *The Importance of Being Earnest*, which character posed as Jack Worthing's fictitious younger brother Ernest, in order to discover the identity of Cecily, the donor of a cigarette-case?

STARTER 100

Usually having a selling area of at least 4,645 square metres, what name is given to a very large shop selling a wide range of products which is larger than a supermarket?

BONUS 100

A. David Lloyd George, while Chancellor of the Exchequer in 1915, said that Britain was fighting three foes; Germany, Austria and which substance, which he said was the greatest foe?

B. In the film *Never Give a Sucker An Even Break*, which comedian said, "I was in love with a beautiful blonde once ... she drove me to drink. That's the one thing I'm indebted to her for"?

C. Which brain-addled television cleric's limited vocabulary included the word "Drink" on virtually every opportunity?

9

How Do We Know the
Answers Are Right?

Verifying the questions is a crucial part of the *University Challenge* production process, and it is co-ordinated by Sara Low, who has under her wing a team of around twenty fact-checkers. Sara runs her team from a vicarage in Bushey Heath – she's married to a vicar – and most of her team are people she has encountered through her congregation. They are intelligent, well-educated people with time on their hands, who relish the opportunity to exercise their minds and are happy to spend hours browsing through their local libraries in search of authoritative sources. "I'm never happy with anyone who thinks that a question like 'What is the capital of France?' doesn't need verifying," says Sara. "That's no good to anyone. We all know what the capital of France is, but I need people who are prepared to get down a couple of encyclopaedias and check and double-check it. You must never just accept an answer because you think you know it."

And check they do. Most will have a collection of reference books at home, and will be used to scouring their local libraries. In the case of two of the more senior verifiers, who are old enough to be the grandmothers of the students taking part in the programme, they visit their local Our Price record store to quiz the staff on questions about Marilyn Manson's lyrics.

Making sure the answer is right is the easy part, and there is far more to verification than that. Most of our questions will offer a series of facts as clues to the answer. They must all be checked as well. Every single word of every question is checked, double-checked and, sometimes, triple-checked against different sources to the one

148

the question-setter has used. Each word, if it is acceptable, has a neat black stroke through it. Changes we might consider making are marked by a black asterisk; changes we must make, otherwise the question is either unsafe of simply wrong, are highlighted in red. Grammar is checked, ambiguities weeded out. If there are acceptable alternative answers to the one given, the question will either be reworded in such a way as to exclude them, or the alternatives will be listed against the answer. It is only with this level of thoroughness that the programme can present questions at an appropriate level of difficulty. There's little point in presenting a badly-written or poorly researched set of questions to someone who may well be studying for a doctorate in that subject.

Their attention to detail is exemplary. For example, a few pages of corrections on a question-setter's work points out that we can't say that Matilda was the only daughter of Henry I; we have to say she was his only *legitimate* daughter. There's a line which says that rattlesnakes belong to the sub-family *crotalus*, but we should change it to say that they belong to a sub-family of the family *crotalidae*, otherwise the question won't work. And Shakespeare's play is called *The Winter's Tale* – our question-setter has called it *A Winter's Tale*, which was a song by David Essex!

Once a member of her team has finished work on a batch of questions, they are returned to Sara for her final checks and, as she says, "To sort out the really grisly ones." These will be the ones that can only be checked by trying to get through to the Post Office on the Falkland Islands, or renting a video of *The Man Who Shot Liberty Valance* and watching the entire film to check one line.

Sara is loathe to rely on the Internet as a source. Whilst checking a quotation attributed to Vita Sackville West, she found several sites confirming the attribution, but even more giving another name. She phoned Sissinghurst and spoke to Vita's son, Nigel Nicholson, who didn't recognise the quote as his mother's, but instead suggested another question. Often the old-fashioned approach is the best.

How, we wonder, do they work in such detail without – to put it politely – going bonkers? We suspect they occasionally give their brains a rest by working on the questions for *The Weakest Link*. But Sara couldn't possibly comment.

The following questions are the kind we'd put in a third-round match. These are the quarter-finals. Our twenty-eight qualifying teams have been whittled down to just eight.

QUARTER-FINAL QUESTIONS

STARTER 101

What name was given to a light, open, one-horse vehicle, seating only one person, supposedly by an English physician who wanted to sit alone?

BONUS 101

Three questions on a German city:

A. Which German city is the largest in Hessen, is famous for its Annual Book and Motor Car Fairs, and was the birthplace of Goethe in 1749?
B. The Frankfurt School, a group of researchers associated with the Institute for Social Research founded in 1923, applied which political philosophy to a radical interdisciplinary social theory?
C. The architect Margarethe Schüette-Lihotzky, who died in January 2000 aged 102, was a pioneer in the ergonomic design of what? About 10,000 apartments in Frankfurt benefited from the installation of her designs in the 1920s.

STARTER 102

In which classic science fiction film does Commander Adams land his United Planets Cruiser on Altair-4, which features a green sky, pink sand and two moons, where he is greeted by Robby the Robot?

BONUS 102

Three questions on Scotland:

A. Which Scottish word for a promontory is thought to originate from the old Norse word for a snout?
B. Which Mull is Scotland's southernmost point?
C. Which island, off the west coast of Mull, is famous for its caves, in particular Fingal's Cave?

STARTER 103

The comic opera *Béatrice et Benedict* was the last work by which romantic composer, best known for his *Symphonie Fantastique?*

BONUS 103

Three questions on trains in films:

A. Based on Ethel Lina White's novel *The Wheel Spins*, which 1938 Hitchcock film is set largely on a train, and features the cricket fanatics Charters and Caldecott?

B. Which cult film of 1974 concerns a transit police officer, played by Walter Matthau, and a gang led by Robert Shaw who take hostage the passengers on a New York subway train?

C. In which Ealing comedy of 1952 is a branch railway line threatened with closure, and taken over by local villagers as a private concern?

STARTER 104

The *Systeme International d'Unites*, whose units are called SI units, defines fundamental units in which all other units can be expressed. What are these other units called in the SI system?

BONUS 104

Three questions on "Robertsons":

A. Which film director used the name "Bob Robertson" for the release of his first successful feature in the Western genre, the name also being a tribute to his father, who made the first Italian Western in 1913 as Roberto Roberti?

B. The Canadian-born Robbie Robertson was guitarist with which group, noted for their recordings with Bob Dylan? Their farewell performance was filmed by Martin Scorsese under the title *The Last Waltz.*

C. What was unique in British history about the military career of Sir William Robertson, commissioned in 1888 and created Field Marshal in 1920?

STARTER 105

In chemistry, what property of an element indicates the number of atoms of hydrogen which will combine or displace one atom of that element?

BONUS 105

Three questions on titles:

A. In the poem by Edward Lear, what provided the "single, lurid light" that moved through the vast and gloomy dark, as he searched for his lost love?

B. "The Man in Lincoln's Nose" was an early title suggestion for which film of 1959, directed by Alfred Hitchcock?

C. Which 17th-century French soldier and writer is described thus, in a play of 1897: "Above his toby ruff he carries a nose – ah, good my lords, what a nose is his. When one sees it one is fain to cry aloud 'Nay, 'tis too much' "?

STARTER 106

In mathematics, for a straight-line graph of Y against X, what is the value of Y if X is ten, the slope of the graph is one and the intercept on the Y axis is five?

BONUS 106

Three questions on crustaceans:

A. What is the emblem of St James the Great, worn by some of those who have made the pilgrimage to his shrine at Santiago de Compostella?

B. In a work first published in 1917, which poet wrote of, quote: "Restless nights in one-night cheap hotels,/And sawdust restaurants with oyster-shells?"

C. The equiangular spiral of a snail's shell is one example from the natural world of a structure which obeys the principles of which number sequence, identified by Leonardo Pisano?

STARTER 107

What unit of pressure is equal to ten to the five pascals, and is approximately equal to atmospheric pressure at sea level?

BONUS 107

Three questions on courage and parts of the body:

A. Also meaning "courage", what name is given to the heart, liver and lungs of a slaughtered animal, which are to be used as food?

B. Which term, used particularly for the lower end of the alimentary canal, can, in the plural, mean "courage"?

C. Fearing a Spanish invasion, at which port in Essex did Queen Elizabeth I declare to a detachment of soldiers: "I know I have the body of a weak and feeble woman, but I have the heart and stomach of a king?"

STARTER 108

What term is given to the tissue of the mammalian body which stores fat?

BONUS 108
Three questions on English regional dishes:

A. In which Derbyshire town was a now-famous dish first made by accident, in around 1860, when a cook spread an egg mixture over jam, rather than into pastry?
B. Alternatively called "Yorkshire pennies", liquorice cakes are still made in which town in West Yorkshire?
C. Which town in the English Lake District has, since the mid-19th century, produced a hard, crystalline confection, flavoured with mint?

STARTER 109

Mountaineer Reinhold Messner, rally driver Ari Vatanen, footballer Paolo Rossi, actress Gina Lollobrigida and singer Dana were among the candidates for what during 1999?

BONUS 109
Three questions on the monarchy:

A. Of the six British kings called George, three did not succeed a George; George I was one; who were the other two?
B. Of the kings of England called Henry, three were sons of a King Henry; who were they?
C. Of the eight kings of England called Edward, two reigned for less than one year; who were they?

STARTER 110

From the Latin for "a keel", which verb means to turn a ship on its side for cleaning or repair, but can also refer to swift, uncontrolled movement?

BONUS 110
Three questions on a Roman god:

A. In Roman religion, who was the god of commerce and merchants; he is sometimes represented holding a purse, although he is usually given the attributes of his Greek counterpart and portrayed wearing winged sandals?

B. Who, on 5 May 1961, travelled in the Mercury Space Capsule Freedom 7 to become the first American to travel in space?

C. Which West Country town's local papers include the *Mercury*, whose contributors have included Jeffrey Archer's mother, Lola, who wrote a column called "Over the Tea Cups"?

STARTER 111

During 1999, following a challenge by Will Shortz of the *New York Times*, a team of computer scientists in North Carolina devised Proverb, a program which can solve what, with greater speed and accuracy than humans?

BONUS 111

Three questions on a Lincolnshire town:

A. What name is shared by the Republic of Ireland's smallest county and a town in Lincolnshire?

B. Margaret Wintringham, who won a by-election in Louth in 1921, was the first woman to enter the House of Commons to be born in which country?

C. Which controversial public figure was MP for Louth from 1969 to 1974?

STARTER 112

Which eight-word common proverb emerges from the translation of the Latin phrase *Amicus certus in re incerta cernitur*?

BONUS 112

Three questions linked by a surname:

A. Whose report into the Stephen Lawrence case was published in February 1999?

B. In 1762, James MacPherson issued the epic poem *Fingal*, followed by *Temora* the following year, which he alleged were translations from the Gaelic of which legendary poet?

C. A MacPherson strut is a component commonly used in which part of a car?

STARTER 113

The Bronze Doors, the Arch of the Bells and the Via di Porta

Angelica are the three public entrances to which city on the western bank of the River Tiber?

BONUS 113

Three questions on icosahedron:

A. A regular icosahedron is a figure with 20 regular faces; what precise shape is each face?
B. How many vertices does it have?
C. How many edges?

STARTER 114

In July 1945 scientists set off the first atomic bomb at which test site in New Mexico?

BONUS 114

Three questions about a rock star:

A. What name is the Latinized form of the name of the 6th century Welsh saint Aelfyw, and was familiarized by the success of a rock performer, born in 1935?
B. With which reptile did Frank Skinner appear in London's West End, in Lee Hall's comedy *Cooking With Elvis*?
C. In 1986, which veteran rock performer said of Elvis Presley, "The dead son of a gun is still riding on my coat-tails"?

STARTER 115

The musical term *sul ponticelo* instructs the performer to play with the bow as close as possible to which part of the instrument?

BONUS 115

Three questions on Internet search engines:

A. Which Internet search engine was named when two unrelated words were written next to each other on a white board; taken together, they mean "the view from above"?
B. Supposedly giving direct answers to direct questions, which search engine takes its name from a fictional "Gentleman's Gentleman"?
C. Which search engine has a name deriving from that of a family of predatory spiders common to North America, and refers to the "spidering" technology behind it?

STARTER 116

Which US writer, noted for her novels depicting Black American heritage, won the Pulitzer Prize for her 1987 work *Beloved*, and in 1993 became the first black woman to receive the Nobel Prize for Literature?

BONUS 116
Three questions on the architect John Nash:

A. In which London Park is Cumberland Terrace, intended to face a royal palace which was never built?

B. In which London street does the Theatre Royal still retain Nash's Corinthian portico, although its interior was completely rebuilt at the beginning of the 20th century?

C. What is the name of the church in Langham Place, near Broadcasting House, which was also designed by Nash?

STARTER 117

Who declared himself the only Oscar-winner to be as bald as the statuette when he collected the best actor award in 1956 for a musical role he was to perform over 4,000 times in his career?

BONUS 117
Three questions on a 16th-century figure:

A. Who became Lord Chancellor on the fall of Cardinal Wolsey in 1529?

B. More was accused of treason for his alleged interest in the prophecies of Elizabeth Barton, a Kentish servant girl who was declared a genuine visionary after a diocesan investigation; by what name did she become known?

C. Three pages of revisions to a manuscript of the play *Sir Thomas More*, variously dated about 1593 or 1601, are thought to be whose only surviving literary manuscript?

STARTER 118

Which German Ambassador to Britain had a surname shared by his great-great uncle who was made a Field-Marshal in Bismarck's army as reward for his success in the Austro-Prussian and Franco-Prussian wars?

BONUS 118
Three questions on mechanics:

A. In mechanics, what may be defined as the product of the magnitude of a force applied to move an object, and the displacement produced in the direction of the force?
B. Similarly, what is expressible as the product of the magnitude of a force applied to move an object, and the speed of the object in the direction of the force?
C. And finally, what may be defined as the magnitude of a force multiplied by the time for which the force is applied?

STARTER 119

Thought to have been built by Postnik Yakovlev, what is the popular name for the building officially called the Cathedral of the Intercession of the Virgin by the Moat, after the moat which once ran beside the Kremlin in Moscow?

BONUS 119

Three questions on the earth's atmosphere:

A. What is the lowest region of the earth's atmosphere, whose upper boundary is about ten to fifteen kilometres about the Earth's surface?
B. After nitrogen and oxygen, which is the most abundant gas of the Earth's atmosphere?
C. What is the most obvious manifestation of the fact that shorter-wavelength light from the sun is scattered to a greater degree by the molecules of the atmosphere?

STARTER 120

What term is applied to any key on a computer keyboard that can be pressed alone or in combination with others but is always marked with an "F" and a numeral?

BONUS 120

Three questions on children:

A. What name did Friedrich Froebel give to the "school for the psychological training of little children by means of play" which he opened in Blankenburg in Thuringia in 1837?
B. Who composed the song-cycle *Kindertotenlieder* between 1901 and 1904?
C. According to the motto of conservative German nationalists, embraced by the Nazis, which allocated a purely domestic role to women, what went with *Kinder* and *Kirche*?

STARTER 121

Which is the only African country to have a coastline on both the Atlantic Ocean and the Mediterranean Sea?

BONUS 121

Three questions on capital cities:

A. Which former Soviet Republic moved its capital city from Almaty in 1997 to Astana, whose name means "capital" in the local language?
B. Which city was called Pei-P'ing, meaning "Northern Peace", between 1368 and 1644, but was then given a new name meaning "Northern Capital"?
C. The capital of Mongolia, whose name now means "Town of the Red Hero", was called "Niislel Hureheh" in 1991 meaning "Capital Monastery"; what is its present name?

STARTER 122

Which word can mean either a first draft of a diplomatic document or the correct formal or diplomatic procedure?

BONUS 122

Three questions on units:

A. Which unit of loudness of sound measures the intensity of sound relative to a reference tone of known intensity and frequency, the reference tone usually having a frequency of 1 kilohertz?
B. Which unit of illuminance is equal to 10,000 lux, or one lumen per square centimetre?
C. A photon may be regarded as a discrete packet or quantum of electromagnetic energy; what analogous name is given to a quantum of vibrational energy in a crystal lattice?

STARTER 123

In an 1899 issue of *International Geography*, Hugh Robert Mill introduced which word to accompany "lithosphere", "hydrosphere" and "atmosphere"?

BONUS 123

Three questions on medical terms:

A. What familiar expression refers to the condition *Globus hystericus*, describing a sensation occurring in conditions of acute anxiety, emotional tension or depression?

B. What name is given to the small, isolated, U-shaped bone situated at the root of the tongue?
C. More prominent in men than in women, the Adam's Apple is the name commonly given to a projection of the thyroid cartilage of which organ at the front of the neck?

STARTER 124

Which north Atlantic seabird of the petrel family takes its name from a combination of the Icelandic words for "foul" and "gull"?

BONUS 124

Three questions on the surface of the moon:

A. Uniquely given the status of an ocean, what name is given to the largest of the so-called "seas" or "maria" on the lunar surface?
B. The terrace-walled crater of around 32 kilometres in diameter, near the heart of Oceanus Procellarum, is named after which German astronomer who formulated the laws describing the motion of planets in their orbits?
C. Which term is used to describe any of the bay-like features of the moon's surface, such as "Roris" at the edge of Oceanus Procellarum, and "Iridium" at the edge of Mare Imbrium?

STARTER 125

Which four words constitute the title of Chapter One of *Alice's Adventures in Wonderland*?

BONUS 125

Three questions on copyright:

A. The American singer-songwriter Loudon Wainwright III claimed in March 2000 that lyrics from his song "I Am The Way" had been included in "Jesus In A Camper Van", a track by which recording artist?
B. Stefan Avalos, the director of the low-budget American movie *The Last Broadcast*, claimed "definite influence" but not "all-out theft" of material in which other cult film of 1999, about a group of young film-makers?
C. Against which British children's writer did the American author Nancy Stouffer file a suit in 2000, alleging that details in one of her own stories had been copied?

STARTER 126

Alexander, Ivan, Peter and Romeo are linked by whom in a musical context?

BONUS 126

Three questions on Mayors of New York:

A. Who served as the Mayor of New York City from 1978 to 1989, being re-elected in 1981 largely for his success in handling New York's financial problems and saving the city from bankruptcy?
B. Which democrat was New York's first black Mayor, and proposed the so-called "Doomsday Budget" in 1991, calling for cuts of $1.5 billion in municipal services?
C. Who was David Dinkins' opponent in 1989, defeated by only 47,000 votes, the narrowest margin to that date? He succeeded in his bid to become Mayor in 1994.

STARTER 127

What term describes the flag of a foreign country in which a ship has been registered in order to avoid taxation in its real country of origin?

BONUS 127

Three questions on medicine:

A. Nociceptors are nerve endings specifically concerned with response to which type of sensation?
B. Which group of peptides occur naturally in the brain, and are normally produced in response to pain?
C. Pain felt at a site other than that at which the source or causal factor operates is commonly described by which term?

STARTER 128

Botev Peak is the highest point of which range of mountains, known locally as Stara Planina and stretching eastwards across Bulgaria from the Serbian frontier to the Black Sea?

BONUS 128

Three questions on popular music:

A. Which American folk group included Pete Seeger and Lee Hays, disbanded between 1952 and 1955 after McCarthyite blacklisting, and were the subject of the 1981 film biography *Wasn't That A Time?*
B. Which traditional African song was recorded by The Weavers in

1950, and subsequently became a British hit for Karl Denver and for The Tokens and Tight Fit, when it was re-titled "The Lion Sleeps Tonight"?

C. Dedicated to The Weavers, *Tapestry* was recorded in 1970 and was the debut album of which singer-songwriter, born in New York State in 1948?

STARTER 129

A powder used to thicken petrol for use in war is known by what name, which also applies to the resultant jellied fuel which clings to everything it touches and burns violently?

BONUS 129
Three questions on the cosmetics industry:

A. *My Life of Beauty* is the autobiography of which cosmetics manufacturer, born in what is now Poland in 1870, whose fortune of around $100 million originated with a face cream mixed to a family formula?

B. Which Canadian-born beautician and businesswoman manufactured a range of over 300 cosmetics, and also owned a string of racehorses, one of which won the Kentucky Derby in 1947?

C. Starting with a face cream produced by her uncle, which New York businesswoman founded her own cosmetics company in 1946, later introducing the "Aramis" range for men and "Clinique" for women?

STARTER 130

The Hundred Years War ended in 1453 in the time of Henry VI, and began during the reign of which English monarch?

BONUS 130
Three questions on magnetism:

A. What name is given to a permanently magnetized deposit of magnetite, the ore of iron first used as a compass by the Chinese in the second millennium BC?

B. Also called the Magnetic Equator, what name is given to the imaginary line where a compass needle balances horizontally, the attraction of the north and south magnetic poles being equal?

C. Which term is used to describe the angle at a particular point on the Earth's surface between the direction of the geographical or true north, and the magnetic north pole?

STARTER 131

When conductor Herbert von Karajan said, "All else is gaslight", he was referring to what innovation, unveiled by Sony at the Japan Audio Fair of 1980?

BONUS 131
Three questions on cows in mythology:

A. The dun cow of Dunsmore Heath was, according to legend, slain by which Anglo-Danish hero?

B. In Scandinavian mythology, what name was given to the cow that nourished Ymir, the father of the evil giants, who drank from the four milky streams which flowed from her udders?

C. In Egyptian mythology, which goddess was the daughter of Ra and the wife of Horus, and was often represented as a star-studded cow, or a woman with a cow's head?

STARTER 132

The overland transport of a boat, and/or its cargo, from one navigable waterway to another is known by what term?

BONUS 132
Three questions on music in cinema:

A. The American composer Paul J. Smith spent most of his career working on music for films made by which Chicago-born producer, who set up his own small studio in the 1920s?

B. Which song was voiced by Cliff Edwards and performed by Jiminy Cricket in the 1940 animated feature film *Pinocchio*, and became the Disney organization's theme song?

C. The soundtrack of which film included part of "The Pastoral Symphony", the results, according to contemporary reports, having inspired an emotional Disney to exclaim, "This will *make* Beethoven!"?

STARTER 133

According to both Homer and Tennyson, Odysseus encountered which fabulous people who lived on "a flowery food" that caused those who ate it to forget their own country and want to live always in a dream-like state?

BONUS 133
Three questions on bridges in literature:

A. Which bridges are referred to in the title of the novel by Robert James Waller, which was published in 1992 and became one of the world's best-selling works of fiction?
B. The defects of which bridge were pointed out in verse with the words "Your central girders would not have given way,/At least many sensible men do say,/Had they been supported on each side with buttresses,/At least many sensible men confesses"?
C. The spectacle of crowds flowing over which bridge prompted T.S. Eliot's line: "I had not thought death had undone so many"?

STARTER 134

Which complex, naturally-occurring chemicals are linked together by bonds between the sugar and phosphate groups to form the building blocks of nucleic acids such as DNA and RNA?

BONUS 134

Three questions on radio astronomy:

A. Which American radio engineer, after whom a unit of radio emission strength is named, picked up the first radio signals from space while working on reception interference problems in 1931, publishing his findings the following year?
B. Which Brighton-born radio astronomer developed the use of interferometers, a technique employing separate radio telescopes to achieve better resolution in the same observed distant object?
C. Pulsars were discovered in 1967 by Jocelyn Bell and Anthony Hewish at which radio astronomy observatory on the outskirts of Cambridge?

STARTER 135

Established in 1872 as a railhead on the Santa Fé Trail, which settlement gained a reputation as a rowdy frontier town and was known as the "Cowboy Capital"?

BONUS 135

Three questions on theatre:

A. Having financed the opening of the Abbey Theatre in Dublin, which theatre manager bought the Gaiety Theatre in Manchester where she ran her own repertory company until 1917?
B. Harold Brighouse, a member of the Manchester school of writers encouraged by Horniman at the Gaiety, was the author of which play, filmed by David Lean in 1954 with Charles Laughton in the title role?

C. Married to the actor and director Lewis Casson, which actress was a leading member of Horniman's company, and also played the title role in the first English performance of Shaw's *Saint Joan*?

STARTER 136

"I wish Martin was my surname, for my own is not a pretty one and takes a long time to sign." So said which eponymous Dickens character?

BONUS 136
Three questions on systems of exchange:

A. What word derives from a Native American term for "gift", and refers to a system of giving away or destroying property as a means of demonstrating social status?
B. What word of Algonquin origin is used is for the seashell beads formerly used as a means of exchange among Native American people?
C. Kula, the ceremonial system of exchanging gifts of red shell necklaces and white shell bracelets, is a traditional practice among Trobriand Islanders and other groups of which South Pacific country?

STARTER 137

Which province in the Gulf of St Lawrence is separated from the mainland by the Northumberland strait and is sometimes referred to by the initials PEI?

BONUS 137
Three questions on sporting fathers and sons:

A. The son of Sir Stanley Matthews, also named Stanley, represented Great Britain at which sport?
B. What is the surname of the father and son who rode the Grand National winners L'Escargot in 1975 and Bobby Jo in 1999?
C. Christopher, the cricketer who captained England in 1988, is the son of which batsman, whose 114 tests included 27 as captain?

STARTER 138

Derived from the Chinese words for "three" and "plank", what name is given to a small, flat-bottomed boat propelled by oars?

BONUS 138

Three questions on Atlantic Islands:

A. Which Atlantic Island group lies west of Senegal and has its capital at Praia, on São Tiago?
B. Fully independent since 1975, Cape Verde had previously been a territory of which European country?
C. In 1981, Cape Verde abandoned constitutional proposals to unite with which other former Portuguese colony on the African mainland, south of Senegal?

STARTER 139

When Stephen Potter popularized the term "Gamesmanship" he defined its meaning as "The art of winning games without actually ..." what?

BONUS 139

Three questions on a household implement:

A. Published in 1575, which English verse comedy is attributed to William Stevenson and concerns the loss of a household implement and its reappearance in the breeches of the manservant, Hodge?
B. "Adam's Needle" is a name given to which tropical plant, characterized by long strap-like leaves tapering to sharp points, and popularized as a house plant in the UK in the 1960s?
C. "Saint Wilfred's Needle", the narrow passage of which it was formerly believed that only women who were virgins could pass through, is to be found in the crypt of which cathedral in north Yorkshire?

STARTER 140

How are Hunk, Zeke and Hickory better known in a 1939 film based on a novel by Frank Baum?

BONUS 140

Three questions on chemistry:

A. Used to identify elements present in a substance, the flame test depends for its results upon which variable property of the flame produced?
B. What colour flame is produced when sodium burns?
C. Which soft, waxlike, silver-white metallic element burns with a distinctive lilac flame?

STARTER 141

The Earl of Kent a faithful follower of which of Shakespeare's eponymous characters, serving him in disguise after being banished from his kingdom?

BONUS 141

Three questions on a writer:

A. Which writer, music critic and caricaturist, born in Prussia in 1776, was the author of *The Nutcracker and the Mouse King*, used by Tchaikovsky as the basis for a ballet?
B. A fairy story by Hoffmann provided the plot for which ballet by Delibes?
C. Inspired by Hoffmann's work and his colourful personality, *Les Contes d'Hoffmann* is an opera by which Cologne-born composer?

STARTER 142

Usually serving as an anchor for the handrail, what name is given to the upright post either at the foot of a stairway, at its landings or at its top?

BONUS 142

Three questions about bishops:

A. What name is given to the two conflicts of 1639 and 1640 between the Scottish covenanters and Charles I, which resulted in defeat for the English?
B. Henry Bishop, born in 1786, was a prolific composer of operas, but is better remembered for which 19th-century popular song whose words, by JH Payne, begin, "Mid pleasures and palaces / Tho' we may roam"?
C. The first woman to be consecrated as an Anglican bishop was Barbara Harris, appointed in 1989 by the Episocopal Church of the United States as the Bishop of which state?

STARTER 143

Green-skinned with slitted eyes, a small body and a huge head and generally resembling a monstrous human foetus, which "treen" from the planet Venus was the deadly foe of comic strip hero Dan Dare?

BONUS 143

Three questions on health in the USA:

A. Founded in Philadelphia in 1847, which American organization was established to "Promote the science and art of medicine and the betterment of public health"?
B. Available to those in the US over the age of 65, which health scheme draws from a combination of payroll taxes, premiums and tax revenues to provide help for the elderly in paying medical bills?
C. Both the Medicare and Medicaid health care schemes were passed by Congress as part of the "Great Society" programme of which US president?

STARTER 144

Which two-letter word, described as the northern English form of "Oh", is included in the latest edition of *The Concise Oxford Dictionary*?

BONUS 144

Three questions on spices:

A. Michelle Stephenson was a founder member of which pop group, quitting in August 1994 shortly after the other members changed its name from "Touch"?
B. The Spice Islands is a former name for which province of Indonesia, lying between Sulawesi in the west and New Guinea in the east?
C. Allspice is an evergreen tree native to tropical America and the West Indies, producing a fruit known as allspice, Jamaican pepper or, more commonly, by which other name?

STARTER 145

From the French for "to stereotype", what word describes a trite expression which has lost its cutting edge?

BONUS 145

Three questions on theatre in literature:

A. The eponymous hero of which novel by Charles Dickens supports himself and his companion Smike by working for a time as an actor in the company of Vincent Crummles?
B. The amateur enthusiasts Jess Oakroyd, Inigo Jollifant and Miss Trant came together to set up which small theatrical company, in a JB Priestley novel of the same name?
C. An amateur theatrical production of *Lovers' Vows* is planned in which novel of 1814, much to the consternation of the novel's heroine, Fanny Price?

STARTER 146

Called *The Silver Locusts* in Britain, which Ray Bradbury work established his reputation as a science fiction writer?

BONUS 146

Three questions linked to a railway station:

A. "The Drain" is a name which has been popularly associated with the direct underground link built in 1899 between The Bank in the City of London and which major rail terminus?
B. Founded in 1836, the Waterloo Cup is the major event in English coursing, and is staged annually at Altcar near Southport over a three-day period in which month of the year?
C. The Waterloo Gallery, housing many paintings captured from the French during the Peninsular War, is part of which house, built by Robert Adam at Hyde Park Corner?

STARTER 147

The North Italian provinces of Emilia and Lombardy produce two distinct kinds of which hard, granular cheese?

BONUS 147

Three questions on wishful thinking:

A. What name was given to the Children's Temperance movement founded in 1855 from various societies originating in the United Kingdom in the 1840s?
B. "Hope," depicted as sitting blindfolded on the globe, plucking the string on a broken lyre, is a work by which London-born portrait painter, whose sculpture *Physical Energy* is in Kensington Gardens?
C. Who, in *An Essay on Man*, published in 1733, wrote, "Hope springs eternal in the human breast,/Man never is but always to be blest"?

STARTER 148

Those who reigned in Ireland between the 3rd and 12th centuries were accorded which title a purely nominal one which did not necessarily give them authority over other kings?

BONUS 148

Three questions on pestilence:

A. The Black Death, the 14th-century outbreak of bubonic plague, reached Britain when a ship from Calais brought it to which Dorset port during the summer of 1348?

B. *The Masque of the Red Death*, in which a wealthy prince entertains his guests while a plague rages outside his castle, is a short story by which American writer?

C. Yellow fever, the tropical viral disease formerly prevalent in Africa and the West Indies, is transmitted by what means?

STARTER 149

In 1964, husband-and-wife medical team Vincent Dole and Marie Nyswander developed long-term therapy which aimed to help people overcome some types of narcotic addiction by using what as a substitute?

BONUS 149

Three questions linked to skin complaints:

A. *Phacochoerus aethiopicus* is the zoological name for which large animal of the African plains, named after the tough excrescences on its face, below the eyes?

B. According to Walpole's *Anecdotes of Painting*, which portrait painter was instructed by Oliver Cromwell to "Remark all these roughnesses, pimples, warts and everything as you see me, otherwise I will never pay a farthing for it"?

C. Thomas Wart is a country soldier recruited by Falstaff in which play by Shakespeare?

STARTER 150

Which fictional land has Archenland and Calormen to the south, Ettinsmoore to the north and can only be visited by select children?

BONUS 150

Three questions on epistolary novels:

A. Who wrote the epistolary novel *Evelina*, first published anonymously in 1778, in which the eponymous heroine is ultimately recognized as the rightful heir of Sir John Belmont?

B. Which of Jane Austen's novels developed from an epistolary sketch entitled *Elinor and Marianne*?

C. "Mr B" is amongst the correspondents whose letters comprise the material of which novel, whose author, Samuel Richardson, presents himself as the editor?

10

Who Watches?

"Why," asked a letter from one of our viewers, "does it say at the end of the programme that Jeremy Paxman speaks with the voice of Jim Pope? Why doesn't he use his own voice? It's very puzzling. In my mother's nursing home, they speak of little else."

This initially baffling letter arrived from a viewer a couple of years ago. The credits on the programme did, of course, begin with the words: *presented by Jeremy Paxman*, followed by *with the voice of Jim Pope*. Once we figured out our viewer's confusion we wrote back to explain that it was Jim Pope's voice we heard announcing the name of the team and the team member who buzzed in to answer starter questions. The voice-over has always been an essential part of the grammar of the programme, but Jim's contribution went far beyond that. As the voice of *University Challenge* for twenty-seven years until his death in 2001, he was a very gentlemanly presence in the studio, a friend to the production team and something of a cult figure among our students. Recently, the role has been taken over by Roger Tilling, a man only just out of his twenties but which an extraordinarily rich and mature voice, redolent of Dundee cake and leather armchairs.

But who, beyond our baffled letter-writer, watches *University Challenge*? We are popular in closed communities, it seems. We are told we are very big in prisons, and there is also a convent where the programme is something of a weekly highlight for a closed community of nuns. As far as the more conventional television audience goes, it turns out that students are not the biggest section of the audience. The main body of our audience is at least a generation older than the average student, and around forty per cent of the programme's audience is over sixty – a surprisingly mature audience for a channel which, at the time of writing, also transmits *The Simpsons* and *The New Adventures of Superman* and puts *University Challenge* in an hour's slot with the iconoclastic American import *Malcolm in the Middle*.

We also suspect our audience is reasonably conservative, in outlook at least (we've no idea about their politics), because they clearly expect students to maintain certain standards. The fact they were allowed to smoke on screen in the Sixties brought sacks of complaining letters, and those students who forgot themselves and picked their noses on screen (and you know who you are) also received a post-bag they will not have forgotten in a hurry. Student scruffiness has always bothered our audience; even as late as 1980, when punk fashions had been a familiar sight on the high-street for three years, one student was ferociously taken to task for appearing wearing *a collarless shirt*. Of course, some students deliberately dressed to provoke a reaction; in the Sixties, one student chose to wear a kind of knitted beret in the hope of shocking the bourgeoisie into a terminal decline, clearly believing that 'Disgusted of Tunbridge Wells' was a regular viewer of the programme. Again in 1980, four mature members of a team were told *very* firmly by the post-bag to get proper jobs and stop sponging off the State, the invariable P.S. being that Granada should have known better than to encourage them by allowing them on the programme.

The tension between what an older generation expects, and what a younger generation can do, is a large part of the programme's appeal. Our viewers are probably the people who have little difficulty solving the toughest broadsheet crosswords; our players are more likely to be found around the *Who Wants To Be A Millionaire* quiz machine in their students' union.

What follows are questions we would allocate to the semi-final stage of the contest. By now, the twenty-eight competing teams have been whittled down to just four. If they can beat their opponents on questions like these, they will be through to the final.

SEMI-FINAL QUESTIONS

STARTER 151

What name did Virgin Publishing give to their imprint introduced in 1993 and specializing in erotic fiction written for women
by women?

BONUS 151

Three questions on literature:

A. In 1474, the first book printed in English by William Caxton was
a translated history of which city?
B. In the play by Christopher Marlowe, which title character is referring to Troy when he speaks of "The topless towers of Ilium"?
C. Sergeant Francis Troy is killed by the obsessive John Boldwood in
which novel of 1874?

STARTER 152

To which EU country was Norman Tebbit referring when he said
that being its Prime Minister was "like being chairman of
Basingstoke District Council"?

BONUS 152

Three questions on Greek mythology:

A. According to Greek mythology, which hero killed his wife and
children in a fit of madness, and as penance was ordered to serve
King Eurystheus for 12 years?
B. Which of the 12 labours did Hercules perform for Augeas, the
king of Elis, by diverting the course of a river?
C. Ten of Hercules' labours involved animals or monsters – can you
name either of the other two labours?

STARTER 153

The historian Hugh Trevor-Roper, who gained notoriety in 1983
when he certified the forged *Hitler Diaries* to be genuine, took
which title when he was created a life peer in 1979?

BONUS 153

Three questions on ravens:

A. In which mythology did the ravens Huginn and Muninn, meaning "mind" and "memory", sit on the shoulders of one of the principal gods?
B. Which of Shakespeare's tragic heroes urges on the actors of a play-within-a-play with the words: "Come, the croaking raven doth bellow for revenge"?
C. Which television series of 2000 featured an albino crow playing a white raven called "Mister Chalk"?

STARTER 154

Which American president was the first and, to date, the only one to hold the office without having been elected either president or vice-president?

BONUS 154

Three questions on natural history:

A. What is the more familiar name of the creature with the dialect names "porwiggle" and "polliwog"?
B. "Tadpole", "hooded", "pistol", "coral" and "fairy" are varieties of which aquatic creature?
C. Which writer created the characters of Mr Tadpole and Mr Taper, both politicians, in his 1844 novel *Coningsby*?

STARTER 155

The name of the American jockey Tod Sloan is thought to be the origin of a cockney rhyming slang expression meaning what?

BONUS 155

Three questions on world music:

A. Which south-east Asian country is the home of gamelan percussion music?
B. From which country did "Janissary Music" originate in the 17th century?
C. Combining rock, blues and cajun influences, with which of the southern states of America is zydeco primarily associated?

STARTER 156

Which British writer and entertainer was the niece of Nancy Astor, took the surname by which she became known on her marriage in 1929 and is particularly remembered for her portrayal of the policewoman Ruby Gates in the *St Trinians* film series?

BONUS 156

Three questions on the Euro:

A. When 11 countries fixed their exchange rates against the euro in January 1999, which was the only currency where a single unit was worth more than one euro?
B. Which country's unit of currency had the lowest value at that point, with 1,936 being worth one euro?
C. The UK, Denmark and Sweden chose not to join the euro at that time; which other EU member wanted to join, but could not meet the financial criteria?

STARTER 157

What is the title of TS Eliot's poem in six parts, first published in 1930, of which Part Two opens with the line: "Lady, three white leopards sat under a juniper-tree"?

BONUS 157

Three questions linked by a name:

A. In which country was the Geraldine League formed in the 1530s, with the ultimate aim of overthrowing English rule?
B. Which politician chose Geraldine Ferraro as his running-mate in 1984, when standing for the US presidency against Reagan and Bush?
C. Which European country was ruled by King Zog and Queen Geraldine from 1928, until they were forced into exile in 1939?

STARTER 158

Vostok 6 completed 48 orbits of the earth between 16 and 19 June 1963; who was its famous passenger?

BONUS 158

Three questions linked by an insect:

A. Which insect of the order *orthoptera* was nicknamed "wart-biter" in southern England, and was used as a folk remedy to bite off warts?
B. Which German composer's "helicopter quartet", performed in Amsterdam in 1995, used four helicopters from The Grasshoppers, the Dutch Air Force display team, along with the Arditti Quartet?
C. In which cult television series of the 1970s was David Carradine, playing a Buddhist monk, often addressed as "Grasshopper" by his mentor?

STARTER 159

Which historical play by Goethe has as its title character a Flemish aristocrat who was beheaded in 1568 after defying Philip II of Spain, and has an overture and incidental music written for it by Beethoven?

BONUS 159

Three questions linked by a name:

A. Born in 1852, which Irish writer was the patron of WB Yeats, was one of the founders of Dublin's Abbey Theatre and herself wrote or translated some 40 plays?
B. In 1231, Pope Gregory IX created which judicial institution to combat heresy?
C. Who directed the films *Gregory's Girl* and *Gregory's Two Girls*, made nearly 20 years apart?

STARTER 160

Philip II, who was King of Spain from 1556 to 1598, ruled which country as Philip I from 1580 to 1598?

BONUS 160

Three questions on poetry about England:

A. What is the title of Robert Browning's poem which begins, "Oh, to be in England, now that April's there"?
B. Which of the Romantic poets wrote about his journeying, "I travelled among unknown men,/In lands beyond the sea; nor, England! did I know till then/What love I bore to thee"?
C. And which poet wrote in 1912: "God! I will pack and take a train,/And get me to England once again!/For England's the one land, I know,/Where men with splendid hearts may go"?

STARTER 161

Which painter's depiction of the Virgin Mary was denounced as "sick and offensive" by the New York Mayor Rudi Giuliani in September 1999, before the opening of the Sensation exhibition at the Brooklyn Museum of Art?

BONUS 161

Three questions linked by a name:

A. Which former US Senator for New Jersey was a candidate for the democratic nomination for President in 2000, and was formerly a professional basketball player and Olympic gold medallist?
B. Dame Beatrice Lestrange Bradley, psychiatric Adviser to the Home Office, appears in over 60 detective novels by which author?
C. The schoolmaster Bradley Headstone attempts to murder Eugene Wrayburn in which work of 1865, the last complete novel by Charles Dickens?

STARTER 162

Which word prefixes the names of compounds containing copper in its plus-one oxidation state?

BONUS 162

Three questions on:

A. King Olaf of Norway was one of only a few foreigners admitted to which 16-member order of chivalry, whose chapel is in St Giles' Cathedral, Edinburgh?
B. What is the motto of the Order of the Thistle? You can answer in either Latin or English.
C. In *A Midsummer Night's Dream*, which "rude mechanical" asks the fairy Cobweb to find him a humble-bee on top of a thistle, and bring him the honeybag?

STARTER 163

Released in 1933, which film concerns its title character's obsession with the starlet Ann Darrow, whom he encounters on Skull Island?

BONUS 163

Three questions on historical events:

A. Which decade of which century saw all of the following take place: the defeat of James II's forces at the Battle of the Boyne; the Salem Witch Trials; and the publication of John Locke's essay *Concerning Human Understanding?*
B. Which decade of which century saw the publication of Dickens' *Oliver Twist*; the start of the first Opium War in China; and the ascension to the throne of Queen Victoria?
C. Which decade saw Frederick Barbarossa become Holy Roman Emperor; Henry II become King of England; and Adrian become Pope, the only Englishman ever to do so?

STARTER 164

What meteorological phenomenon is measured by an udometer, a device more familiarly known as a pluviometer?

BONUS 164

Three questions on locusts:

A. The name of which marine crustacean is a corruption of the Latin "locusta"?
B. What pen-name was used by Nathan Weinstein, the American author of *The Day of the Locust* and *Miss Lonelyhearts?*
C. Which Canadian actor starred in the 1974 film *The Day of the Locust*, following his appearances in *Don't Look Now* and *Klute?*

STARTER 165

Spashaya Krasavitsa and *La Belle au Bois Dormant* are respectively the original Russian and French titles of which ballet, choreographed by Pétipa with music by Tchaikovsky?

BONUS 165

Three questions linked by an ancient civilization:

A. Which Greek city state was destroyed by the Visigoths in 395 AD, and was the site of the Byzantine city of Lacadaemon?
B. What name was given to the state-owned serfs of Sparta, who revolted against Archidamus II in 466 BC?
C. Sparta, Mississippi, is the setting for which film of 1967, starring Sidney Poitier as the detective Virgil Tibbs who helps the bigoted local sheriff to solve a murder?

STARTER 166

Bound to an eternally-revolving fiery wheel as punishment for his attempted seduction of Hera, the mythological King Ixion of Thessaly is said to have been the forefather of which race of creatures?

BONUS 166

Three questions on literature:

A. In which play by TS Eliot is the hero, Colby Simpkins, employed by Sir Claude Mulhammer, his job description being the title?
B. Who wrote *The Confidential Agent* in 1939, one of several thrillers that he called "Entertainments"?
C. Who was the author of the crime novels *LA Confidential, American Tabloid* and *The Black Dahlia*?

STARTER 167

What name is given to the incident in 1618, in which Protestants of the Bohemian national council ejected two Roman Catholic members from a window of Hradcany Castle, thus challenging the religion and authority of the Hapsburg Emperors?

BONUS 167

Three questions on buildings:

A. Which building in Buenos Aires is the equivalent of the "Istana" in Singapore, and the "Palacio de la Revolucion" in Cuba?
B. In which European city is the "Palacio de Belem" the official presidential residence?
C. Which palace, named after one of Rome's seven hills, is the official home of Italy's President?

STARTER 168

Jacinth is a reddish-orange gem variety of which mineral?

BONUS 168

Three questions linked by a name:

A. Which fashion designers produced the wedding dress worn by Diana, Princess of Wales on her wedding day in July 1981?

B. Immanuel was the first name of which philosopher, born in 1724 and the author of the treatise on metaphysics entitled *Critique of Pure Reason?*

C. Emmanuel Goldstein's *The Theory and Practice of Oligarchical Collectivism* is a banned book in the society described in which work of fiction, first published in 1949?

STARTER 169

In anatomy, the haunch bone is the wide, curving bone forming each side of the upper part of the hip bone in the pelvis, and is more properly known by which name?

BONUS 169

Three questions about mountains:

A. Which major mountain system includes areas called the Shickshocks, the Berkshires and the Catskills?

B. Who wrote the best-selling book about walking the Appalachian scenic trail, called *A Walk in the Woods*, published in 1997?

C. The highest peak in the Appalachians in Mount Mitchell, in which state?

STARTER 170

Which English king was murdered at Corfe Castle in 978 by supporters of his stepmother Elfrida, and was canonized in 1001?

BONUS 170

Three questions about maidens:

A. Which King of Scotland was 11 years old when he succeeded his grandfather David in 1153, died unmarried, and was nicknamed "The Maiden"?

B. The *Snow Maiden*, first performed in 1882, is an opera by which Russian composer, born in 1844?

C. The song "Prithee, Pretty Maiden, Will You Marry Me", is sung by the poet Grosvenor to his childhood sweetheart, the village milk-maid, in which operetta by Gilbert and Sullivan?

STARTER 171

In Italian cooking, what name is given to coarsely-ground cornmeal, often cooled after cooking, to be sliced and then fried or toasted?

BONUS 171

Three questions on Austerlitz:

A. The Battle of Austerlitz in December 1805 saw one of Napoleon's greatest victories, and was fought on a site in which present-day country?
B. Shortly before Austerlitz, which Russian Emperor took overall control of the Russian and Austrian forces from General Kutuzov, and lost to a smaller French army?
C. Which film star, born with the surname Austerlitz, was 60 years old when he played his first serious dramatic role, as a nuclear physicist in *On The Beach* in 1959, and 75 when nominated for an Oscar for *The Towering Inferno*?

STARTER 172

Sometimes called vergeboards, the projecting boads placed against the inside of the gable of a building to conceal the ends of the horizontal roof timbers are more commonly known by which name?

BONUS 172

Three questions on literature:

A. Which author wrote three science fiction novels with a strongly Christian attitude, beginning in 1938 with *Out of the Silent Planet*?
B. Matthew Gregory Lewis was the author in 1796 of which sensational Gothic novel, greatly influenced by German romanticism?
C. Wyndham Lewis, the novelist and artist, was a founder in 1914 of *Blast*, a Vorticist review; which American poet, born in 1885, was his co-founder?

STARTER 173

Referred to in the title of a song by Harry Lauder, which Scottish term of Gaelic origin describes a drink taken by guests or travellers immediately before departure?

BONUS 173

Three questions on a name:

A. In which novel by Max Beerbohm do all the young men of Judas College, Oxford, fall madly in love with the Warden's niece?
B. In 1813, who wrote a long poem about Zuleika, the Pacha's daughter, entitled *The Bride of Abydos: A Turkish Tale?*
C. In Muslim tradition, Zuleika is the wife of an Egyptian called Potiphar, named in the Bible as the employer of which Israelite?

STARTER 174

Part of the super-order *Commelinidae*, which widespread mono-cotyledonous plants, with around 9,000 species, belong to the family *gramineae?*

BONUS 174

Three questions on railways:

A. Which preserved standard-gauge passenger railway line was founded in Sussex in 1959, and runs between Sheffield Park Station and Kingscote?
B. Dating from 1896, the only rack-and-pinion system in Britain carries steam passenger trains over four-and-a-half miles to the summit of which mountain?
C. Which 15-inch gauge miniature railway runs for 13-and-a-half miles along the Kent coast, using one-third scale locomotives?

STARTER 175

Which general term describes the sensory feedback from muscles, tendons and joints, informing the brain of the movements made by the body or limbs, and their position in space?

BONUS 175

Three questions on biblical dances:

A. According to Mark's Gospel, who was so pleased by his daughter's dancing at his birthday feast that he allowed her to name her reward, and was asked for the head of John the Baptist?
B. According to Exodus, who fashioned the golden calf before which, during the absence of Moses on Mount Sinai, the people of Israel danced naked?
C. Who, in the Second Book of Samuel, brought the Ark of the Covenant to Jerusalem, dancing "With all his might before the Lord", "girded with a linen ephod"?

BONUS 176

In the *Nibelungenlied*, who is the husband of Brünhild and the brother of Kriemhild, by whom he was beheaded in revenge for Siegfried's murder?

BONUS 176

Three questions on poetry:

A. Which poet's works were collected in the Twickenham edition?
B. Which of Pope's poems contains the lines: "Know then thyself, presume not God to scan;/The proper study of mankind is man."?
C. Who was the poet and friend of Pope, who became an enemy after a bitter quarrel in 1727 which led to venomous personal attacks in verse including *The Dunciad* and *Epistle to Dr Arbuthnot*?

STARTER 177

The pronunciation of which Hebrew word was used by Jephthah at the ford of the River Jordan as a test to detect the fleeing Ephraimites who had been in battle with his own men of Gilead?

BONUS 177

Three questions on Second World War conferences:

A. Which was the first Second World War Allied conference to which Stalin was invited?
B. At which of the Second World War conferences did the Soviet Union agree to declare war on Japan?
C. Who were the Big Three who attended the Potsdam Conference in July 1945?

STARTER 178

Auriga, the northern constellation between Perseus and Gemini, is otherwise known by which name?

BONUS 178

Three questions on the Cold War:

A. Who was the US Secretary of State during the Cuban Missile Crisis?

B. How is the unsuccessful invasion of Cuba in 1961, when most of
    the 1,500 Cuban exiles who took part were captured or killed,
    better known?
C. What was the name of the US pilot shot down over the USSR in
    1960, an incident which effectively sabotaged the subsequent
    Paris Summit between Kruschev and Eisenhower?

STARTER 179

Which broad term is used to describe the ethnographic and
geographical region of the Pacific which includes the islands of
New Guinea, the Bismarck Archipelago, the Solomons, Vanuatu,
New Caledonia and sometimes Fiji?

BONUS 179

Three questions on medieval bankers:
A. Name the German family of bankers who, during the 16th
    century, financed Charles V's candidacy as Holy Roman
    Emperor?
B. Which artist decorated the Arena Chapel, financed by the Italian
    banker Enrico Scrovengi in atonement for crimes of usury?
C. What was the name of the powerful Italian merchant and bank-
    ing family whose emblem was three *palle* or balls, supposedly a
    pun on the family name because of their resemblance to pills?

STARTER 180

Coming into prominence in the 8th century BC and establishing
a system of powerful city states, the people of which ancient country occupied an area between the Arno and Tiber rivers, a region
roughly corresponding to the modern Tuscany?

BONUS 180

Three questions on the Incas:
A. What was the capital city of the Inca Empire?
B. Which Spanish adventurer arrived in Peru in 1532 and effectively
    heralded the end of the Inca empire?
C. In which modern South American country is the Inca town of
    Macchu Picchu?

184   UNIVERSITY CHALLENGE: THE FIRST 40 YEARS

STARTER 181

Based on the novel by William Trevor, *Felicia's Journey* is a film by which Egyptian-born director, who grew up in Canada?

BONUS 181

Three questions on ancient China:

A. What was the name of the monument designed to provide ritual protection for the tomb of the Emperor Shih Huan-Ti?
B. Who was the scholar who lived from 551–479 BC and provided the basis for religious belief and conduct in ancient China?
C. What was the principal religion of China during the T'ang Dynasty?

STARTER 182

The music for the ballet *Scaramouche*, first performed in 1922, was written by which composer, not usually associated with ballet music, who was born at Tavastehus in Finland in 1865?

BONUS 182

Three questions on churches and sects:

A. Which is the religion which believes that the new Jerusalem will be built on the American continent and whose prophets include Enos, Nephi and Moroni?
B. Who is the present leader of the movement founded in 1931 by the honourable Elijah Muhammed and which demonstrated a show of strength in the Million Men March in Washington on 16 October 1995?
C. Where in 1825 were the Plymouth Brethren founded by Dr Edward Cronin and John Nelson Darby?

STARTER 183

Honouring the Roman Emperor, what name was given by Herod Antipas in around 20 AD to the Sea of Galilee?

BONUS 183

Three questions on early cinema:

A. What was the name of the so-called "Film Magician" who attended the first screening of the Lumière Cinematographe and whose films included *A Trip to the Moon* and *An Up-To-Date Conjurer*?
B. What was the name of DW Griffith's pioneering epic of 1915,

accused by many of racism, which featured some of the earliest examples of cross-editing for dramatic effect?

C. What was the 1922 film by Robert Flaherty, often credited as the first documentary?

STARTER 184

Originally designed to measure the diameter of the sun, which astronomical instrument has been used subsequently to determine the angular distance between two celestial objects in close proximity?

BONUS 184

Three questions on Frank Capra films:

A. What was the Frank Capra film which won the Oscar for best film in 1934 and which paired Clark Gable and Claudette Colbert?

B. Frank Capra's film *Lost Horizon*, based on a James Hilton novel, gave the language which name, meaning "an ideal world", where there is no suffering or old age?

C. In Frank Capra's best-loved film, *It's A Wonderful Life*, who played the part of Mr Potter, the curmudgeonly businessman and slum-owner?

STARTER 185

What power is dissipated by a 100 ohm resistor carrying a current of five amps?

BONUS 185

Three questions on Poets Laureate:

A. When the title became official, who was the first to hold it?

B. Who was the Poet Laureate from 1813 to 1843, whose first major work in office was *A Life of Horatio Nelson*?

C. Cecil Day-Lewis, Poet Laureate from 1968 to 1972, was noted for his translations of which Latin poet?

STARTER 186

What name is commonly given to a convex polyhedron with one face, the base, a convex polygon and all the vertices of the base joined by edges to one other vertex, the apex, thus making all the other faces triangular?

BONUS 186

Three questions linked by a name:

A. Who was married first to a French, then to an English king, by whom she was imprisoned for her part in the rebellion of her sons, two of whom became Kings of England?
B. The writer Elinor Glyn, who earned a reputation in the 1920s for risqué novels, coined which fashionable one-word phrase meaning sex appeal?
C. The sisters Elinor and Marianne Dashwood appear in which early 19th-century novel?

STARTER 187

Which British electrical engineer invented the mnemonics, using the fingers and thumb of one hand, for relating the relative directions of magnetic field, current and force in electrical machines?

BONUS 187

Three questions on modern American writers:

A. Garrison Keillor first came to popular attention with a collection of stories all beginning with the line, "It has been a quiet week in …" which fictional midwestern town?
B. *Postcards* and *The Shipping News* were successful novels by which American author?
C. Which novel by Pete Dexter was filmed in 1991 and starred Dennis Hopper in the title role?

STARTER 188

The town of Metz in France, the German cities of Stuttgart and Munich, Lake Balaton in Hungary and the cities of Bucharest and Karachi all shared what specific distinction on Wednesday, 11 August 1999?

BONUS 188

Three questions on American composers:

A. Name the composer who died in 1990 and whose works include the operetta *Candide*, the ballet *The Dybbuk* and the musicals *On The Town* and *West Side Story*?
B. In 1938 Aaron Copland composed the music for a ballet based on the life of which American folk hero?
C. Name the songwriting brothers whose hits include "I Got Rhythm" and "I Got Plenty of Nothin' "?

STARTER 189

Derived from the old English word meaning "proclamation", which plural noun is used for an announcement of intended marriage?

BONUS 189

Three questions on muses:

A. What was the name of Sir Philip Sidney's sonnet sequence inspired by his hopeless love for Penelope Devereux, married against her will to Lord Rich?
B. What was the pseudonym given by Jonathan Swift in poems and letters to Esther Johnson, with whom he formed a lifelong attachment, and to whom some believe he was secretly married?
C. Who fell in love at the age of nine with the woman he immortalized as Beatrice?

STARTER 190

Reflecting the name of the country before 1989, what is the official language of the union of Myanmar?

BONUS 190

Three questions on the city of Bath:

A. What was the Roman name for the city of Bath, referring to the goddess of water who had a shrine there?
B. Who wrote the 18th-century comedy set in Bath which centres on the love affair between Captain Absolute and Lydia Languish?
C. What is the name of the 18th-century novel by Tobias Smollett which describes the Bramble family's tour of England and which includes a lengthy stay in Bath?

STARTER 191

Which word for a brief pithy saying is derived from the Greek words for "from" and "a limit"?

BONUS 191

Three questions on writings:

A. In which English town did John Bunyan serve the prison sentence during which he wrote the *Pilgrim's Progress*?
B. Which Catholic martyr wrote *A Dialogue of Comfort Against Tribulacion* while imprisoned in the Tower of London?
C. Who was arrested in 1649 after he produced a series of controversial pamphlets including *Eikonoklastes* and *A Ready and Easy Way to Establish a Free Commonwealth*?

STARTER 192

The word "piggin", meaning a small drinking vessel, occurs in the expression "piggin and wassail". Which common pub name is a corruption of this phrase?

BONUS 192

Three questions on utopias and dystopias:

A. How did Samuel Butler arrive at the title of his Utopian work *Erewhon*?
B. In which 18th-century novel does the eponymous hero visit the imaginary city of El Dorado?
C. In George Orwell's *1984*, what name has been given to Great Britain?

STARTER 193

The name *Les Pieds Noirs*, argued to derive from the early settlers' black boots which much impressed the indigenous population, is still applied to the French former colonial inhabitants of which country?

BONUS 193

A question about musicians:

With what instruments are the following associated:
A. Yo Yo Ma?
B. Isaac Stern?
C. Martha Argerich?

STARTER 194

What, to a stamp collector, does the abbreviation UN/M stand for?

BONUS 194

Three questions on conductors:

A. In 1999, Simon Rattle left the City of Birmingham Symphony Orchestra to take up the conductorship of which orchestra?
B. Born in 1899, which conductor is most closely associated with the Halle Orchestra.
C. Name the principal conductor of the Berlin Philharmonic from 1955 to 1989 who was forbidden to work from 1945 to 1947 because of his associations with the Nazi Party?

STARTER 195

Which tune is referred to in the Stationers' Company register in 1580, where it is called "a new northern dittye" and is also mentioned twice in Shakespeare's *The Merry Wives of Windsor*? It is popularly believed to have been written by Henry VIII.

BONUS 195

Three questions on South American writers:

A. Name the Peruvian writer whose first novel was *The House of the Spirits*?
B. What is the English title of Gabriel Garcia Marquez's first novel, published in 1955?
C. What is the literary style associated with writers such as Allende and Marquez, characterized by introducing elements of fantasy into everyday situations?

STARTER 196

Often mistakenly called the "loud pedal", what is the correct name for the right-hand pedal on a pianoforte?

BONUS 196

Three questions on space travel:

A. What was the name of the space mission which saw the first manned flight around the moon?
B. What was the name of the astronaut who remained in the command module during the Apollo 11 moon landing?
C. What was the name of the novel by Tom Wolfe which described the experiences of the first American astronauts?

STARTER 197

Which now obsolete name for the lands and islands of the eastern Mediterranean comes from the French for "rising"?

BONUS 197

Three questions on psychiatry:

A. Name the German psychiatrist born in 1840 who is best known for his work on sexual aberrations?
B. What was the name of Sigmund Freud's 1900 publication which argued that the repressed desires of the subconscious are manifested during sleep?

C. What name did Carl Jung give to his psychiatric theories to distinguish them from Freud's psychoanalysis?

STARTER 198

What is the common name for *pastinaca sativa*, a member of the *umbelliferae* family which has been cultivated since ancient times for its tapering edible root, and which can be boiled, braised, roasted, puréed, candied or made into wine?

BONUS 198

Three questions on India:

A. The Act for Better Government of India of 1858 replaced whose rule with that of the British Crown?
B. Who was the leader of the Indian Muslim League from 1937, whose demands for a separate Muslim state led to the creation of Pakistan, of which he was the first Governor-General?
C. What is the English translation of the Hindi word *Satyagraha*, a technique developed by Mahatma Gandhi as a political tool used against the British?

STARTER 199

Which Greek biographer and philosopher, born around 46 AD, was the author of *Parallel Lives*, a collection of biographies of Greek and Roman figures later used as a source by Shakespeare?

BONUS 199

Three questions on dogs in literature:

A. The dog Flush, whose story was told in a biography by Virginia Woolf, belonged to which Victorian literary figure?
B. What was the name of the dog in Jerome K. Jerome's novel *Three Men In A Boat*?
C. To which schoolboy hero did the dog Jumble belong?

STARTER 200

The diet of *larus argentatus*, despite its familiar name, does not consist entirely of one species of fish; in fact, it will eat almost anything, including domestic rubbish. How is this seabird usually known?

BONUS 200

Three questions on the Mafia:

A. In 1931 FBI officer Elliott Ness successfully brought charges of tax evasion against which notorious gangster?
B. What was the trade union of which Jimmy Hoffa, imprisoned in 1967 for corruption and accused of Mafia associations, was president?
C. Who was the Attorney-General who, during the 1960s, led a campaign against organized crime bosses including Sam Giancana and Jimmy Hoffa?

11

Final Questions – and the University Challenge Puzzle

Chaos Theory, the S.T.W. Conjecture, holography, the physical constant of proportionality, the author of Topographica Hibernica, Greeks bearing gifts and a novel by Muriel Spark are among the diverse subjects coming up in the questions in the next and final section. They are the kind of questions our brainiest, fastest students will come up against if they make it through to the last match of the series. We wish you good luck with them.

You will, of course, find the answers to these questions at the back of the book. But we thought it might be fun to set you another, slightly tougher challenge, this time with *no* answers. It's always fun to see over the course of a series which of our teams is the brainiest – but who, out of all the people reading this book, is the smartest? Let's find out.

This is your challenge

You are about to see a series of eleven questions. First, you have to answer them all correctly. Once you have done that, another challenge presents itself. Your eleven answers, taken together with the clues we've given you in this chapter, will give you everything you need to solve our puzzle.

We want to know who can solve the puzzle first. If you think you've cracked it, please write to us. You should send your solution, and your name and address, to: University Challenge Puzzle, Granada Television, Quay Street, Manchester M60 9EA. Of course this is still *University Challenge*, not *The $64,000 Dollar Question*, so there's no cash prize, not even $64, but we'd be delighted to announce your triumph on screen.

Good luck!

1. Who, in 1805, asked for the map to be rolled up?

2. Who had his back to the wall in 1918?

3. Which dead language became official by a constitution of 1950?

4. Look to windward – wasn't that George III?

5. Which Maths teacher was in his element?

6. What steadies the stream's current?

7. How do you measure where thy father lies?

8. Another name for the *Fennecus zerda*?

9. What kind of record could be called a 78?

10. What borders I, W, C, A, and N, touching NM at the SE? .

11. Daphne? Don't let's ask.

Not too tough, we hope. We look forward to hearing from you.

Now for some questions of the level of difficulty we would reserve for the two teams which make it to the final.

FINAL QUESTIONS

STARTER 201

The grave of the 19th-century writer Edward Fitzgerald bears a rose tree grown from a cutting taken from one which grew on the tomb of which Persian writer, born in the 11th century?

BONUS 201

Three questions linked by a word:

A. Which theatre, known for its non-stop variety revues in which comedians such as Harry Secombe and Tony Hancock made their debuts, was the only London theatre to remain open during the Blitz of 1941, adopting the slogan "We Never Closed"?

B. In which 17th-century fictional work does the eponymous hero shout at a group of windmills: "Though ye flourish more arms than the giant Briareus, ye have to reckon with me"?

C. In December 2000, the world's first offshore multi-megawatt wind turbines were officially opened off the coast of which English county?

STARTER 202

The largest computation ever performed, with an accumulated 50,000 years of computer time spanning over 200 countries, the "Seti at Home Screensaver Project" is part of the on-going search for what?

BONUS 202

Three questions on being fat:

A. Which American feminist author and therapist wrote the anti-dieting classic *Fat Is A Feminist Issue?*

B. Which English actress said in 1991: "Life, if you're fat, is a mine-field – you have to pick your way, otherwise you blow up"? She has appeared as Lady Whiteadder in the television series *Blackadder*, and starred in the one-woman stage show *Dickens' Women*.

C. "I'm fat, but I'm thin inside. Has it ever struck you that there's a thin man inside every fat man, just as they say there's a statue inside every block of stone?" Which author wrote these lines in his 1939 novel *Coming Up For Air?*

STARTER 203

Which word derives from a Hindi term meaning "ripe" or "substantial", and has come to be used as a colloquial expression meaning genuine and of good quality?

BONUS 203

Three questions on a game:

A. What was described by the British conservative politician Lord Mancroft as "a game, which the English, not being a spiritual people, have invented in order to give themselves some conception of eternity"?
B. In 1990, which former Foreign Secretary described the difficulties caused by Margaret Thatcher's anti-European views as being "like sending your opening batsmen to the crease only for them to find … that their bats have been broken … by the team captain"?
C. Which politician, speaking in 1990 about Britain's immigrant population, offered his controversial concept of the "cricket test", saying "Which side do they cheer for? Are you still looking back to where you came from or where you are"?

STARTER 204

Described as one of the most difficult problems in mathematics and believed to have been solved in 1999, the S.T.W. Conjecture links elliptic curves and modular forms. Which mathematician first proposed some of the ideas behind the conjecture, and is represented by the letter T?

BONUS 204

Three questions linked by a word:

A. From a Greek word for "vast chasm" or "void", what word, now used to mean disorder and confusion, was sometimes personified in Greek mythology as the first created being, from which came the primeval deities Gaia, Tartarus and Erebus?
B. Chaos theory attempts mathematically to describe irregular, unpredictable systems, and from the early 1960s led Benôit Mandelbrot to develop which branch of geometry, concerned with irregular patterns which are in some way similar to the whole?
C. The now obsolete genus *chaos* was created by Linnaeus to accommodate which organisms, whose many different species include *armallaria ostoyae*, an individual example of which was, in 1992, identified as the world's largest living thing?

STARTER 205

Who is being described? The recipient, in 2000, of a "Lifetime Achievement" award from *Loaded* magazine, he made his television debut as a guest on the David Nixon magic show, and his sidekicks have included the actors Rodney Bewes, Derek Fowlds and Roy North?

BONUS 205
Three bonus questions:

A. Which geological epoch has a Greek name meaning "entirely new", and is the second and current epoch of the Quaternary period? It began around 10,000 years ago and marks the period in which the glaciers retreated, the climate became warmer and human society developed from the primitive?
B. The class *Holothuroidae* include the long, spiny-skinned marine animals which are dried and eaten as a delicacy in Japan and Taiwan, and are known by what common name?
C. Which Hungarian-born scientist developed the theory of holography in 1947, while working to improve the resolution of an electron microscope?

STARTER 206

The American techno DJ Richard Hall uses what stage name, indicating that he is a descendant of the writer Herman Melville?

BONUS 206
Three questions on pasta:

A. Which type of stuffed pasta is formed into a shape which, according to popular belief, was modelled on the navel of Venus?
B. The name of which thin, spaghetti-like pasta means literally "little worms"?
C. The eating of pasta was denounced in the 1930s by the Italian poet Filippo Marinetti, as part of the manifesto of which early 20th-century political movement?

STARTER 207

St Crispin, whose day is celebrated on Agincourt Day, 25 October, is the patron saint of which trade?

BONUS 207
Three questions on laws:

A. What term, meaning "harsh" or "severe", is derived from the name of the Athenian politician of the 7th century BC who was the first to codify the laws of the city-state, which were notorious for their severity?
B. The term *lex talionis* refers to a retaliatory punishment also referred to by which familiar term, deriving from the Book of Exodus, Chapter 21, Verse 24?
C. The Abolition of Death Penalty Act of 1965 abolished capital punishment for murder in England and Wales, but until the 1990s it was still by law the punishment for high treason, burning down naval dockyards, and which other offence?

STARTER 208

What name derived from the Old High German for "company", and was applied to the association of north German cities formed in 1241 as a trading alliance, later functioning as an independent political, military and naval power?

BONUS 208
Three questions on a politician:

A. Which British Prime Minister was described by the economist John Maynard Keynes as "this extraordinary figure of our time, this syren, this goat-footed bard, this half-human visitor to our age from the hag-ridden magic and enchanted woods of Celtic antiquity"?
B. In 1909, when Lloyd George was Chancellor of the Exchequer, which body did he deride as "a body of 500 men, chosen accidentally from among the unemployed"?
C. In 1912, Lloyd George became involved in a financial controversy when he purchased 1,000 cheap shares in which wireless company, before they went on sale to the public at a much higher rate?

STARTER 209

The physical constant of proportionality, which has a value of 6.672 times ten to the minus 11 newton metres squared per kilogram squared, is usually denoted by which upper case letter?

BONUS 209
Three questions on losing one's mind:

A. In a play by Shakespeare, which character's madness becomes apparent as she sings: "He is dead and gone, Lady,/He is dead and gone,/At his head a grass-green turf;/At his heels a stone."

B. The song "Losing My Mind" was written by Stephen Sondheim for which stage musical, which began its first New York run in 1971, and concerned the reunion of a group of retired performers?

C. In a film of 1968, who, or what, confesses: "My mind is going. There is no question about it. I can feel it", before starting to sing "Daisy, Daisy"?

STARTER 210

Roughly meaning in Latin "a bit cut off", what name is given to the part of a cone or pyramid which lies between the base and a parallel plane?

BONUS 210

Three questions on peace:

A. Which organization has as its motto words adapted from Isaiah: "Nation Shall Speak Peace Unto Nation"?

B. According to the Gospel of Matthew in the King James version: "Blessed are the peacemakers, for they shall be called ..." – what?

C. On his return from the Congress of Berlin in 1878, who declared "Lord Salisbury and myself have brought you back peace – but a peace, I hope, with honour"?

STARTER 211

The runes or "matchstick signs" known as futhark, from the first six letters of the alphabet in Scandinavian countries, are known by what name when used by their Celtic counterparts, especially in Ireland?

BONUS 211

Three questions on oils:

A. Used for centuries as a medication by Australian Aborigines, which powerful antiseptic oil has been popularized in cosmetic preparations such as shampoos and skin cleansers, and is derived from the leaves and twigs of the tree *melaleuca alternifolia*?

B. The essential oil neroli, which is used in perfumery, is distilled from the flowers of which fruit tree?

C. A native of northern Mexico and the southwestern USA, the leathery-leaved shrub *simmondsia chinensis*, also called the goat nut, yields which high-quality oil, which since the 1980s has been used extensively in soaps, moisturizers and hair conditioners?

STARTER 212

Pronouncing the name of which of its suburbs is a class shibbo-leth in Birmingham, with so-called working-class speakers empha-sizing the first syllable and giving the second syllable a short "I" sound, while the upwardly mobile emphasize the second syllable as a long "A"?

BONUS 212

Three questions on religion:

A. Which long-running BBC TV programme was first broadcast in 1961, its presenters having included Alan Titchmarsh, Toyah Wilcox, Harry Secombe and Diane Louise Jordan?
B. What is the title of the song of praise which, according to Luke's gospel, is sung by the Virgin Mary on her visit to her sister Elizabeth after the annunciation, and is used in the liturgy of some Christian churches in the form of a canticle?
C. Which two Latin words, taken from a phrase meaning "now lettest thou thy servant depart", are used as the title of Simeon's song of praise on the presentation of the infant Jesus in the temple, this song also being traditionally used in evening liturgical services?

STARTER 213

Which three-word phrase, frequently encountered during the Second World War, is believed to have originated with a shipyard inspector in Quincy, Massachusetts, who chalked it on the inside of ships' hulls to show that a check had been made by him?

BONUS 213

Three questions on unwelcome gifts:

A. Which Roman poet of the first century BC was the author of the lines, "Do not trust the horse, Trojans. Whatever it is, I fear the Greeks even when they bring gifts"?
B. "God answers sharp and sudden on some prayers,/And thrusts the thing we have prayed for in our face,/A gauntlet with a gift in't." Which 19th-century poet wrote these lines in *Aurora Leigh*, her work of 1856?
C. Which Edinburgh-born novelist, in her autobiographical work of 1992 entitled *Curriculum Vitae*, said that "From my experience of life, I believe my personal motto should be 'Beware of men bear-ing flowers' "?

STARTER 214

Which country is a crescent-shaped island containing 54 cities sited at least 24 miles apart, each of less than 100,000 people, and was created in a work of fiction which first appeared in 1516?

BONUS 214

Three questions on novels about war:

A. Erich Remarque served as a German soldier in the First World War, and was deprived of his German nationality after writing which book, considered to be one of the first anti-war novels?
B. The pilot Yossarian is the central character in which 1961 novel, satirizing the madness of war and military bureaucracy?
C. Who is the author of the *Regeneration Trilogy*, concerned in part with the First World War experiences of Siegfried Sassoon and Wilfred Owen?

STARTER 215

At the height of the American Civil War, which author did Abraham Lincoln greet with the words, "So you're the little woman who wrote the book that made this great war," referring to her anti-slavery novel of 1852, *Uncle Tom's Cabin?*

BONUS 215

Three questions on topographers:

A. Which 2nd-century Greek geographer and historian was the author of *Description of Greece*, which, as a guide to the topography and remains of Ancient Greece, is still considered an invaluable source?
B. Which early medieval cleric and chronicler was the author of *Topographia Hibernica*, covering the natural history, marvels and early events of Ireland, and the *Itinerarium Cambriae*, on the topography of Wales?
C. Which novelist and pamphleteer was the author in the 1720s of the three-volume *Tour Through The Whole Island of Great Britain*, a guide-book giving a first-hand account of the state of the country, gleaned from his many travels?

STARTER 216

In Matthew's gospel, which monetary unit, equal to 3,000 shekels, features in the parable of a man going abroad who shares his money among his servants for them to invest?

BONUS 216

Three bonus questions:

A. In Freudian psychology, what term refers to the element of the human mind which represents the conscious processes concerned with reality?
B. Edo was the former name of which Asian capital city, which was renamed in 1868 and which in 1923 was severely damaged by an earthquake?
C. Brian Eno, who has been credited with creating the genre of "ambient music", was an original member of which British art rock band of the 1970s, being their keyboardist and technical adviser?

STARTER 217

Containing variations on the tune of his song "Die Forelle", what is the English title of Schubert's piano quartet in A major, D667, composed in 1819?

BONUS 217

Three questions on birds:

A. Which migratory British bird comprising the genus *Hirundo* is called the Hirondelle in heraldry?
B. Which black bird of the crow family, having a long red bill and red legs, appears on the arms of the County Council of Cornwall and, according to Cornish legend, became the home for King Arthur's spirit after his death?
C. Which bird was regarded as sacred in early Celtic and Druidic traditions, although in later folk customs in England and Ireland it was ritually hunted and killed on St Stephen's Day? It has the Latin name *troglodytes troglodytes*.

STARTER 218

Which English city takes its name from an 11th-century construction ordered by Robert Curthouse, eldest son of William the Conqueror, on his return from a raid into Scotland, and built on the site of the Roman fort of Pons Aelius?

BONUS 218

Three questions on language:

A. What word, derived from Arabic, is given to an area of shifting sand dunes in the Sahara?
B. What is the literal meaning of the Latin word "ergo"?
C. What is the common name of the grain *secale cereal*, which is used for bread, fodder and a type of whisky, and which is the main victim of the fungal disease ergot which attacks the plant's kernels, making it highly poisonous?

STARTER 219

Derived from a mythical Greek king, what name did Anders Ekberg give to the silvery-grey metallic element of group 5B he isolated in 1802, because of the teasing difficulty he had in dissolving its oxide in acids?

BONUS 219

Three questions on food preservation:

A. Lyophilization, literally meaning "easily dissolved", is the technical term for which method of preservation, used for some foods such as coffee, and also for drugs and organic archaeological remains?
B. Which American businessman and inventor developed the processes for food preservation he encountered while working as a fur-trader in Labrador in 1912 and 1916, and became associated with the freezing of foods in small packages for retail?
C. What is the common name of potassium or sodium nitrate, which is added as a preservative to cured meats and helps to produce their characteristic pink colour?

STARTER 220

Andrew Motion's *In A Perfect World* was the first poem to be written by a Poet Laureate in honour of which organization, founded in 1868?

BONUS 220

Three questions on divination:

A. In Ancient Rome, haruspicy was supposedly a method of predicting the future based on the examination of what?

B. The girdle of Venus and the plain of Mars feature in which method of fortune-telling, also known as chiromancy?

C. In "The Burial of the Dead", the first part of TS Eliot's *The Waste Land*, what form of divination is practised by Madame Sosostris?

STARTER 221

Also known as Alpha Boötes, which star is an orange giant and the fourth brightest star in the night sky, its name deriving from the Greek meaning "guardian of the bear", and referring to its position in relation to the tail of Ursa Major?

BONUS 221

Three questions on a Greek playwright:

A. *The Acharnians*, written in 425 BC, is the earliest of which Greek playwright's 11 comedies to have survived intact?

B. Which philosopher is lampooned in Aristophanes' play *Clouds*, in which he runs an academy called The Phrontisterion, or "Thinking Shop", where instruction consists of making a wrong argument sound right?

C. In which play by Aristophanes do all the women of Greece unite and declare a sex strike until their menfolk make peace?

STARTER 222

Which British lexicographer was, with his brother Francis, the author of *The King's English* and editor of *The Concise Oxford Dictionary*, although his most famous work, first published in 1926, is *Modern English Usage*?

BONUS 222

Three questions on Christ's Apostles:

A. Which two of the 12 Apostles of Jesus were brothers, the sons of Zebedee, and were known collectively as Boanerges, meaning "sons of thunder"?

B. Which of the Apostles, also known as Thaddeus, is venerated as the saint of lost or desperate causes?

C. Which Apostle, also known as "the zealot" or "the Canaanean", was, according to some sources, martyred by being cut in half longitudinally with a saw, the instrument now being one of his chief iconographic symbols?

STARTER 223

Aphrodite Terra, close to the equator, and Ishtar Terra, in the north, are two of the chief areas of highland on which planet, the rotation of which is longer than its year?

BONUS 223
Three questions on lines of poetry:

A. Which poem was written by the American Unitarian lay preacher Julia Ward Howe in 1862, and set to the tune of "John Brown's Body"? It became the semi-official Civil War song of the Union Army, and has as its first line: "Mine eyes have seen the glory of the coming of the Lord".
B. "Drink to me only with thine eyes, and I will pledge with mine" are the opening lines of *To Celia* by which English playwright and poet, who was renowned for his masques for the court of King James I?
C. "The voice of your eyes is deeper than all roses/Nobody, not even the rain, has such small hands," are the closing lines of *Somewhere I Have Never Travelled* by which American poet, born in 1894 and noted for his avoidance of capital letters?

STARTER 224

The Torino Scale runs from nought to ten, and indicates the degree of potential threat from what form of hazard?

BONUS 224
Three questions on US Presidents:

A. Which General and later President of the US had the original first name Hiram, although he later dropped it?
B. Which assassinated President was a student, English teacher and finally, from 1857–60, Principal of Hiram College, Ohio?
C. In the 1912 presidential election, Hiram Johnson stood on the Progressive Party ticket as the running-mate of which former Republican President?

STARTER 225

In the early hours of New Year's Day 2000, a painting by Paul Cézanne, "Auvers-sur-Oise", was stolen from which English museum?

BONUS 225
Three questions on the deaths of legendary kings:

A. Which legendary English king was, according to Geoffrey of

ier of King Lear, and was dashed to pieces
ly above the Temple of Apollo?
, King Arthur received his death wound at
a around the year 540 at the hands of which
is nephew, who was also slain there?
King of Ulster was the uncle of Cuchulainn,
:d when a slingshot buried deep in his head
ied to avenge the crucifixion of Christ?

1880s, Otto von Bismarck engaged in an
l conflict with the Vatican, as he attempted
irch to the state in a campaign known by

BONUS 226

Three questions on linguistics:

A. From the Greek words for "equal" and "tongue", what name is given to a line on a map delimiting the area in which a given linguistic feature occurs?
B. Coined by the anthropologist Bonislaw Malinowski, what expression is used to indicate speech used to convey feelings of general sociability, as opposed to information or ideas?
C. What form of modality is used in the sentence "He must know that; he's got a degree in physics," where the word "must" expresses a judgement about the truth of a proposition?

STARTER 227

Which short story, considered a classic of the horror genre, was first published in 1902 and adapted for the stage the following year, its author being WW Jacobs?

BONUS 227

Three questions on the transience of life:

A. "And life is given to none freehold, but is leasehold for all," were the words of which Epicurean poet of the first century BC?
B. In his *Ecclesiastical History of the English People,* what image did the Venerable Bede evoke to compare "the present life of men on earth … with that time which to us is uncertain"?
C. The phrase "In the midst of life we are in death", from the *Book of Common Prayer,* had its final word altered to what in a parody by the American humorist Ethel Watts Mumford?

STARTER 228

What word derives from the Greek for "most new" and refers to the first epoch of the Quaternary period, during which the Great Ice Age occurred?

BONUS 228

Three questions on 4th-century church history:

A. The doctrines of which Alexandrian priest, declared a heretic at the Council of Nicaea in 325, denied that Jesus was of the same substance as God and held instead that he was only the highest of created beings?
B. Consecrated Bishop by the Arian Eusebius of Nicomedia in 341, Ulfilas translated the Bible into which east Germanic language, his translation providing the major surviving textual source of this extinct tongue?
C. Ulfilas's translation included all of the Old Testament with the exception of which two books, which he is said to have omitted because "… the Gothic tribes … were in more need of restraints to check their military passions than of spurs to urge them on to deeds of war"?

STARTER 229

What standard strength of spirit or alcohol was originally defined as the minimum concentration of alcohol which will burn when mixed with an equal quantity of gunpowder, and is now defined as equivalent to 57.1 per cent of alcohol by volume at 10.6 degrees celsius in the UK, and 50 per cent at 15.6 degrees Celsius in the US?

BONUS 229

Three questions on a Japanese province:

A. Which peninsula and former province of the southern Japanese island of Kyushu gives its name both to a cream-coloured porcelain, first manufactured there by Korean artisans in the 16th century, and to a variety of tangerine?
B. Sparked off by the Richardson incident of 1862, in which a British merchant was killed by Samurai from Satsuma, the Anglo-Satsuma War culminated in a brief bombardment of which city, sometimes known as the "Naples of the East"?
C. Satsuma became a major participant in which political movement

of 1869 which resulted in the overthrow of the Tokugawa Shogunate and the establishment of Japan as an industrial and military power?

STARTER 230

Which group of chemicals are used for treating sheep against parasites, have been identified by researchers as a potential health risk to humans, and are referred to as OPs?

BONUS 230

Three bonus questions:

A. Taking its name from a Greek letter, which figure of speech refers to a reversal in the order of words of two otherwise parallel phrases, for example, "Never let a fool kiss you, or a kiss fool you"?
B. In a work of 1958, which satirist made the caustic observation that "the man who is denied the opportunity of taking decisions of importance begins to regard as important the decisions he is allowed to take".
C. The author of numerous works on naval history, of which fictional naval hero did Parkinson publish a biography in 1970?

STARTER 231

For the chemical reaction A plus B gives C plus D, where A and B are concentrations of reactants, and C and D are concentrations of products, what is given by C times D divided by A times B?

BONUS 231

Three questions linked by a word:

A. What term was given by the historian Karl Wittfogel to a culture having an agricultural system dependent upon large-scale, state-managed systems of irrigation and flood control?
B. Invented by Ktesibios of Alexandria in the 3rd century BC and used until medieval times, the hydraulis was an early form of what musical instrument?
C. His instruments described by Mozart as "magnificent beyond measure", what was the name of the German organ-builder whose grand pipe organ of the Frauenkirche in Dresden was played by Bach soon after its dedication in 1736?

STARTER 232

From the Latin for "spring", what name is given to the stimulation of flowering in some plants by exposure to low temperature?

BONUS 232

Three questions on Greek personalities:

A. Which Greek philosopher is said to have lived in a tub and, when asked by Alexander the Great if he could help him in any way, replied, "Move out of the sun so you don't cast a shadow on me"?

B. Described by Sherlock Holmes in the story of *The Greek Interpreter* as a collection of "the most unsociable and unclubbable men in town", what were members of the Diogenes Club forbidden from doing?

C. The 2nd-century writer Diogenes Laertius is best known for his biographies of which eminent figures?

STARTER 233

Which Nobel Prize-winning zoologist described the dance-like movements made by hive bees as they communicate with each other?

BONUS 233

Three questions on the economist John Kenneth Galbraith:

A. An in-depth look at the industrial age, what 13-week television series, later followed by a book of the same name, was presented by Galbraith in 1976?

B. What two-word term usually describes the economic theory associated with the Reagan years, and referred to by Galbraith as the "Horse-sparrow theory" – in other words, if one feeds the horse enough oats, some will pass through to the road for the sparrows?"

C. In which country did Galbraith serve, at his own request, as US Ambassador from 1961 to 1963?

STARTER 234

Which battle of 1916, at a fortified city on the upper Meuse river, became a symbol of French military determination inspired by Pétain's declaration "Ils ne passeront pas!", or "They shall not pass"?

BONUS 234

Three questions linked by the ox:

A. The "Ox Minuet" by Ignas Xavier von Seyfried is based on the legend that which composer, of whom von Seyfried was a pupil, wrote a minuet for a butcher who gave him an ox in return?
B. From the Greek meaning "ox hunger", what name is given to the eating disorder in which large amounts of food are consumed in a short time, often followed by depression?
C. Ox-bow lakes, formed when a river's meandering loops enlarge through erosion and eventually become cut off, are known in Australia by what Aboriginal name, meaning "dead water"?

STARTER 235

The process used for the transformation of anything humanly readable into a form which can be used by a computer is referred to by the initials OCR. What do these initials stand for?

BONUS 235

Three questions linked by facial hair:

A. The surname "Pogonatus", given to the 7th-century Byzantine Emperor Constantine IV, referred to what physical feature, also noted in the bynames of Count Baldwin IV of Flanders and Fidel Castro?
B. The bearded vulture *gypaetus barbatus* is Europe's largest bird of prey and is also known by what German name, reflecting its choice of victim?
C. Who, as he placed his head on the executioner's block in 1535, is reputed to have drawn aside his beard and said, "This hath not offended the king"?

STARTER 236

What word derives from the Latin for "thread" and "seed", refers to a style of jewellery known in the ancient world, and means an openwork decoration of very fine wires and tiny metal balls soldered into a design?

BONUS 236

Three questions on geology:

A. What type of rock is a finely-grained, sometimes glassy, basic igneous rock, generally found in the form of lava flows, such as those forming the Giant's Causeway in Antrim?
B. What type of rock has a banded structure, and is formed during high-grade regional metamorphism? It is generally fairly coarse-grained, and can contain large clots or "eyes" of very coarse crystals of feldspar and quartz.
C. What type of rock is of a detrital sedimentary formation, of the argillaceous group, with a well-marked bedding plane fissility? This rock does not form a plastic mass when wet, although it may disintegrate when immersed in water.

STARTER 237

Which nickname originated with Geoffrey IV, Count of Anjou, and was given to the royal dynasty which held the English throne from the reign of his son, Henry II, to Richard III?

BONUS 237

Three questions linked by an animal:

A. The American blues singer and songwriter Chester Arthur Burnett, whose recordings include "Smokestack Lightnin'" and "Little Red Rooster", earned himself which stage name because of his habitual falsetto vocal call?
B. The writer Tom Wolfe, author of the 1988 novel *The Bonfire Of the Vanities*, was a founder, in the 1960s, of which form of writing, which brought fiction's methods to reportage?
C. Wolfram is an alternative name for which hard, heavy, grey-white, metallic element? It has the symbol W, and the highest melting point of any metal.

STARTER 238

The reported appearance in 1917 of the Virgin Mary to a group of children led to the establishment of a shrine at which town in central Portugal?

BONUS 238

Three questions on astronomy. On each case, identify the planet of our solar system from the description given.

A. Which planet has an equatorial diameter of just over 4,880 kilometres, making it the second smallest in the solar system? It is just over 58 million kilometres from the sun, and one year lasts nearly 88 earth days.
B. Which planet is 778 million kilometres from the sun, and has an equatorial diameter of 142,800 kilometres, making it the largest in the solar system? One year lasts nearly 12 earth years.
C. Which planet's equatorial diameter is 6,787 kilometres, is 228 million kilometres from the sun and has a year lasting 687 earth days?

STARTER 239

With its origins in the Kamakura period around the 13th century, the code of conduct adopted by the Samurai class of Japan is known by which term, meaning "way of the warrior"?

BONUS 239

Three questions on SI units:

A. What SI prefix is given to units which are multiples of ten to the 12?
B. Units with the SI prefix "EXA-" are multiples of ten to what power?
C. Units with the SI prefix "FEMTO-" are multiples of ten to what minus power?

STARTER 240

What name was given to the fastening which bound together the yoke and beam of a chariot dedicated to Zeus, the fastening being designed by Gordius and ultimately cut apart by Alexander the Great?

BONUS 240

Three questions on fundamental values: which fundamental values are expressed as the following, in SI units?

A. 1.01325 times ten to the five pascals?
B. 9.80665 metres per second squared?
C. 8.31434 JK^{-1} mol^{-1}?

STARTER 241

Which country was, in its ancient era, divided into administrative regions called "Nomes", each identified by an emblematic god? Latterly, there were 22 nomes in the upper division, and 20 in the lower.

BONUS 241

Three questions on martial arts:

A. Which Japanese martial art teaches self-defence and offence without weapons, was originally practised by the Samurai, and has developed into the modern sport of judo?

B. Which martial art is an unarmed combat derived from Kempo, which is in turn a form of the Chinese shaolin, and became popular in the West in the 1950s?

C. Which of the martial arts is essentially non-violent and non-competitive, is based on the principle of the harmony of "Ki" or energy, and combines elements of ju-jitsu and karate, while never using force to oppose force?

STARTER 242

Whose body, along with those of John Bradshaw and Henry Ireton, was removed from its burial place, taken to Tyburn and displayed there after the Restoration in 1660?

BONUS 242

Three questions on Native American people:

A. Which nomadic Native American people of the Great Plains, led by their chiefs Crazy Horse and Sitting Bull, defeated Custer at the Battle of Little Bighorn in 1876, after the US government broke the terms of their resettlement treaty?

B. Which Native American people, formerly of the south Appalachians, sided with Britain in the War of Independence and were subsequently punished, under the orders of President Andrew Jackson, by being transported to a reservation in Oklahoma by a forced march known as "The Trail of Tears"?

C. Geronimo, who spent the last years of his life as a prosperous Christian farmer and a national celebrity, formerly led which tribe against US federal troops and encroaching white settlers in Arizona?

STARTER 243

Which word can mean both a scree slope formed from frost-shattered rocks, and the ankle bone?

BONUS 243

Three questions on a fish:

A. Which jawless fish is a member of the family *petromyzontidae*, and feeds on other fish by fixing itself by its round mouth to its host and boring into the flesh with its toothed tongue?
B. In a tradition lasting from the reign of King John until 1917, which town made an annual presentation to the reigning monarch of a lamprey pie, the lampreys being caught in the nearby River Leadon?
C. *A Surfeit of Lampreys* is the tenth in a series of novels featuring Inspector Roderick Alleyn, the creation of which New Zealand-born crime writer, who died in 1982?

STARTER 244

Successor to Isaac Newton as President of the Royal Society, which Irish-born British physicist bequeathed to the nation the collections and library which formed the nucleus of the British Museum?

BONUS 244

Three questions on the sciences:

A. In physics, according to the standard model, the electron, muon and tau, and their neutrinos, comprise which class of elementary particles which interact via the electro weak force and gravity, but are not affected by the strong interaction?
B. Leptospirosis, an infectious disease communicated by animal urine and prevalent in rats, is also known by which common name, after the German physician who first described it?
C. Leptocephalus is the transparent oceanic larva of which fish, which migrates over 2,000 miles across the Atlantic from breeding grounds near the West Indies to reach European fresh waters, where it becomes an adult?

STARTER 245

Which three Latin words mean an unexpected power or event saving a seemingly hopeless situation, and derive from the convention in ancient Greek theatre of a god making an entrance in a play by means of a crane?

BONUS 245

Three questions on astronomy:

A. In astronomy, what term derives from the name of the French mathematician who predicted its existence in 1772 and is given to a point in space at which a small body, under the gravitational influence of two larger ones, will remain approximately at rest relative to them, each system of two heavy bodies having theoretically five such points?

B. Lagrange also predicted the location of two groups of asteroids, near the stability points of a three-body system formed by the sun, Jupiter, and the asteroids; what name was later given to this asteroid system, and to any object occupying the equilateral Lagrangian points of other pairs of bodies?

C. The Lagrangian Function is a quantity which characterizes the state of a physical system; in mechanics, this is expressed in what simple equation?

STARTER 246

Usually depicting elegantly-dressed young people engaged in outdoor entertainment, the "Fête Galante" is a type of genre painting developed by which French Rococo artist, born in 1684, whose painting include "The Embarkation for Cythera"?

BONUS 246

Three questions on patterns of lines:

A. Which ancient Chinese book of divination is based on 64 hexagrams, or patterns of six lines, which are traditionally generated by throwing yarrow stalks or coins?

B. Named after the Viennese scientist who discovered them in 1808, the Widmanstatten pattern of lines are formed by bands of kamacite and taenite, and appear when a cross-section of which objects are etched with weak acid?

C. Over 2,000 years old, indecipherable from ground level but recognizable from the air as around seventy images of plants and animals, the Nazca lines cover nearly 500 square kilometres in the southern part of which country?

STARTER 247

First excavated in the 1930s, which deep cleft in the Serengeti plains of northern Tanzania yielded the bones of gigantic extinct mammals, prehistoric stone tools and the remains of *homo habilis*?

BONUS 247

Three questions on famous quotations:

A. According to Thomas Hobbes in his 1651 work *Leviathan*, what are: "Wise men's counters, they do but reckon by them; but they are the money of fools"?
B. Who wrote in the preface to his work of 1770: "I am not yet so lost in lexicography, as to forget that words are the daughters of earth, and that things are the sons of heaven"?
C. Which American politician, standing for the Democrats against Eisenhower, said in a campaign speech in Denver, Colorado, in 1952: "Man does not live by words alone, despite the fact that sometimes he has to eat them"?

STARTER 248

In architecture, what name is given to that part of a cruciform-planned church which projects out at right angles from the main body of the building, usually between the nave and the chancel?

BONUS 248

Three questions on poetry:

A. The Story of the Three Bears was first printed in 1837 in *The Doctor*, a miscellany by which English poet, who also wrote the poems *The Old Man's Comforts and How He Gained Them* and *The Cataract of Lodore*, and produced a children's edition of the *Morte d'Arthur*?
B. Southey's *The Old Man's Comforts* was parodied by which Victorian children's writer in his poem *You Are Old, Father William*?
C. Which poem in Carroll's *Alice's Adventures in Wonderland* is a parody of Isaac Watts' moralistic poem against idleness and mischief, entitled *How Doth The Little Busy Bee*?

STARTER 249

Which film of 1955 was directed by Ingmar Bergman, and set on a country estate in turn-of-the-century Sweden. Influenced by Shakespeare's *A Midsummer Night's Dream*, it in turn influenced the Broadway musical *A Little Night Music* and the Woody Allen film *A Midsummer Night's Sex Comedy*.

BONUS 249

Three questions on the Commonwealth:

A. Which Australian state, annexed for Britain by James Cook, was part of New South Wales until it became a separate colony in 1851, became a state in 1901 and has Melbourne as its capital?
B. The Victoria Falls, named after Queen Victoria by David Livingstone in 1855, are on the River Zambezi on the border of which two countries?
C. Bounded by Uganda, Kenya and Tanzania, Lake Victoria is Africa's largest lake and was named after the Queen in 1858 by which British explorer, whose claim that it was the source of the Nile was disputed by fellow-explorer Richard Burton?

STARTER 250

"Equivalent Eight", made of bricks stacked in two layers to form a rectangle, was purchased by the Tate Gallery in 1972, and is a controversial work of 1966 by which American minimalist sculptor?

BONUS 250

Three questions on African lakes:

A. Which lake of the Great Rift Valley is the deepest in Africa, and has ports in Burundi and Zambia?
B. Which salt-water lake of the Great Rift Valley is sited mainly in Kenya, with its northern shoreline in Ethiopia? Archaeological remains discovered on its shores by Richard Leakey prove it to have been an early human hunting-ground.
C. Lake Malawi, formed in a section of the Great Rift Valley, is bordered by Malawi, Tanzania and which other East African country?

12

The Answers

STARTER 1
A. "FIDDLER ON THE ROOF" (by Jerry Brock, Sheldon Harnick, Joseph Stein)
BONUS 1
A. CALIFORNIA
B. HONG KONG (horses are exercised on the flat roofs of the surrounding tower blocks!)
C. JACQUELINE SUSANN

STARTER 2
A. CONFESSION
BONUS 2
A. *CRIME AND PUNISHMENT* (Dostoyevsky, 1866)
B. "THE MIKADO" ("My object all sublime, I shall achieve in time, to let the punishment fit the crime, the punishment fit the crime.")
C. SOLES OF THE FEET

STARTER 3
A. CORKAGE
BONUS 3
A. (AUSTRALIAN) ABORIGINES (the islands are off the coast near Darwin)
B. (PAPUA) NEW GUINEA
C. FAROES / FAEROE ISLANDS (Danish: Faeroerne)

STARTER 4
A. "PAINT YOUR WAGON"
BONUS 4
A. "I DON'T LIKE MONDAYS" (Boomtown Rats)
B. PRINCE / THE ARTIST FORMERLY KNOWN AS, etc (he used the pseudonym "Christopher")
C. NEW ORDER

STARTER 5
A. ST. MARTIN'S
BONUS 5
A. FAMILY HEALTH SERVICES AUTHORITY
B. OCCUPATIONAL HEALTH SERVICE
C. CONTROL OF SUBSTANCES HAZARDOUS TO HEALTH

STARTER 6
A. TOM SAWYER

BONUS 6
A. HORIZON
B. GLEYING
C. UNDECOMPOSED LITTER

STARTER 7
A. (HENRI) TOULOUSE-LAUTREC

BONUS 7
A. N.K.V.D.
B. THE GREAT PURGES / THE PURGE TRIALS
C. (SERGEI) KIROV (or KOSTRIKOV) (a Secretary of the Politburo's Central Committee; his assassination may have been at Stalin's instigation)

STARTER 8
A. SUE MacGREGOR

BONUS 8
A. KATHY BURKE
B. GARY OLDMAN
C. *SID AND NANCY*

STARTER 9
A. MAFIA [accept COSA NOSTRA]

BONUS 9
A. BABYLONIA
B. IRAQ
C. ALEXANDER THE GREAT (THE THIRD)

STARTER 10
A. A.M. / A.C. (Assembly Member, Aelod O'r Cynulliad)

BONUS 10
A. "THE MAN WITH NO NAME"
B. G.K.CHESTERTON
C. SAMUEL GOLDWYN (although many of the "Goldwynisms" were scripted by his press office)

STARTER 11
A. CARLISLE UNITED

BONUS 11
A. *THE LITTLE PRINCE*
B. DENNIS BERGKAMP
C. ERICA JONG

STARTER 12
A. MADISON SQUARE GARDEN

BONUS 12
A. SHADOWFAX
B. BANQUO'S GHOST (Act 3, Scene 4)
C. K.D. LANG

STARTER 13
A. ALDERNEY
BONUS 13
A. TROMBONE
B. PIANO (he also made harpsichords before making pianos)
C. FLUTE

STARTER 14
A. THREE
BONUS 14
A. MAHOGANY
B. HICKORY
C. SYCAMORE (Acer pseudoplatanus)

STARTER 15
A. BATH
BONUS 15
A. JULY 31ST (Lammas is August 1st)
B. BURUNDI
C. UXBRIDGE

STARTER 16
A. LION
BONUS 16
A. REVENGE
B. *KIND HEARTS AND CORONETS*
C. BYRON

STARTER 17
A. MAPLE
BONUS 17
A. THEA MUSGRAVE
B. AUSTRALIA (in South Australia)
C. JOHN ARDEN

STARTER 18
A. 38 PENCE
    (1p + 2p + 5p + 10p + 20p)
BONUS 18
A. "ART FOR ART'S SAKE"
C. *THE YELLOW BOOK*
A. "A LILY" (the flower particularly associated with the movement)

STARTER 19
A. STATEN ISLAND
BONUS 19
A. GEORGE II (during the War of the Austrian Succession)
B. GEORGE ORWELL / ERIC BLAIR
C. THE NARNIA STORIES / CHRONICLES OF NARNIA

STARTER 20
A. TOM JONES (*Tom Jones, A Foundling*, Henry Fielding, 1749)
BONUS 20
A. *PRIDE AND PREJUDICE* (Pemberley being Mr Darcy's home)
B. SUSAN HILL
C. LORD PETER WIMSEY

STARTER 21
A. TRAMPOLINING
BONUS 21
A. MILLION INSTRUCTIONS PER SECOND
B. GARBAGE IN, GARBAGE OUT (GIGO)
C. MUSICAL INSTRUMENT DIGITAL INTERFACE

STARTER 22
A. SPRING CLEANING (Kenneth Graeme's novel)
BONUS 22
A. VOORTREKKER MONUMENT
B. HENRY THE NAVIGATOR
C. SANTIAGO

STARTER 23
A. SIR PAUL McCARTNEY
BONUS 23
A. OEDIPUS
B. BLINDNESS
C. ANTIGONE

STARTER 24
A. INTERNATIONAL BANK FOR RECONSTRUCTION AND DEVELOPMENT
BONUS 24
A. BELL ROCK
B. CANTERBURY
C. SYLVIA PLATH

STARTER 25
A. ECHO SOUNDER
BONUS 25
A. NICCI FRENCH

B. EMMA LATHEN
C. TERRY VENABLES

STARTER 26
A. MADONNA
BONUS 26
A. RHODESIAN RIDGEBACK
B. NORWAY (usually called the Norwegian Elkhound)
C. GAZELLE (the Gazelle-hound)

STARTER 27
A. 5/9 (FIVE-NINTHS)
BONUS 27
A. MINNIE THE MINX
B. PLUG (Percival Proudfoot Plugsley, of the Bash Street Kids)
C. LITTLE PLUM

STARTER 28
A. RICKSHAW (last seen in the city during the German occupation)
BONUS 28
A. LLADRO (Juan, Jose and Vicente Lladro)
B. (GLASS) PAPERWEIGHTS
C. ALESSI

STARTER 29
A. EARTH or SOIL
BONUS 29
A. ALEXANDER THE SECOND
B. THE THIRTEENTH
C. EXCLUSIONISTS

STARTER 30
A. HELENA BONHAM CARTER
BONUS 30
A. TWENTY-THIRD ("…my three and twentieth year". From "On His Having Arrived at the Age of Twenty-Three", his Sonnet No.7 of 1645)
B. PSI
C. "HE RESTORETH MY SOUL:" (continuing "He leadeth me in the paths of righteousness for his name's sake")

STARTER 31
A. CZECHOSLOVAKIAN
BONUS 31
A. DOVER
B. DAVID COPPERFIELD
C. *THE COOK'S TALE*

STARTER 32
A. THEIR ROYAL HIGHNESSES
BONUS 32
A. CARNAC
B. SEAHENGE (in the news for the debate on whether they should be moved
    for their own protection)
C. *TIME TEAM*

STARTER 33
A. 324
BONUS 33
A. SUGAR RAY ROBINSON
B. HIGH COMMISSIONER FOR HUMAN RIGHTS
C. AMANDA DONOHOE

STARTER 34
A. KNIGHT
BONUS 34
A. THE ATRIA / THE RIGHT AND LEFT AURICLES
B. MITRAL VALVE (the Latin: *mitra*)
C. SYSTOLE

STARTER 35
A. SINEAD O'CONNOR
BONUS 35
A. (JEAN-BAPTISTE) LULLY
B. MOLIÈRE
C. (MARC-ANTOINE) CHARPENTIER

STARTER 36
A. KING COBRA
BONUS 36
A. PLYWOOD
B. CHIPBOARD
C. MEDIUM DENSITY FIBREBOARD

STARTER 37
A. CATION
BONUS 37
A. MAO TSE-TUNG
B. AUGUST STRINDBERG
C. DAVID HUME

STARTER 38
A. BRITISH FILM INSTITITUE / B.F.I.
BONUS 38
A. U.S. SPACE MISSION / SPACE SHUTTLE (the shuttle Columbia)

B. ELLEN MACARTHUR (in the yacht Kingfisher)

C. CATHY FREEMAN (of Australia)

STARTER 39
A. MANNA

BONUS 39
A. ANTHONY COMSTOCK

B. GEORGE BERNARD SHAW

C. THOMAS BOWDLER

STARTER 40
A. FROTTAGE

BONUS 40
A. MARE NOSTRUM (literally "our sea")

B. OMERTA

C. SUFFOLK (THE SUFFOLK ANT-LION)

STARTER 41
A. FAKE BLOOD

BONUS 41
A. GENE HACKMAN

B. ALAN J. PAKULA

C. *THE RAINMAKER*

STARTER 42
A. *THINGS CAN ONLY GET BETTER*

BONUS 42
A. DILL or DILL WEED (from the Norse "dilla")

B. MINT or MENTHA

C. SAGE

STARTER 43
A. (TENOR) SAXOPHONE

BONUS 43
A. "NO FEAR"

B. CHIHUAHUA

C. HIP HOP

STARTER 44
A. CORVETTE

BONUS 44
A. CROOK

B. THALLIUM

C. COMEDY

STARTER 45
A. CORAL
BONUS 45
A. BRISBANE (named after Sir Thomas Brisbane)
B. KENYA
C. BRAZIL (after São Paulo and Rio de Janeiro)

STARTER 46
A. *A CLOCKWORK ORANGE* (Anthony Burgess; a drastic form of aversion therapy)
BONUS 46
A. BACKBONE or SPINE or VERTEBRAL COLUMN
B. AXIS
C. THORACIC VERTEBRAE (accept DORSAL VERTEBRAE)

STARTER 47
A. CARDIFF
BONUS 47
A. STRAWBERRY
B. "THESE FOOLISH THINGS"
C. JEROME K. JEROME

STARTER 48
A. "STRAWBERRY FIELDS" ("Strawberry Fields Forever" was a double-A side with "Penny Lane" in 1967)
BONUS 48
A. ETHER
B. DOC HOLLIDAY (John Henry Holliday)
C. STEVE MARTIN

STARTER 49
A. SNOWY (*Le Petit Vingtieme* was the children's supplement to *Le Vingtieme Siecle*)
BONUS 49
A. CASTEL SANT'ANGELO
B. WILLIAM THE FIRST (THE CONQUEROR) (the sarcophagus burst when they tried to squeeze his body in)
C. GRANADA

STARTER 50
A. MOTHER TERESA
BONUS 50
A. *ANDERBY WOLD*
B. MARGARET RUTHERFORD
C. CHARLES KINGSLEY (*The Water Babies*)

STARTER 51
A. MARTIN LUTHER KING [Jr.]

BONUS 51
A. TOKYO ROSE
B. AXIS SALLY
C. HANOI HANNAH

STARTER 52
A. M
BONUS 52
A. OLIVER REED
B. BELA LUGOSI
C. BRANDON LEE

STARTER 53
A. TELEVISION
BONUS 53
A. BENJAMIN BRITTEN
B. "JUBILEE"
C. "ORLANDO"

STARTER 54
A. JUMBO JET
BONUS 54
A. LAHAR (20th c., of Japanese origin)
B. PUNJAB (Karachi's population is 12.1m, Lahore's is 6.4m)
C. SIKHISM (Lahina was also known as Angad)

STARTER 55
A. TENPIN BOWLING
BONUS 55
A. THE WALKER BROTHERS
B. THE RIGHTEOUS BROTHERS
C. THE DOOBIE BROTHERS

STARTER 56
A. ST. PETERSBURG
BONUS 56
A. FREDERICK WINSLOW TAYLOR (known as "The Father of scientific management")
B. DOUGLAS McGREGOR
C. ABRAHAM MASLOW

STARTER 57
A. SLUG
BONUS 57
A. GEORGE BERNARD SHAW
B. (SAINT) JOSEPH OF ARIMATHEA (Luke 23:50)
C. THEODORE ROOSEVELT (the term "Square Deal" being associated with his political record, of course)

STARTER 58
A. OFLAG

BONUS 58
A. ANTHONY SHER
B. BARBARA WINDSOR
C. MARTIN AMIS (his autobiography *Experience*)

STARTER 59
A. KITTEN

BONUS 59
A. "DON'T GIVE UP YOUR DAY JOB"
B. "OFF THE TOP OF MY HEAD"
C. "WAKE UP AND SMELL THE COFFEE"

STARTER 60
A. HANGING GARDENS

BONUS 60
A. JERRY SPRINGER
B. OPRAH WINFREY
C. RICKI LAKE

STARTER 61
A. SNOW WHITE

BONUS 61
A. CRIBBAGE
B. BAT AND TRAP
C. PETANQUE

STARTER 62
A. HAMMER FILMS

BONUS 62
A. KIRCHHOFF (Gustav Robert Kirchhoff, 1824-1887)
B. THEVENIN
C. NORTON

STARTER 63
A. NEEDLES

BONUS 63
A. THEY WERE ALL HIGHWAYMEN
B. WILLIAM PLUNKETT
C. JOHNNY LEE MILLER and ROBERT CARLYLE

STARTER 64
A. JOHN DOE ("John Doe" and "Richard Doe" were the names of fictional
   plaintiff and defendant in common law acts of dispossession)

BONUS 64
A. ALEXANDRE DUMAS
B. THE LORD CHAMBERLAIN
C. MARY, QUEEN OF SCOTS

STARTER 65
A. JAMES JOYCE
BONUS 65
A. C & A
B. B & Q
C. J.M.C. (John Mason Cook)

STARTER 66
A. SPORES
BONUS 66
A. LEONARDO DA VINCI (it worked, fortunately)
B. STONEHENGE
C. RA (followed by RA 2, which completed the journey. N.B., NOT Kon-Tiki,
   which was the craft on the 1947 expedition from Peru to Polynesia)

STARTER 67
A. SPAT
BONUS 67
A. TOP LEVEL DOMAIN (i.e., such as dot com)
B. DOT ORG
C. UNIVERSAL RESOURCE LOCATOR

STARTER 68
A. "THE REST IS SILENCE"
BONUS 68
A. CRIBBAGE
   SHOVE HALFPENNY
   DOMINOES
   DARTS
   BILLIARDS
   SKITTLES
   BAGATELLE

STARTER 69
A. JUGGERNAUT
BONUS 69
A. -1
B. -j
C. 1

STARTER 70
A. THE ROYAL SCOTS
BONUS 70
A. THE PITUITARY
B. WATER LEVELS (ADH, i.e., Anti-diuretic hormone or vasopressin, controls
   water re-absorption by kidney tubules)
C. DIABETES INSIPIDUS

STARTER 71
A. MORECAMBE BAY
BONUS 71
A. *NIGHTEEN EIGHTY-FOUR*
B. GEORGE WASHINGTON
C. HORACE

STARTER 72
A. LEVIATHAN
BONUS 72
A. PTARMIGAN
B. CAPERCAILLIE
C. BLACK GROUSE or BLACK GAME

STARTER 73
A. SIR EDWARD HEATH
BONUS 73
A. MARIE CURIE (her daughter was Irène Joliot-Curie)
B. DARWIN (in their book *The Power of Movement in Plants*)
C. BRAGG

STARTER 74
A. SLOW HEART RATE (usually less than 60 beats per minute)
BONUS 74
A. FIR
B. SPRUCE
C. SCOTS PINE (not just pine because the species name is specific)

STARTER 75
A. 12/51
BONUS 75
A. A PONY
B. £100 (i.e. A TON)
C. A MONKEY

STARTER 76
A. A WOMAN / MOTHER ("God our Father and our Mother")
BONUS 76
A. ZEPHYR (from Zephuros)
B. JOB (Job, 1:19)
C. BELIZE (The former capital was Belize City)

STARTER 77
A. [DOMESTIC] DOG
BONUS 77
A. THE NATIONAL RAIL ENQUIRIES SERVICE

B. CRIMESTOPPERS
C. NHS DIRECT

STARTER 78
A. CHARISMA
BONUS 78
A. PETER CAREY
B. SIR SIDNEY NOLAN
C. MICK JAGGER

STARTER 79
A. IRON (A method of making pure iron from pig iron; "puddled" meaning stirred)
BONUS 79
A. DINOSAUR
B. METEORITE IMPACT (AND ITS SUBSEQUENT DUST CLOUD) (his theory published in 1981)
C. KENNETH BRANAGH

STARTER 80
A. SAMUEL PEPYS
BONUS 80
A. DIPHTHERIA
B. TRACHEOTOMY / TRACHEAOSTOMY
C. BELA SCHICK (The Schick Test)

STARTER 81
A. DAVID BAILEY
BONUS 81
A. SIGMUND FREUD
B. GEORGE, LORD BYRON
C. JOHN HENRY (later CARDINAL) NEWMAN

STARTER 82
A. NERO
BONUS 82
A. SARIN (or GB)
B. C.S. GAS (Corson and Stoughton)
c) MUSTARD GAS (also known as Distilled Mustard [HD])

STARTER 83
A. THE COMEDY STORE
BONUS 83
A. ANTWERP
B. JONATHAN SWIFT
C. JERSEY

STARTER 84
A. GEORGE BEST

BONUS 84
A. ON TO ITS BACK (and then try and force its head and neck downwards)
B. OPEN YOUR WINDOW (which then enables you to open your door when under water)
C. DIG A SMALL HOLE AND SPIT INTO IT (because your saliva will fall downwards)

STARTER 85
A. EUROVISION SONG CONTEST

BONUS 85
A. *A MIDSUMMER NIGHT'S DREAM* (1:1; line 134)
B. POLONIUS (in *Hamlet* 2:2; line 90)
C. *THE MERCHANT OF VENICE* (in the casket opened by the Prince of Morocco; 2:7; line 65)

STARTER 86
A. RING ROADS

BONUS 86
A. CHEESES
B. ZOROASTER
C. BELGIUM

STARTER 87
A. BIRMINGHAM

BONUS 87
A. TITHONUS
B. *GULLIVER'S TRAVELS* (Swift's *Travels into Several Remote Nations*)
C. JAMES HILTON (in *Lost Horizon*)

STARTER 88
A. STEFFI GRAF

BONUS 88
A. MIRIAM MAKEBA
B. DHARAMSALA
C. AUNG SAN SUU KYI

STARTER 89
A. PITTSBURGH

BONUS 89
A. *THE WOMAN IN WHITE*
B. SARAH WOODRUFF
C. GUDRUN and URSULA BRANGWEN

STARTER 90
A. DAME EDNA EVERAGE

BONUS 90
A. ROSA BUD
B. NICHOLAS NICKELBY
C. DAVID COPPERFIELD

STARTER 91
A. ROGER TAYLOR
BONUS 91
A. GREG DYKE
B. HELEN BOADEN
C. LEONARD SLATKIN

STARTER 92
A. REEVES
BONUS 92
A. SPIKE LEE
B. RICHARD PRYOR
C. CHRIS ROCK

STARTER 93
A. DAVID NIVEN
BONUS 93
A. SAUDI ARABIA
B. HAILE MARIAM MENGISTU
C. PARAGUAY

STARTER 94
A. ORANGUTAN
BONUS 94
A. MESSINA
B. LUXEMBOURG
C. AMSTERDAM

STARTER 95
A. IRIS
BONUS 95
A. HYPOGLYCAEMIA (N.B. NOT HYPERGLYCAEMIA which is the opposite –
   an excess of sugar in the blood, a condition also accompanying diabetes
   melitus)
B. FAINTING
C. INHALATION

STARTER 96
A. "STAIRWAY TO HEAVEN"
BONUS 96
A. ROSS STRETTON
B. BOB KILEY
C. ZIMBABWEAN

STARTER 97
A. FORTHWITH
BONUS 97
A. BLACKFRIARS BRIDGE (the Dominican Friars who removed there from Holborn)
B. LAMBETH BRIDGE (from "Loamhithe")
C. PRINCE ALBERT (the Albert Bridge)

STARTER 98
A. CULTURE
BONUS 98
A. SCORE AN INTERNATIONAL GOAL (the first fixture having had a nil-nil result)
B. SOCCER (Asked if he was going to play rugger, he replied, "No, I am going to play soccer")
C. AUSTRIA and HUNGARY

STARTER 99
A. PRIME RATE
BONUS 99
A. "FRÈRE JACQUES"
B. BARBARA TRAPIDO
C. ALGERNON / ALGY (MONCRIEFF)

STARTER 100
A. HYPERMARKET
BONUS 100
A. DRINK
B. W.C. FIELDS (Sometimes quoted as, "A woman drove me to drink. I never had the courtesy to thank her for it")
C. FATHER JACK (in the comedy series *Father Ted*)

STARTER 101
A. SULKY
BONUS 101
A. FRANKFURT (AM MAIN)
B. MARXISM
C. KITCHEN

STARTER 102
A. "FORBIDDEN PLANET"
BONUS 102
A. MULL
B. MULL OF GALLOWAY
C. STAFFA

STARTER 103
A. HECTOR BERLIOZ

BONUS 103
A. *THE LADY VANISHES*
B. *THE TAKING OF PELHAM 123*
C. *THE TITFIELD THUNDERBOLT*

STARTER 104
A. DERIVED UNITS (i.e. derived from the seven base units and the two
   supplementary units)

BONUS 104
A. SERGIO LEONE (concerned that American audiences would not go to see a
   Western made in Italy by Italians)
B. THE BAND
C. BEGAN HIS CAREER AS AN ENLISTED MAN (or PRIVATE)

STARTER 105
A. VALENCY

BONUS 105
A. THE LUMINOUS NOSE OF THE DONG ("The Dong With A Luminous
   Nose", searching for his Jumbly Girl)
B. *NORTH BY NORTHWEST* (referring to the climactic scene on
   Mt Rushmore)
C. CYRANO DE BERGERAC (in Rostand's play; the character Ragueneau is
   speaking)

STARTER 106
A. 15

BONUS 106
A. (SCALLOP) SHELL
B. TS ELIOT ("The Love Song of J. Alfred Prufrock", from *Prufrock and
   Other Observations*)
C. FIBONACCI (SEQUENCE)

STARTER 107
A. THE BAR

BONUS 107
A. PLUCK
B. GUTS
C. TILBURY

STARTER 108
A. ADIPOSE TISSUE

BONUS 108
A. BAKEWELL
B. PONTEFRACT
C. KENDAL

STARTER 109
A. EUROPEAN PARLIAMENTARY ELECTIONS
BONUS 109
A. GEORGE V & GEORGE VI (succeeded Edward VII & Edward VIII
respectively)
B. HENRY V, HENRY VI & HENRY VIII (wrong answers: Henry I was the son of
William the Conqueror / Henry II of Geoffrey Plantagent / Henry III of
King John / Henry IV of John of Gaunt / Henry VII of Edmund Tudor)
C. EDWARD V & EDWARD VIII (Duke of Windsor) (reigned 77 days & 325 days.
Wrong answers: Edward I – 35 yrs / Edward II – 20 yrs / Edward III – 50
yrs / Edward IV – 22 yrs / Edward VI – 6 yrs /Edward VII – 9 yrs)

STARTER 110
A. CAREEN
BONUS 110
A. MERCURY
B. ALAN B SHEPARD JR.
C. WESTON-SUPER-MARE

STARTER 111
A. CROSSWORD PUZZLE
BONUS 111
A. LOUTH
B. GREAT BRITAIN (ENGLAND) (the first woman Liberal MP. She won the
by-election caused when her husband Tom died in the Commons library)
C. JEFFREY ARCHER

STARTER 112
A. A FRIEND IN NEED IS A FRIEND INDEED
BONUS 112
A. (SIR WILLIAM) MACPHERSON (OF CLUNY)
B. OSSIAN (Oisin)
C. SUSPENSION (Accept shock absorbers)

STARTER 113
A. VATICAN CITY
BONUS 113
A. EQUILATERAL TRIANGLE
B. 12
C. 30

STARTER 114
A. ALAMOGORDO
BONUS 114
A. ELVIS (St Elvis was a cousin to St David, and Bishop of Munster in Ireland)
B. A TORTOISE
C. JERRY LEE LEWIS

STARTER 115
A. THE BRIDGE

BONUS 115
A. ALTA VISTA (the words "Palo Alto" and "vista" were written close together)
B. ASKJEEVES
C. LYCOS (from *lycosidae*, the wolf spiders)

STARTER 116
A. TONI MORRISON
BONUS 116
A. REGENT'S PARK
B. HAYMARKET (Haymarket Theatre Royal; NOT, of course, Theatre Royal
    Drury Lane)
C. ALL SOULS

STARTER 117
A. YUL BRYNNER (For *The King and I*)
BONUS 117
A. SIR / SAINT THOMAS MORE
B. MAID or NUN OF KENT (sometimes prefixed MAD, FAIR or HOLY)
C. WILLIAM SHAKESPEARE

STARTER 118
A. VON MOLTKE
BONUS 118
A. WORK
B. POWER
C. IMPULSE

STARTER 119
A. ST BASIL'S CATHEDRAL (In Red Square)
BONUS 119
A. TROPOSPHERE (height varies according to latitude)
B. ARGON
C. THE SKY IS BLUE

STARTER 120
A. FUNCTION KEY
BONUS 120
A. KINDERGARTEN
B. GUSTAV MAHLER ("Songs on the Deaths of Children")
C. "KÜCHE" (Kitchen; [Children, Church, Kitchen])

STARTER 121
A. MOROCCO
BONUS 121
A. KAZAKHSTAN (The city was known as Aqmola, meaning "white grave" until
    May 1998)
B. BEIJING (PEKING)
C. ULAN BATOR

STARTER 122
A. PROTOCOL

BONUS 122
A. PHON
B. PHOT
C. PHONON

STARTER 123
A. BIOSPHERE

BONUS 123
A. "A LUMP IN THE THROAT"
   (NOT "a frog in the throat", which is not caused by acute anxiety etc)
B. HYOID BONE
C. LARYNX
   (if they answer "voice box", press for the correct term)

STARTER 124
A. FULMAR

BONUS 124
A. OCEANUS PROCELLARUM (or OCEAN OF STORMS)
B. (JOHANNES) KEPLER
C. SINUS

STARTER 125
A. "DOWN THE RABBIT-HOLE"

BONUS 125
A. ROBBIE WILLIAMS
B. *THE BLAIR WITCH PROJECT*
C. J.K. ROWLING (author of the "Harry Potter" series, of course)

STARTER 126
A. SERGE PROKOFIEV

BONUS 126
A. ED KOCH
B. DAVID DINKINS
C. RUDY GIULIANI

STARTER 127
A. FLAG OF CONVENIENCE

BONUS 127
A. PAIN (accept NOXIOUS / LIKELY TO DAMAGE TISSUES OF THE BODY)
B. ENDORPHINS (accept ENKEPHALINS, BETA-ENDORPHIN, DYMORPHIN)
C. REFERRED PAIN

STARTER 128
A. BALKAN MOUNTAINS

BONUS 128
A. THE WEAVERS

B. "WIMOWEH"

C. DON MCLEAN (NOT Carole King, who had an album called *Tapestry* released the following year)

STARTER 129

A. NAPALM

BONUS 129

A. HELENA RUBENSTEIN

B. ELIZABETH ARDEN (born Florence Nightingale Graham)

C. ESTÉE LAUDER (born Josephine Esther Mentzer)

STARTER 130

A. EDWARD THE THIRD (The war began in 1337)

BONUS 130

A. LODESTONE

B. THE ACLINIC LINE

C. ANGLE OF DECLINATION or THE MAGNETIC VARIATION

STARTER 131

A. COMPACT DISC

BONUS 131

A. SIR GUY OF WARWICK ("On Dunsmore heath I alsoe slewe / A monstrous wyld and cruell beast / Calld the Dun-cow of Dunsmore heath";)

B. AUDHUMLA

C. HATHOR (NOT Isis, whose iconography came to feature the cow's horns and head as her cult was increasingly identified with Hathor's. Isis was Horus' mother)

STARTER 132

A. PORTAGE

BONUS 132

A. WALT DISNEY

B. "WHEN YOU WISH UPON A STAR"

C. *FANTASIA*

STARTER 133

A. LOTUS-EATERS or LOTOPHAGI

BONUS 133

A. *THE BRIDGES OF MADISON COUNTY*

B. THE TAY BRIDGE (William McGonagall's poem on the disaster of 1879)

C. LONDON BRIDGE (in "The Waste Land")

STARTER 134

A. NUCLEOTIDES

BONUS 134

A. KARL JANSKY

B. (SIR) MARTIN RYLE

C. THE MULLARD (RADIO ASTRONOMY OBSERVATORY)

STARTER 135
A. DODGE CITY

BONUS 135
A. ANNIE HORNIMAN
B. *HOBSON'S CHOICE*
C. DAME SYBIL THORNDIKE (for whom Bernard Shaw wrote the part)

STARTER 136
A. MARTIN CHUZZLEWIT

BONUS 136
A. POTLATCH
B. WAMPUM
C. PAPUA NEW GUINEA

STARTER 137
A. PRINCE EDWARD ISLAND

BONUS 137
A. LAWN TENNIS (in the Davis Cup)
B. CARBERRY (Tommy and son Paul. Tommy also trained the 1999 winner)
C. COLIN COWDREY

STARTER 138
A. SAMPAN

BONUS 138
A. CAPE VERDE [ISLANDS]
B. PORTUGAL
C. GUINEA-BISSAU

STARTER 139
A. CHEATING

BONUS 139
A. *GAMMER GURTON'S NEEDLE*
B. YUCCA
C. RIPON CATHEDRAL

STARTER 140
A. THE SCARECROW, THE [COWARDLY] LION AND THE TIN MAN (In *The Wizard of Oz*)

BONUS 140
A. ITS COLOUR
B. ORANGE-YELLOW
C. POTASSIUM

STARTER 141
A. KING LEAR

BONUS 141
A. E.T.A. HOFFMANN (Ernst Theodor Amadeus Hoffmann)

B. *COPPELIA*
C. JACQUES OFFENBACH

STARTER 142
A. NEWEL POST
BONUS 142
A. THE BISHOPS' WARS
B. "HOME, SWEET HOME" (from the opera "Clari, Maid of Milan", though the tune had been previously published by Bishop as "Sicilian Air")
C. MASSACHUSETTS

STARTER 143
A. THE MEKON
BONUS 143
A. THE A.M.A. / AMERICAN MEDICAL ASSOCIATION
B. MEDICARE (NOT Medicaid, which is a state-operated scheme covering some medical expenses of the poor)
C. L.B. JOHNSON (in 1965, though Truman was the original sponsor of the schemes)

STARTER 144
A. EE
BONUS 144
A. THE SPICE GIRLS
B. THE MOLUCCAS / MALUKU
C. PIMENTO

STARTER 145
A. CLICHÉ
BONUS 145
A. *(THE LIFE AND ADVENTURES OF) NICHOLAS NICKLEBY*
B. *THE GOOD COMPANIONS*
C. *MANSFIELD PARK*

STARTER 146
A. *THE MARTIAN CHRONICLES*
BONUS 146
A. WATERLOO STATION
B. FEBRUARY
C. APSLEY HOUSE (Owned by Wellington from 1817)

STARTER 147
A. PARMESAN
BONUS 147
A. BAND OF HOPE
B. G.F. WATTS (George Frederick Watts)
C. ALEXANDER POPE

STARTER 148
A. HIGH KING

BONUS 148
A. MELCOMBE REGIS
B. EDGAR ALLEN POE
c. MOSQUITO BITE (the bite of the mosquito *aedes aegypti*, either between humans or between monkeys and humans)

STARTER 149
A. METHADONE

BONUS 149
A. WARTHOG
B. SIR PETER LELY
C. *HENRY THE FOURTH PART TWO*

STARTER 150
A. NARNIA

BONUS 150
A. FANNY BURNEY (later Madame D'Arblay)
B. *SENSE AND SENSIBILITY*
C. *PAMELA*

STARTER 151
A. BLACK LACE

BONUS 151
A. TROY ("Recuyell (ie. compilation) of the Histories of Troye")
B. "DOCTOR FAUSTUS"
C. *FAR FROM THE MADDING CROWD* (Thomas Hardy)

STARTER 152
A. LUXEMBOURG

BONUS 152
A. HERCULES or Herakles
B. CLEANSING HIS STABLES (THE AUGEAN STABLES) (the river washed out the stables of the king's herd of oxen)
C. To get the GIRDLE OF HIPPOLYTA, Queen of the Amazons; to get the GOLDEN APPLES OF THE HESPERIDES

STARTER 153
A. [BARON / LORD] DACRE OF GLANTON

BONUS 153
A. NORSE MYTHOLOGY (they perched on Odin's shoulders)
B. *HAMLET* (Act 3, Scene 2; the players of "The Mousetrap")
C. *GORMENGHAST* (based on Mervyn Peake's writings)

STARTER 154
A. GERALD FORD (appointed vice-president on Spiro Agnew's resignation)

BONUS 154
A. TADPOLE (also "polliwig" and "purwiggy")
B. SHRIMP
C. BENJAMIN DISRAELI

STARTER 155
A. [TO BE] ALONE
BONUS 155
A. INDONESIA
B. TURKEY (from military bands)
C. LOUISIANA

STARTER 156
A. JOYCE GRENFELL
BONUS 156
A. Republic of IRELAND (the Punt) (the Euro was worth about 79p)
B. ITALY (the lira)
C. GREECE

STARTER 157
A. "ASH-WEDNESDAY"
BONUS 157
A. IRELAND (after Gerald, heir to the Earldom of Kildare)
B. WALTER MONDALE (Senator for Minnesota)
C. ALBANIA

STARTER 158
A. VALENTINA TERESHKOVA (the first woman in space)
BONUS 158
A. GRASSHOPPER
B. (KARLHEINZ) STOCKHAUSEN
C. *KUNG FU*

STARTER 159
A. EGMONT
BONUS 159
A. Lady AUGUSTA GREGORY
B. THE (PAPAL) INQUISITION (not, of course, the Spanish Inquisition, established by a Papal Bull of Sixtus the Fourth in 1478)
C. BILL FORSYTH ('81, '99 respectively)

STARTER 160
A. PORTUGAL
BONUS 160
A. "HOME THOUGHTS FROM ABROAD"
B. WILLIAM WORDSWORTH (in one of the "Lucy" poems)
C. RUPERT BROOKE (in "The Old Vicarage, Grantchester")

STARTER 161
A. CHRIS OFILI

BONUS 161
A. BILL BRADLEY
B. GLADYS MITCHELL
C. *OUR MUTUAL FRIEND*

STARTER 162
A. CUPROUS / CUPREOUS

BONUS 162
A. ORDER OF THE THISTLE
B. "NEMO ME IMPUNE LACESSIT" / "Nobody provokes me with impunity"
    (inscribed around the rim of some pound coins)
C. BOTTOM (whilse being courted by Titania)

STARTER 163
A. KING KONG

BONUS 163
A. 1690s (1690, 1692, 1692)
B. 1830s (1837, 1839, 1837)
C. 1150s (1152, 1154, 1154)

STARTER 164
A. RAINFALL

BONUS 164
A. LOBSTER
B. NATHANAEL WEST (1903-1940)
C. DONALD SUTHERLAND

STARTER 165
A. "SLEEPING BEAUTY"

BONUS 165
A. SPARTA
B. HELOTS
C. *IN THE HEAT OF THE NIGHT*

STARTER 166
A. CENTAURS

BONUS 166
A. *THE CONFIDENTIAL CLERK*
B. GRAHAM GREENE
C. JAMES ELLROY

STARTER 167
A. THE DEFENESTRATION OF PRAGUE

BONUS 167
A. CASA ROSADA (they are all the Official Residence of the President)
B. LISBON
C. QUIRINAL

STARTER 168
A. ZIRCON
BONUS 168
A. DAVID & ELIZABETH EMANUEL
B. KANT
C. *NINETEEN EIGHTY-FOUR*

STARTER 169
A. ILIUM
BONUS 169
A. APPALACHIANS
B. BILL BRYSON
C. NORTH CAROLINA

STARTER 170
A. (ST EDWARD THE MARTYR
BONUS 170
A. MALCOLM (IV)
B. (Nikolay Andreyevich) RIMSKY-KORSAKOV
C. "PATIENCE" ([the name of the milkmaid] in the duet, "Hey Willow Waly O!")

STARTER 171
A. POLENTA
BONUS 171
A. CZECH REPUBLIC (at Slavkov u Brna in Moravia)
B. ALEXANDER I
C. FRED ASTAIRE

STARTER 172
A. BARGEBOARDS
BONUS 172
A. C.S.LEWIS
B. *THE MONK*
C. EZRA POUND

STARTER 173
A. DOCH-AN-DORIS
BONUS 173
A. "ZULEIKA DOBSON"
B. LORD BYRON
C. JOSEPH (Potiphar's wife tries unsuccessfully to seduce him)

STARTER 174
A. GRASSES
BONUS 174
A. THE BLUEBELL RAILWAY
B. SNOWDON (the Snowdon Mountain Railway in Llanberis)
C. THE ROMNEY, HYTHE AND DYMCHURCH RAILWAY

STARTER 175
A. KINAESTHESIS or KINAESTHESIA
BONUS 175
A. HEROD (ANTIPAS) (daughter is unnamed in Mark's Gospel, identified by
    Josephus as Salome)
B. AARON
C. DAVID (an ephod being a priest's vestment)

STARTER 176
A. GÜNTHER
BONUS 176
A. ALEXANDER POPE
B. ESSAY ON MAN "EPISTLE II"
C. LADY MARY WORTLEY MONTAGU

STARTER 177
A. SHIBBOLETH
BONUS 177
A. TEHERAN
B. YALTA
C. STALIN, ATTLEE, TRUMAN

STARTER 178
A. THE WAGGONER / THE CHARIOTEER
BONUS 178
A. DEAN RUSK
B. BAY OF PIGS
C. GARY POWERS

STARTER 179
A. MELANESIA
BONUS 179
A. FUGGERS
B. GIOTTO
C. MEDICI

STARTER 180
A. ETRURIA
BONUS 180
A. CUZCO
B. FRANCISCO PIZARRO
C. PERU

STARTER 181
A. ATOM EGOYAN
BONUS 181
A. TERRACOTTA ARMY
B. CONFUCIUS
C. BUDDHISM

STARTER 182
A. JEAN SIBELIUS
BONUS 182
A. LATTER-DAY SAINTS [MORMONS]
B. LOUIS FARRAKHAN
C. DUBLIN

STARTER 183
A. LAKE TIBERIAS
BONUS 183
A. GEORGES MELIES
B. *BIRTH OF A NATION*
C. *NANOOK OF THE NORTH*

STARTER 184
A. HELIOMETER
BONUS 184
A. *IT HAPPENED ONE NIGHT*
B. SHANGRI-LA
C. LIONEL BARRYMORE

STARTER 185
A. 2500 WATTS [2.5 KILOWATTS]
BONUS 185
A. JOHN DRYDEN
B. ROBERT SOUTHEY
C. VIRGIL

STARTER 186
A. PYRAMID
BONUS 186
A. ELEANOR OF AQUITAINE
B. IT
C. *SENSE AND SENSIBILITY*

STARTER 187
A. [SIR JOHN AMBROSE] FLEMING
BONUS 187
A. LAKE WOBEGON
B. E. ANNIE PROULX
C. PARIS TROUT

STARTER 188
A. ALL EXPERIENCED TOTALITY DURING THE SOLAR ECLIPSE
BONUS 188
A. LEONARD BERNSTEIN
B. BILLY THE KID
C. GEORGE AND IRA GERSHWIN

STARTER 189
A. BANNS
BONUS 189
A. ASTROPHEL AND STELLA
B. STELLA
C. DANTE ALIGHIERI

STARTER 190
A. BURMESE
BONUS 190
A. AQUAE SULIS
B. SHERIDAN
C. *HUMPHRY CLINKER*

STARTER 191
A. APHORISM
BONUS 191
A. BEDFORD
B. THOMAS MORE
C. JOHN MILTON

STARTER 192
A. PIG & WHISTLE
BONUS 192
A. "NOWHERE" BACKWARDS
B. *CANDIDE*
C. AIRSTRIP ONE

STARTER 193
A. ALGERIA
BONUS 193
A. CELLO
B. VIOLIN
C. PIANO

STARTER 194
A. UNMOUNTED MINT
BONUS 194
A. BERLIN PHILHARMONIC
B. SIR JOHN BARBIROLLI
C. HERBERT VON KARAJAN

STARTER 195
A. "GREENSLEEVES"
BONUS 195
A. ISABEL ALLENDE

B. *LEAF STORM*
C. MAGIC REALISM

STARTER 196
A. SUSTAINING [PEDAL]
BONUS 196
A. APOLLO 8
B. MICHAEL COLLINS
C. *THE RIGHT STUFF*

STARTER 197
A. LEVANT
BONUS 197
A. RICHARD KRAFT-EBBING
B. *THE INTERPRETATION OF DREAMS*
C. ANALYTICAL PSYCHOLOGY

STARTER 198
A. PARSNIP
BONUS 198
A. THE ENGLISH EAST INDIA COMPANY
B. MUHAMMAD ALI JINNAH
C. NON-VIOLENT RESISTANCE

STARTER 199
A. PLUTARCH
BONUS 199
A. ELIZABETH BARRETT BROWNING
B. MONTMORENCY
C. WILLIAM BROWN

STARTER 200
A. HERRING GULL
BONUS 200
A. AL CAPONE
B. TEAMSTERS' UNION
C. ROBERT KENNEDY

STARTER 201
A. OMAR KHAYYAM (Fitzgerald being the translator of the Rubaiyat)
BONUS 201
A. THE WINDMILL THEATRE
B. *DON QUIXOTE DE LA MANCHA* (Cervantes, Chapter 8, the "tilting at windmills" episode)
C. NORTHUMBERLAND

STARTER 202
A. (SEARCH FOR) EXTRA-TERRESTRIAL INTELLIGENCE
BONUS 202
A. SUSIE ORBACH (first published in 1978)
B. MIRIAM MARGOLYES (quoted in the *Observer*, 1991)
C. GEORGE ORWELL

STARTER 203
A. PUKKA (from *pakka*)
BONUS 203
A. CRICKET (in *Bees In Some Bonnets*, 1979)
B. (GEOFFREY) LORD HOWE (resigning as Deputy Prime Minister; Foreign
    Secretary 1983-89)
C. NORMAN TEBBIT (interviewed in the *Los Angeles Times*, reported in the
    Telegraph 20.4.90)

STARTER 204
A. (YUKATA) TANIYAMA
BONUS 204
A. CHAOS
B. FRACTAL (GEOMETRY)
C. FUNGI

STARTER 205
A. BASIL BRUSH
BONUS 205
A. HOLOCENE (following the Pleistocene. *Holo*, the whole, entirety; *kainos*, new)
B. SEA CUCUMBERS (NB: also called COTTON-SPINNERS / TREPANG /
    BECHE-DE-MER)
C. DENNIS GABOR (born in Budapest, 1900, worked in the UK from 1933)

STARTER 206
A. MOBY
BONUS 206
A. TORTELLINI (supposedly invented by the 19th-century Florentine Guiseppe
    Ceri, inspired by a vision of Venus)
B. VERMICELLI
C. FUTURISM (from *The Futurist Handbook*; from the belief that it made
    people sluggish)

STARTER 207
A. SHOEMAKING (strictly, also glovemaking, lace-making, tanning)
BONUS 207
A. DRACONIAN (from Draco)
B. "AN EYE FOR AN EYE" (or more correctly "EYE FOR EYE") (Verse 24: "Eye
    for eye, tooth for tooth, hand for hand, foot for foot,")
C. PIRACY (WITH VIOLENCE) (ie., if accompanied by acts endangering life,
    or by an assault with intent to murder)

STARTER 208
A. HANSEATIC LEAGUE
BONUS 208
A. DAVID LLOYD GEORGE (in *Essays in Biography* (1933) "Mr Lloyd George")
B. THE HOUSE OF LORDS
C. MARCONI COMPANY (known as the "Marconi Scandal")

STARTER 209
A. G (It is known as the gravitational constant)
BONUS 209
A. OPHELIA (in Act Four of *Hamlet*)
B. "FOLLIES"
C. HAL 9000 (accept HAL) (the rogue computer in the film *2001: A Space Odyssey*)

STARTER 210
A. FRUSTRUM
BONUS 210
A. THE BBC (from Isiah 2,4: "Nation shall not lift up sword against nation," words adapted by Montague John Rendall, on the BBC's first board of governors)
B. "THE CHILDREN OF GOD" (Chapter 5, verse 3)
C. BENJAMIN DISRAELI (the Congress having revised the terms of the Treaty of San Stefano, which had ended the Russo-Turkish War)

STARTER 211
A. OGAMS or OGHAM
BONUS 211
A. TEA TREE (of the family Myrtaceae; used as a tea by Captain Cook to prevent scurvy)
B. (BITTER or SEVILLE) ORANGE (after the Italian Anna Maria de la Trémoille, 17th-century princess of Nerola, whose favourite perfume it was)
C. JOJOBA

STARTER 212
A. EDGBASTON
BONUS 212
A. *SONGS OF PRAISE*
B. MAGNIFICAT (ANIMA MEA DOMINUM / MY SOUL DOTH MAGNIFY THE LORD) (from Luke 1: 46-48)
C. NUNC DIMITTIS (from Luke, 2: 29-32)

STARTER 213
A. "KILROY WAS HERE"
BONUS 213
A. VIRGIL (PUBLIUS VERGILIUS MARO) (in the Aeneid, book 2, line 48)
A. ELIZABETH BARRETT BROWNING
C. DAME MURIEL SPARK

STARTER 214

A. UTOPIA

BONUS 214

A. *ALL QUIET ON THE WESTERN FRONT* (*Im Westen Nichts Neues*, 1929)
B. *CATCH-22* (by Joseph Heller)
C. PAT BARKER (*Regeneration, The Eye In The Door, The Stone Road*)

STARTER 215

A. HARRIET BEECHER STOWE

BONUS 215

A. PAUSANIAS
B. GERALD OF WALES (or GIRALDUS CAMBRENSIS, GIRALDUS DE BARRI)
C. DANIEL DEFOE

STARTER 216

A. TALENT

BONUS 216

A. EGO (the Id is that governed by irrational and instinctive forces, the
   Superego is that concerned with moral conscience)
B. TOKYO
C. ROXY MUSIC

STARTER 217

A. THE "TROUT QUINTET"

BONUS 217

A. SWALLOW
B. CHOUGH (*Pyrrhocorax pyrrhocorax*, formerly prolific along Cornwall's
   coasts)
C. WREN (St Stephen's Day, December 26, was also traditionally called
   Wrenning Day; sacred in Celtic / Druidic tradition, and on the Isle of Man)

STARTER 218

A. NEWCASTLE (UPON TYNE)

BONUS 218

A. ERG (the Arabic "irk")
B. THEREFORE
C. RYE

STARTER 219

A. TANTALUM

BONUS 219

A. FREEZE-DRYING
B. (CLARENCE) BIRDSEYE
C. SALTPETRE (helps preserving salt to penetrate the meat and produces stable
   pink colour)

STARTER 220

A. TRADES UNION CONGRESS

BONUS 220

A. ENTRAILS (OF SACRIFICIAL ANIMALS)
B. PALMISTRY / PALM READING / CHIROMANCY
C. CARTOMANCY / READING PLAYING (OR TAROT) CARDS ("the wisest
   woman in Europe / With a wicked pack of cards." Some of the cards
   described are Eliot's invention and not part of the standard Tarot pack)

STARTER 221

A. ARCTURUS

BONUS 221

A. ARISTOPHANES
B. SOCRATES
C. *LYSISTRATA*

STARTER 222

A. HENRY WATSON FOWLER

BONUS 222

A. JAMES and JOHN (Mark, 3:17)
B. JUDAS (ST JUDAS or ST JUDE) (not Judas Iscariot)
C. SIMON

STARTER 223

A. VENUS

BONUS 223

A. "BATTLE HYMN OF THE REPUBLIC"
B. BEN JONSON
C. E. E. CUMMINGS (Edward Estlin Cummings)

STARTER 224

A. ASTEROID OR COMET IMPACT (WITH THE EARTH)

BONUS 224

A. ULYSSES S GRANT
B. JAMES GARFIELD
A. THEODORE ROOSEVELT

STARTER 225

A. ASHMOLEAN

BONUS 225

A. BLADUD (of the 9th century BC)
B. MORDRED / MODRED / MEDRAUT
C. CONCHOBAR (Conchobar mac Nessa)

STARTER 226

A. KULTURKAMPF

BONUS 226

A. ISOGLOSS
B. PHATIC COMMUNION (e.g "Nice morning, isn't it?")
C. EPISTEMIC MODALITY (as distinct from deontic modality, where the modal
   verb is used to express a command or obligation)

STARTER 227
A. "THE MONKEY'S PAW"

BONUS 227
A. LUCRETIUS
B. A SPARROW FLYING INTO THE HALL AND IMMEDIATELY OUT
C. "DEBT"

STARTER 228
A. PLEISTOCENE

BONUS 228
A. ARIUS
B. GOTHIC
C. BOOKS OF KINGS (1 & 2)

STARTER 229
A. 100 PROOF or 100 PER CENT PROOF

BONUS 229
A. SATSUMA
B. KAGOSHIMA
C. MEIJI RESTORATION

STARTER 230
A. ORGANOPHOSPHATES

BONUS 230
A. CHIASMUS
B. C. NORTHCOTE PARKINSON (in *Parkinson's Law*)
C. HORATIO HORNBLOWER (created by C.S. Forester)

STARTER 231
A. THE EQUILIBRIUM CONSTANT

BONUS 231
A. HYDRAULIC CIVILISATION
B. ORGAN (water pressure was used to stabilize the wind supply)
C. GOTTFRIED SILBERMANN

STARTER 232
A. VERNALISATION

BONUS 232
A. DIOGENES THE CYNIC (also known as Diogenes of Sinope)
B. TALKING TO EACH OTHER (except in the Strangers' Room; the story in
    The Memoirs of Sherlock Holmes)
C. PHILOSOPHERS (author of the ten books of *Lives of Eminent
    Philosophers*)

STARTER 233
A. KARL VON FRISCH

BONUS 233
A. *THE AGE OF UNCERTAINTY*
B. TRICKLE-DOWN (THEORY)
C. INDIA

STARTER 234
A. VERDUN
BONUS 234
A. JOSEF HAYDN (the minuet is often incorrectly called "Haydn's Ox Minuet")
B. BULIMIA (accept BULIMIA NERVOSA / BULIMY / BULIMUS) (strictly, bulimia nervosa is an emotional disorder in which eating is followed by deliberate vomiting and purging)
C. BILLABONG

STARTER 235
A. OPTICAL CHARACTER RECOGNITION
BONUS 235
A. HIS BEARD (both nicknamed "the bearded")
B. LAMMERGEIER (i.e., "lamb vulture")
C. SIR (SAINT) THOMAS MORE (in Bacon's Apophthegms)

STARTER 236
A. FILIGREE
BONUS 236
A. BASALT
B. GNEISS
C. SHALE (argillaceous, ie. that which is made up of clay or silt particles)

STARTER 237
A. PLANTAGENET
BONUS 237
A. HOWLIN' WOLF
B. NEW JOURNALISM
C. TUNGSTEN (Tungsten is extracted from the ore wolfram, or wolframite)

STARTER 238
A. FATIMA
BONUS 238
A. MERCURY
B. JUPITER
C. MARS

STARTER 239
A. BUSHIDO
BONUS 239
A. TERA-
B. 18
C. 15 (ie. minus 15; from the Danish / Norwegian *femten*, fifteen)

STARTER 240
A. THE GORDIAN KNOT

BONUS 240
A. STANDARD ATMOSPHERIC PRESSURE
B. ACCELERATION OF FREE FALL (accept ACCELERATION DUE TO GRAVITY [IN A VACUUM] AT / NEAR THE EARTH'S SURFACE)
C. (MOLAR or UNIVERSAL) GAS CONSTANT

STARTER 241
A. EGYPT

BONUS 241
A. JU-JITSU
B. KARATE (the word is first recorded in English in 1955)
C. AIKIDO

STARTER 242
A. OLIVER CROMWELL

BONUS 242
A. SIOUX (or DAKOTA / LAKOTA)
B. CHEROKEE (The Indian Removal Act of 1830)
C. (CHIRICAHUA) APACHE

STARTER 243
A. TALUS

BONUS 243
A. LAMPREY
B. GLOUCESTER (The presentation is now only made for Coronations and Jubilees)
C. NGAIO MARSH

STARTER 244
A. (SIR) HANS SLOANE

BONUS 244
A. LEPTON (all have antiparticles called anti-leptons)
B. WEIL'S DISEASE (after Dr H. Adolf Weil, 1848-1916)
C. (EUROPEAN) EEL (*leptocephalus*, ie. thin or narrow-skulled)

STARTER 245
A. DEUS EX MACHINA

BONUS 245
A. LAGRANGIAN POINT (or Libration Point or L-Point; Comte Joseph Louis Lagrange, 1736–1813)
B. TROJAN
C. KINETIC ENERGY MINUS POTENTIAL ENERGY

STARTER 246
A. JEAN-ANTOINE WATTEAU

BONUS 246
A. I CHING (or BOOK OF CHANGES)
B. METEORITES (Josep Alois Widmanstatten)
C. PERU

STARTER 247
A. OLDUVAI GORGE
BONUS 247
A. WORDS
B. SAMUEL JOHNSON (in the preface to his *Dictionary of the English Language*)
C. ADLAI STEVENSON

STARTER 248
A. TRANSEPT
BONUS 248
A. ROBERT SOUTHEY
B. LEWIS CARROLL / CHARLES LUTWIDGE DODGSON
C. "HOW DOTH THE LITTLE CROCODILE"

STARTER 249
A. *SMILES OF A SUMMER NIGHT*
BONUS 249
A. VICTORIA
B. ZAMBIA AND ZIMBABWE
C. JOHN SPEKE

STARTER 250
A. CARL ANDRE
BONUS 250
A. LAKE TANGANYIKA
B. LAKE TURKANA (accept LAKE RUDOLF) (the "Turkana Boy" is an almost-complete skeleton 1.6 million years old)
C. MOZAMBIQUE